THE AGING CHALLENGE

Making the Most of Life After 50

To Dawn,
Many thanks
for inviting us to
participate in the
"aging wize" events —
and for performing
with us. It was
a great pleasure to
see + work with
you again.
Best wishes!

William

4-30-15

THE AGING CHALLENGE

Making the Most of Life After 50

Clifton Ware

Birch Grove Publishing

To Jon, David, and Alan
and their loving wives
Sarah, Tamsen, and Colleen

The Aging Challenge: Making the Most of Life After 50
Clifton Ware

ISBN 978-0-9822544-0-0

Manufactured in the U.S.A.

Contents

Chapter 6 — Cultivating Social Connections 142

Chapter 7 — Pursuing a Moderate Lifestyle 166

Chapter 8 — Managing Money and Resources 189

Preface

The Second Half of Life

If you've made it to the second half of life—the better part in many ways—from approximately age 50 to the century mark, this book should offer some relevant information and advice. For certain, the aging process presents many challenges, and the primary goal we all face is learning how to make the most of whatever life tosses our way.

Although there's a big age spread between a relatively young 50-year-old and a 90-something, there are some common life issues shared by all, namely, health status, lifestyle choices, and the inevitable prospect of suffering and dying. The good news is that, depending on your genetic disposition, lifestyle, and overall attitude toward life, it may be possible for a person in relatively good condition at the mid-century mark to enjoy functional mind-body health through the senior years—assuming proactive measures are undertaken early enough to become habitual for the long haul. And for anyone at the far end of the age spectrum, it's never too late to make positive lifestyle changes and improve the quality of life.

For the past quarter of a century I've often pondered aging and death, and have made appropriate decisions, arrangements, and preparations along the way, all of which I discuss in this book. Like many in my generation, my wake-up call came in my mid 40s, when I was struck with the harsh realization that my youth was fading, and I was not far from becoming a senior citizen. I had reached the top of the hill—at least career-wise—and figured I would at best experience a steady mind-body decline for the rest of my life. I figured I could hope only that my decline would resemble a slow slide instead of a steep, unexpected crash. At one point I made a proactive commitment to work at slowing down the aging process, and my wife, Bettye, also took up the cause. We began by initiating self-prescribed physical fitness and nutrition programs. And, upon my reaching the 50-year milestone, we joined the American Association of Retired Persons (AARP) to keep abreast of pertinent information for persons over age 50.

Now, at the ripe age of 72, poised somewhere between the half-century milestone and the goal of living for another decade or so, I feel qualified to share some of the knowledge and skills I've gained about life past 50. As for dying and death, like most aging persons I'm still seeking answers and making preparations. When adversity eventually strikes—as it assuredly will—there's no way of knowing if I will be able to follow through with all my well-formed ideas and intentions. I can only hope that the studying, planning, and actions I've taken will positively influence decisions at the end. Depending on where you are in the aging process, I'm sure you can relate to these thoughts and concerns.

A brief survey of my background would be appropriate at the outset, just so you know who I am and why I've written this book. My socio-economic background is a factor in my overall health and outlook, just as it is for you, the reader. As you read this book, take time to reflect on concerns you have, perhaps jotting down thoughts, questions, plans, or reactions as they come to mind.

My Personal Background and Qualifications

I'm a native of Jackson, Mississippi, where I was fortunate to receive a good public school education, from elementary age through high school. Another major institutional influence was the Methodist church I attended, the second largest in the state. My father was a civil engineer with the city of Jackson, and for most of my childhood my mother owned and managed a small grocery store, where I spent many hours. We were an average family of four, including my sister, Kay, who arrived when I was age 10. Up until age 15 my main interest was art, but when my voice developed, I became a dedicated and very active vocal performer.

My wife, Bettye, and I attended Millsaps College in Jackson, a well-regarded Methodist-affiliated institution. I received a B.A. degree with majors in philosophy and music, while Bettye received a degree in music theory and organ. We married during college and by the time we reached our mid-20s we had been blessed with three sons. Both of us finished masters degrees at the University of Southern Mississippi, she in English literature and I in vocal music. As a musical team, we served several churches, she as organist and children's choir director, and I as a choir and youth director. After receiving my master's degree in music, I taught for one year in a Jackson high school, followed by six years of teaching at the University of Southern Mississippi, during which time I also completed a doctoral program at Northwestern University in Evanston, Illinois. In 1970, after completion of my D.M. degree, we moved to Minneapolis, where for 37 years I taught voice and voice pedagogy at the University of Minnesota, until retiring in May 2007 as professor emeritus.

Between the ages of 15 to around 40, I was a very active semi-professional tenor soloist, performing extensively in recital, oratorio, and opera formats. But upon reaching my mid-40s, it became clear that the once-flourishing young tenor on the block was gradually being replaced by younger tenors on the block. Many performance-oriented workers experience age-discrimination, and in the classical voice performance world it's the sopranos and tenors who feel most of the effects, primarily because most opera roles for these voices feature young characters. To be sure, getting older influenced the choices available in my life's direction.

So, beginning in the early 1980s I went through a somewhat typical mid-life crisis, which required some serious soul-searching. At that point I finally began realizing my career had been set on automatic pilot, determined largely by professional responsibilities and obligations, including performances and teaching duties, plus the needs and family matters we all address. At that time I became more and more aware of my age-related decline in physical conditioning, which I'll discuss in more detail later when we take up health issues. In other words, not only was I getting older but my life was also swinging out of balance. I was certainly not prepared for the looming reality of growing old—and certainly not of dying—two topics no one that age enjoys contemplating.

One common strategy for people involved in public performance professions is to gravitate toward teaching. In my case, I gradually transformed myself from the role of *performer-teacher* to that of *teacher-performer*, and began writing manuals that summarized my ideas about singing. To shorten the story, by the late 1980s I'd written, with Bettye's assistance, a voice manual titled *Voice Adventures*, which we self-published and marketed moderately successfully for a few years. Then, in the early 1990s, Paul Nockleby, who later became my agent and editor, approached me about promoting my book to a major publisher, and I agreed, albeit at first somewhat reluctantly. The results of his search were more rewarding than I ever expected. Through Paul's mediation, McGraw-Hill contracted with us for two books: *Adventures in Singing*, a very successful publication, now in its fourth edition (2008), and *Basics of Vocal Pedagogy* (1998), a widely adopted voice teaching text. A decade later Paul convinced me to write *The Singer's Life: Goals and Roles*, which he published though his company, Birch Grove Publishing (www.birchgrovepublishing.com).

The reason for my mentioning this career as a writer of books about singing is partly to establish my credentials as an authority in that field, but also to point out that the *holistic approach* I've taken in all my books forms the underlying theme for this book as well. In other words, all of my books are concerned with *integrating opposites* and *creating a balanced approach to life,* as well as *making the connections between the health of mind and health of body.*

We can also help ourselves by preparing adequately for the journey and garnering the necessary resources that enable us to cope effectively with the challenges we will face along our way. This book is the result of my own research into the problems and possibilities of getting older. I have written it with the reader in mind. And so it is my hope in sharing my story that you will also spend time reflecting upon your life, including your personal goals, and how you wish to reach your final destination.

We're all aging, and some day our physical existence comes to an end. The overriding question is: *Will we prepare ourselves to age and die gracefully, with full realization of our authentic selves, and having created a meaningful legacy?* This book is based on the story of my quest, and I hope you'll be writing yours as we proceed.

Acknowledgments

Before moving on to the first chapter, I wish to acknowledge some very significant people who helped give birth to this publication. As always, I am deeply indebted to my wife, Bettye, the first-time reader and editor of all my publications. Her affinity for books is reflected in her prolific reading regimen, which easily amounts to more than a hundred books annually. She has loyally waded through many pages of my writings, so I greatly appreciate her generosity of time, effort, and valuable feedback.

Paul Nockleby, my long-time agent, editor, and publisher, is the most influential professional associated with this project. Thanks to Paul and his excellent editorial skill this book was born from a very large manuscript. I hope that this book, like others we have produced together, will also meet the practical needs and interests of the reader.

Another key person is Sara Specht, a communications technologist at the University of Minnesota and a former associate in the School of Music. Sara has created a website originally designed to feature this book, which gradually evolved into a supplementary source of information for readers of all my books. Please visit the site (integralife-balance.com), and write me if you have any comments or observations.

Finally, I wish to thank my entire family for providing inspiration and moral support, with special appreciation due our three sons—Jon, David, and Alan—along with their affable wives. As boomers, they, and a host of aging citizens, will face some of the challenges Bettye and I have so far surmounted. We've learned some valuable life lessons from our aging parents regarding effective coping strategies for our final years, and greatly appreciate their role-modeling throughout our adult years. May we, in turn, serve as role models for our children and grandchildren, and anyone who knows us or reads this book.

1

Laying the Groundwork

A human being would certainly not grow to be seventy or eighty years old if this longevity had no meaning for the species. The afternoon [and winter] of human life must also have a significance of its own and cannot be merely a pitiful appendage to life's meaning. — Carl G. Jung

Yes, dear reader, it's true. We're all aging. Indeed, everyone begins aging at the moment of birth, but the process doesn't really pick up until we stop growing, which occurs sometime in our early-to-mid 20s. By age 30, it's downhill most of the way, although much of our youthful vitality may continue for another decade or so. Fortunately, those of us who are blessed with good genes and enjoyed a healthy lifestyle during our childhood and youth may experience a more gradual aging process, rather than an early onset, that is, providing we take preventive measures. We'll get around to discussing ways to slow down aging—physically and psycho-emotionally—but first we need to grasp the context and significance of the modern-day aging phenomenon.

The Global Aging Phenomenon

It's old news that we are witnessing a global aging phenomenon, what some people call a "senior tsunami". In 1995, for example, the number of people over the age of 60 worldwide increased by more than 12 million, at a rate of more than a million per month. Almost 80 percent of this increase occurred in developing countries. In fact, the fastest growing portion of the population in many countries is the over-75 age group. Less developed countries, including India and China, both of which are making fast economic gains, have even larger aging populations. In the U.S., a whopping 78 million baby boomers begin hitting age 65 in 2011. With retirement will come enormous strains on entitlement programs, especially Social Security and Medicare. By 2030, there will be about 71.5 million older persons in the U.S. (20 percent of the population), more than twice their number in 2000, when people aged 65-plus represented 12.4 percent of the population (AOA 2008).

Not only is the over-50 population increasing, the average life expectancy has been increasing at the rate of approximately 25 years per century since 1850. In the U.S. the average lifespan has increased from less than 50 years in 1900 to 78 years today, and we're not at the top of the longevity list. In Japan, the record-holder for longevity, women can expect to live to 85. More people are also reaching the centennial mark, and their numbers are expected to increase worldwide. Currently, the U.S. boasts a population of more than 40,000 people over the age of 100, up from a mere 2,300 in 1950.

Lifecycle Stages

> There is nothing to be unhappy about the fact that we are, as it were, delivered upon this beautiful Earth as its transient guests for a good part of a century. —Lin Yutang (1937)

Until reaching their mid-twenties, the majority of children and youth the world over are eager to become adults, because that is when they gain more respect, privileges, and control over their lives. Gradually, it begins to dawn on young adults that, although there are real advantages to getting older, there is at least one overriding disadvantage: the body's steady decline. Wisecracks about getting older usually begin with the thirty-year marker ("You can't trust anyone over the age of thirty"), become more pronounced at 40, and decrease gradually thereafter, as respect and sympathy rather than humor is shown to those observing these milestones. Actor Johnny Depp is known to have said upon turning 40 in 2004: "Growing old is fun." I admire his bravado in the face of aging, but I wonder if he'll still think it fun when he reaches the age of 80.

I recall a surprise party on my 40th birthday, which was attended by at least twenty friends and colleagues, in addition to the party's organizer, my wife Bettye, and our three young sons. I don't recall any special celebration at age 50, other than our traditional family gathering, but my 60th birthday was highlighted with a public concert featuring favorite songs, all thematically related to life stages. Our three guitar-playing sons and two daughters-in-law joined Bettye (pianist) and me (vocalist) to perform a few musical selections. The audience also participated by singing a few songs. In 2007, on reaching my 70th birthday and official retirement from the University of Minnesota, our family celebrated by making our debut as the Silver Tones, a band performing "Hit Songs From the 50s".

It's common knowledge there are notable stages in a person's life. The simplest division consists of two stages, with the first half beginning at birth and climaxing at midlife (around 40-50). As Joseph Campbell describes the two stages, in the first half of life we serve society (engagement), and in the second half of life we turn inward (disengagement). The goal in the first half of life is to develop into a responsible adult, to learn and work in a trade or profession, to develop a social network (family, friends), and to serve the greater society. In the second half of life (after we have passed through our 40s and 50s) children gradually move out of their home nest, freeing parents to focus on areas that have been neglected due to earlier challenges associated with building a career, raising a family, and accumulating material possessions, including a stable living situation. Attention turns to mind-body concerns and social issues in the second half of life.

In *Reflections on the Art of Living* (Osbon 1991), Joseph Campbell proposes three stages of late adulthood:

• *Midlife Adulthood* (to 50s). Career-minded persons who have been motivated toward achieving success in their chosen field may face waning expectations of receiving rewards for goals not accomplished. Gradually, as one becomes more concerned with matters of the heart— by focusing more on family and friends instead of achievement or prestige—inappropriate ego issues may be sublimated. Growing older and encountering possible age discrimination, individuals may voluntarily or involuntarily step down from long-term careers to pursue other options. This can be a very stressful period, when children leave the nest, and finances associated with college educational expenses and retirement are strained, especially if a long-term career position is lost. Recent studies indicate that individuals in their 40s are more prone to suicide than any other age, so the midlife crisis phenomenon is most likely real.

• *Senior Adulthood* (to 70s) This empty-nest period offers time for self-reassessment and new beginnings, a "young-old" stage marked by retirement from full-time work, but the possibility of interesting part-time employment, including social service areas for volunteers. This period is the time to prepare for old age and enjoy meaningful activities, such as travel, hobbies, special causes, and increasing attention to family and friends. Unfortunately, this is the period when the body begins its inevitable decline, climaxing typically in the next and final stage.

• *Old Age* (beyond 80s) This final "old-old" stage is associated with surviving mind-body issues and leaving a worthwhile legacy. It is a time for reflecting more profoundly on life, dying and death, and setting one's house in order. Ideally, one has time and inclination to focus on achieving a spiritual transcendence that extends beyond the confines of the physical world. The diminishing of mind-body vitality may be equal (in reverse order) to the growth and development of childhood to youth.

Yet another popular lifecycle division includes three broad stages: youth, middle age, and old age. W. Somerset Maugham seems to have preferred this division. As he wrote in *The Narrow Corner* (1952):

I have always been attracted by the idea of the Brahmans* that a man should devote his youth to study, his maturity to the duties and responsibilities of a householder, and his old age to study, abstract thought, and meditation on the Absolute. [*traditionally, the highest class in India]

It seems reasonable to describe the middle years (ages 40 to 60) as the high-noon of life, when characteristics of youth and old age are in rough equilibrium. Though physical powers are declining, most middle-aged people remain in good health, with few major life-threatening illnesses, capable of easily accomplishing most physical tasks. Mental acumen also remains intact, and, with an added boost from life experiences, a greater sense of emotional maturity is gained, and with that maturity comes wisdom. At this stage most people are fairly secure financially, working careers are firmly established, and social life is still vibrant, especially for couples with children of wide-ranging ages.

Not everyone gets to enjoy these middle decades without challenges to health and prosperity. Sadly, I've witnessed younger relatives, friends, colleagues, and students suffer terminal illnesses or accidents, dying before they were able to enjoy their full day in the sun. I've also known many people who suffer from chronic illnesses and disorders far more serious than my few afflictions. But these have been the exception rather than the rule.

Levels of Human Development

In addition to passing through chronological stages, we also progress through levels of needs, from basic survival to spiritual transcendence. Abraham Maslow (1970) listed the following in his famed "pyramid of needs":

• *Biological*—food, drink, rest, oxygen, sexual expression, and tension release.

• *Safety*—security, comfort, tranquility, and freedom from fear.

• *Attachment*—to love and be loved, including family, friends, and others.

• *Esteem*—competence, self-confidence and self-worth, and respect of others.

• *Cognitive*—knowledge, skills, understanding, and novelty.

• *Aesthetic*—order and beauty.

• *Self-actualization*—potential fulfillment and meaningful goals.

• *Transcendence*—spirituality and cosmic identification.

People of all ages have the same basic needs. If all goes well, by age 50 the first six needs will have been met on a regular basis, but it's possible that the last two—self-actu-alization and transcendence—are still unrealized, the for-mer in terms of feeling one's potential has been fulfilled, and the latter as a sense of deepened spirituality and cos-mic identification.

One of my favorite philosophers, Ken Wilber, describes human growth and development along this axis: precon-ventional, conventional, and postconventional.

• The *preconventional* or *egocentric* level begins at birth, with physical sensory-motor responses, and progresses through a series of psycho-emotional responses that derive from narcissistic, hedonistic, and magic-impul-sive drives typically associated with children up to ages 5-6. Persons who work with children of early ages readily recognize egocentric personality characteris-tics in tiny tots, especially when they reach the "terri-ble two's", when the entire world supposedly revolves around them. As the news media reminds us daily, some adults retain various degrees of egocentric traits, and some even regress to the preconventional level when severely stressed, sometimes with alarming signs of pathology. Because brain development has not reached the rational level, belief systems at the preconventional level are based on a magical, child-like view of reality that typically include a belief in supernatural phenom-ena. Just imagine a Harry Potter type of world.

• The *conventional* or *ethnocentric* level begins some time after age 6-7, when the child begins to take more notice of the feelings of others. This shift from selfish-ness to empathy generally settles in from age 7 to ado-lescence, when children become more conformist and socio-centric, indicating that their interest and con-cern are focused more on others, beginning with fam-ily and peers and moving on to larger groups—tribe, school, and nation. This move from "me" to "us" is often referred to as the "good boy", "nice girl" stage of moral development. As all adults know, adolescents are extremely connected by membership in peer groups that require considerable conformity in terms of appearance, speech, and behavior, epitomized negatively in the formation of gangs. Unfortunately, many people get stuck at this level, with belief systems that are very conservative, based on authority, and committed to absolute interpretations that may or may not be true. On social levels, conventional folk show strong allegiance to their social groups, from family and peers to nation, with a stance of "it's my group or country, right or wrong", a perspective largely founded on traditional myths and folklore.

• The highest developmental level—*postconventional* or *world-centric*—is attained when persons evolve from the conventional or socio-centric level to become rational, highly conscientious individuals. At this level, international organizations came into being, such as the United Nations and the World Council of Churches, with the humanitarian goal of uniting the world's peoples in common causes. It's pertinent to note that most U.S. citizens at the conventional-level tend not to endorse most international organizations, ostensibly because of suspicions that the goals of international social, political, and economic institutions do not serve the best interests of the U.S. and undermine our sovereignty. And it's likely true that most citizens in most countries feel the same way. It's encouraging that many world leaders may be said to have attained the postconventional or world-centric level, even though the general populations they represent remain mostly at the conventional or ethnocentric level.

Wilber goes on to explain that within the general postconventional level, there are two higher-level tiers:

Tier 1—the *pluralistic relativism level*—is represented by highly idealistic and altruistic persons who support such "green" causes as ecology, cultural diversity, and world peace, as exemplified in the general beliefs and behaviors exhibited by many of the 1960s boomer generation. The term "political correctness" is attributed to a segment of individuals at this level, which explains why some critics refer to them as "do-gooders". The extremely tolerant belief that all ideas, beliefs, customs, traditions, and so on are equally valid, that no one has "the truth" (except them) is what Wilber and other critics consider a negative contribution by these well-meaning, sensitive folk. More explanation will be provided later.

Tier 2—the *integral, transcendental, or cosmo-centric level*—is based on autonomous thought and behavior, a belief system and a mystical approach to life that embraces all the truths of the other levels. Individuals at this level are open to receiving new truths based on experiential evidence, including spiritual truths gained through prayer and deep meditation, and, in practice, living a balanced or integrated (non-dual) life. Wilber estimates that less than two percent of the world's population has achieved this highest tier of development, so there's lots of room for more company.

Wilber's perspective helps us see that most of the social problems the world faces are the result of most people's psycho-emotional, social, and moral developmental being stuck at the lower levels. To summarize:

• The *preconventional level* is represented mostly by primitive types of people (most of whom existed in our ancient past) whose behavior stems from natural urges and magical belief systems. Young children also represent this stage.

• The *conventional level* is represented by a majority of the world's citizens, primarily mythic-fundamentalists and nationalists who put their primary allegiance in their socio-ethnic groups, right or wrong. Children typically grow into this level around ages 6-7, as they become more socialized, and remain at this level through adolescence, and if development is checked, may remain at this level for the rest of their life.

• The *postconventional level* is represented by another large segment of population that is primarily world-centric, and located in the most highly developed countries, where scientific and economic progress is valued. Persons who continue gaining greater awareness and understanding of the world through continuing educational life experiences tend to reach this general level, which entails two tiers. For Wilber, the *first tier* is represented by the pluralistic, relativistic "greens", an increasingly influential population, and the *second tier* is represented by a small percentage of enlightened people holding a cosmo-centric perspective, with an integral and balanced approach to life.

Developing Mind-Body Awareness

In working with hundreds of voice students over four decades, I've learned a great deal about how people learn—through observation, trial and error, workshops, readings, and, most importantly, through helping students make positive changes. One instructional challenge has remained: to convince students to use a full-length mirror when practicing—so as to observe their body alignment, mannerisms, attitude, and other visual cues—or to listen attentively to recordings of their practice sessions. Most students consider these assignments distasteful and fail to incorporate them into their regular study schedules. I have gradually come to realize that the reason for their negative responses is most likely because these technological devices—both the low-tech mirror and the high-tech recorder—reveal too much about ourselves. It seems people prefer living in a fantasy world, harboring self-images that may be somewhat deluded, making it harder to accept reality. Moving forward requires clear eyesight and clear thinking.

Psychologist Jean Piaget pioneered research in *cognitive development*, the process of acquiring knowledge through reasoning, intuition, or perception. On a practical level, we first learn how to use our bodies, and then—in order—we learn how to manage objects, symbols, concepts and ideas. If our development continues to the highest level, we move beyond the realm of ideas to the transpersonal or transrational (beyond self and reason).

Piaget's four levels of cognitive development—sensorimotor, preoperational, concrete operational, and formal operational—are considered applicable across all human cultures. It is worth noting that Piaget's levels correspond to Wilber's preconventional (sensorimotor, preoperational), conventional (concrete operational), and postconventional (formal operational) levels discussed earlier.

The conclusion I draw from Joseph Campbell, Abraham Maslow, Ken Wilber, and Jean Piaget is this: *the more knowledge of self and the environment an individual has, the more highly developed his or her level of consciousness.* Developing objective and accurate awareness of what's going on around us—a separate learning experience from that of memorizing factual data, concepts, etc.—requires a highly specialized intelligence and attention. How often do we take time to objectively and dispassionately pay attention to our thoughts and behaviors, thoughtfully analyzing and reflecting, with a non-judgmental attitude and no emotional strings? Most of us are extremely challenged to observe ourselves objectively, and this includes thoughts about our physical appearance.

Techniques for improving body-mind awareness also include Alexander Technique, yoga, and meditation. Highly skilled practitioners in meditation report achieving a higher level of consciousness, described as emptiness or wholeness, a concept difficult to grasp for persons who've never had a mystical experience. The abundance of media reports extolling the mental and physical achievements of Christian, Hindu, and Buddhist practitioners in meditative practices, as well as those skilled in the gentle forms of the so-called martial arts, such as Tai Chi Chuan, Qigong and Karate, demonstrate the capacity of humans to achieve extraordinary mind-body feats.

The Spiritual Dimension

Ever since the Renaissance era, the twilight of modernity, we Westerners have increasingly considered the physical dimension more real than the nonmaterial dimension of mind or spirit. However, no one has been able to dismiss the reality of a nonmaterial realm consisting of ideas and emotions, and their fundamental role in motivating behavior. I'm inclined to consider matter and mind as complimentary manifestations of a single unified material-spiritual reality. As the love-and-marriage song goes: "You can't have one without the other"!

Although many people are reluctant to recognize a spiritual dimension, I suspect their hesitation has to do more with terminology and interpretation than actual denial of spiritual reality. The terms "religion", "faith", and "spirituality" are so rife with meanings that it's easy for misunderstandings to occur. I will assume that most readers recognize some level of spirituality, and are interested in developing to the highest possible level. The point here is that, if an individual hasn't attained a high level of spiritual development in the first five decades of life (a highly difficult achievement due to our typically hectic modern lifestyles), it's still possible to spend one's remaining years in developing a deeper spiritual life. In short, it's never too late, nor is it impossible, as there are plenty of available how-to books and guidelines.

According to Helen Nearing (*Light on Aging and Dying*, 1995), the individual's quest for transcendence follows three stages: the first for learning, the second for household duties and social service, and the third for spiritual growth, which involves exploring one's higher self through meditation, abstract thought, and reflection. This third stage for spiritual growth is often what we can look forward to in retirement.

Any discussion of belief is bound to arouse strong emotions, even from thinkers. But in our quest for truth, it's essential to know what we believe—and why we believe it. So I hope you will consider the information I've proffered as it's intended: an opportunity for us to rethink where we stand regarding our principal beliefs.

Philosopher Bertrand Russell (1956) pictures the human lifecycle as a flowing stream:

> *An individual's human existence should be like a river—small at first, narrowly contained within its bounds, and seeking passionately past boulders and even waterfalls. Gradually the river grows wide, the banks recede, the waters flow more quietly, and in the end, without any visible break they become merged in the sea and painlessly lose their individual being.*

While reading the above summary of stages, needs, and levels, perhaps you have reflected on where you stand regarding each area. Here are some questions to consider: What life stages have you completed, and where are you now? What needs have been met and which ones remain to be fulfilled? What developmental moral, psycho-emotional, or spiritual levels have you achieved? Are you satisfied with the levels you've reached? If not, where would you like to be? I encourage you to think about these questions, and also take time to jot down some thoughts as they come into your mind. You may want to consider keeping a pad and pen available as you continue.

My Personal Quest

I undertook a four-year quest to explore, identify, and clarify my religious beliefs, based on the conviction that they should be substantiated by critical inquiry. So, rather than simply accepting blindly what someone has taught or written, my goal at the outset was to seek the highest understanding possible that dependable, documented evidence could provide. Another guideline I've tried to follow: it shouldn't matter how many people believe a certain aspect or tenet of any religion, only that the belief makes good sense in light of 21st-century knowledge.

As I've indicated, over my lifetime I've spent a lot of time focusing on ultimate life issues through reading, reflecting, and studying, and this book is the accumulated result. As an undergraduate philosophy major, I was introduced to some of the profound life issues discussed by the world's great thinkers. Thankfully, because I was generally well disposed to moderate religious perspectives through my home church, which was mainline Christian in its orientation, there were no spiritual upheavals resulting from my broadening ideological horizons. In completing my philosophy major I took several courses, including history of philosophy and religions, Bible, ethics, logic, and aesthetics. During this period I entertained the idea of becoming a Methodist minister, completed correspondence study for a preacher's license, and worked two years as a youth and music director in a Methodist church.

Shortly after completing the music major, I began a master's program in vocal performance, and my choral director and mentor persuaded me to enter education as a vocal music teacher, and I complied, as teaching better suited my disposition, talents, and interests. For the next decade my life was filled with music, with little time for readings in philosophy and religion, although I did gravitate toward self-help books in search of effective life-coping strategies. It wasn't until reaching a mid-life crisis in my early 40s that I began to read and study more outside the field of music, with a special emphasis on mind-body health.

Integrating Opposites

The historical concept of *dualism* is well documented, especially in Western thought. In contrast, ancient Eastern spiritual traditions (Hinduism, Buddhism) remain grounded primarily in *monism*, a belief that all of reality is one substance, a non-dual reality. This doesn't mean that opposites aren't recognized in Eastern thought, but rather that they are ultimately viewed as one, just as man and wife are symbolically thought to become one in the ideal union of marriage. A cursory observation reveals that opposites abound in nature, in such dissimilar phenomena as body (matter) and mind (spirit), order and chaos, microcosm and macrocosm, birth and death, male and female, day and night (darkness and light), summer and winter (young and old), interior and exterior, hot and cold, means and ends, process and product, being and doing, form and content, positive and negative, cause and effect, and so on.

On one level, dualism is epitomized in the opposite tendencies of romanticism (right-brain characteristics) on one side, and classicism (left-brain characteristics) on the other. Broadly speaking, *romanticism* is associated more with emotionalism, subjectivity, imagination, freedom of expression, and individualism. Persons with romantic tendencies are motivated primarily by strong emotions, and generally tend to use subjective or interpretive procedures in forming conclusions, as creative artists ("feelers") tend to do. In contrast, *classicism* is associated with reason, objectivity, and formal discipline, characteristics that scientists and intellectuals ("thinkers") personify. Eastern versions of romanticism and classicism are found in the concept of yin and yang, with *yin* representing the principle of darkness, negativity, and femininity, and *yang* representing the principle of light, heat, motivation, and masculinity.

These general romantic and classic characteristics are also exhibited in the political and religious arenas, particularly with liberal and conservative groups, as represented in the U.S. by the opposing Democratic and Republican parties, as well as progressive and evangelical Christians. The more extreme political and religious perspectives are evident in the rhetoric and behavior of left-wing liberals on one side, and right-wing fundamentalists on the other. The inability of these opposing groups to communicate effectively is witnessed in the ongoing gridlock among our congressional representatives in addressing and solving serious national issues. The more moderate or centrist political and religious persuasions on both sides—conservative and liberal—may be loosely associated with classicist (conservative) and romanticist (liberal) ideologies.

One of my favorite books is *Zen and the Art of Motorcycle Maintenance: An Inquiry into Values* by Robert M. Pirsig. Although the author's theme is to explore the metaphysics of quality, a second theme running through the book is a modern picture of the classicism-romanticism conflict. In brief, two motorcyclists represent contrasting personality archetypes: *romanticists*, who are primarily interested in considering a subject from a holistic perspective; and *classicists*, who prefer specific knowledge of a subject, in this case motorcycle maintenance. In the book, Pirsig represents the classicist, faithfully committed to riding an older-model motorcycle that he keeps in excellent mechanical condition, simply because he appreciates knowing how all of its mechanical parts function, and enjoys working on it, though he isn't too concerned about its appearance. On the other hand, his companion cyclist—an ardent romanticist—relishes riding his handsome new machine in the open air, and though he shows zero interest in learning about its mechanical nature and working on it, he does like to keep it looking spiffy.

Based on the above description, in addition to the yin-yang characteristics described earlier, it's not surprising that these descriptions are at least partly correlative to stereotypical male and female personalities, with males representing left-brained classicists, and females representing right-brained romanticists. To provide some insight into this dichotomy and illustrate male/female differences, I submit the differences Bettye and I experience in handling spatial relationships. For example, when traveling by auto to desired destinations I have a fairly dependable directional sense, with an ability to visualize spatial relationships and sense where I am relative to the desired destination. If I need concrete directions, I prefer drawing or seeing a map, which I may refer to briefly, since I prefer finding the way according to a mentally visualized map and an innate directional sense. Meanwhile, Bettye insists on having every detail written down in a precise step-by-step format, with printed-out instructions from Internet mapping websites. She absolutely rejects the available printed-out maps, because visual routing tends to confuse her.

Actually, these gender-based spatial characteristics are thought to be genetically founded, presumably as internalized programming that has occurred over the thousands of years our human forebears spent as hunter-gatherers, with men taking long treks into the wilderness in search of game, and women staying close to camp, with such tasks as caring for children and gathering nearby edible plants.

Based on what we know about genetic factors—together with evidence such as the differences Bettye and I exhibit—

I'm convinced that women tend to be more detail oriented, while men are more "big picture" oriented. I want to strongly stress that such gender-specific characteristics may be found in the opposite sex. For instance, some women exhibit excellent spatial skills, and some men don't, as one female graduate student indignantly pointed out one day in class. So, lest I be interpreted as a male chauvinist, let it be known that I believe *all* persons, male and female, should be given every opportunity to develop *all* potentialities, in *all* non-sexual areas of human endeavor.

One aspect of aging is that both sexes tend to take on more of the opposite sex's characteristics, as happens with extra hair growth on women. Emotionally, women may grow more authoritative and outgoing, and men may grow more sensitive and mellow—generally speaking. Personal changes throughout the developmental process may cause temporary discomfort, requiring us to break out of our box, to expand to take in more of the world.

In closing, the following summarizes my belief about the need for integrating opposites to achieve balance and unity:

> *To function optimally in life we must learn to acknow-*
> *ledge, identify, and integrate opposites in everything we*
> *do, a challenge that involves an ongoing commitment*
> *to seeking and discovering a balanced coordination or*
> *integration of opposites in all endeavors and areas of life,*
> *the so-called midpoint, or Middle Path, or Golden Mean,*
> *where equilibrium is created, and dualism is resolved*
> *into a unified non-dual wholeness.*

Process Versus Product and Life's Journey

In the course of daily life we are constantly engaged in the present dimension, even when we're daydreaming about the past or planning our future. Actually, the present is our only dependable contact with reality. All past recollections and future plans exist strictly in our minds—in the ever-present moment. Because our lives can be so hectic, it's apparent that very few of us master the art of living fully in the present, which requires acute mindfulness and awareness. For instance, when someone is speaking to us, we may fail to give complete attention. (I plead guilty! When Bettye volunteers some non-urgent story, or explanation, I occasionally lapse into a superficial listener, and it's embarrassing to realize I'm not giving full attention to the person I consider my best friend.) Of course, one can also be inappropriately focused in the present moment, especially when overlooking past or current behavior, living hedonistically for physical pleasures, or not creating worthwhile future goals.

Making preparations for—and experiencing—a long journey to a desired destination provides a fitting metaphor for the life journey every human being undertakes. The ways life journeys may take vary considerably, some on intimate, winding paths—especially well suited for those who prefer traveling solo—and some on roads that provide more room for kindred spirits to join along. Throughout life we need both paths and roads—perhaps even multilane freeways—depending on where each of us happens to be in progressing toward our final destination. Almost everyone reaches a point in life where the going becomes arduous to negotiate, when our spirits are low, and we struggle to find our way. At other times we feel more comfortable venturing along a wider path (or road) in the company of others, a situation associated with religious communities, when spiritual quests are shared.

I think of students I've known who love taking courses and working toward a degree, yet who prolong the process for years. At the other extreme are students who rush through too quickly, eager to reach their goal. In this regard, I've worked with singers and students who slap-dashed their way through the preparation stage of learning music only to make fellow performers nervous in rehearsals and performances.

In both cases, one-sided individuals fail to grasp the complete picture. Process-oriented people tend to be perfectionists, while product-oriented people tend to focus on their goals, but lack two requisite qualities: patience and perseverance. In promoting the importance of process in achieving mastery (a worthy goal), George Leonard, instructor in the martial art of aikido and author of *Mastery: The Keys to Success and Long-Term Fulfillment*, explains this phenomenon succinctly (Leonard 1992, p. 140):

> *We fail to realize that mastery is not about perfection. It's about a process, a journey. The master is the one who stays on the path day after day, year after year. The master is the one who is willing to try, and fail, and try again, for as long as he or she lives.*

Of course the ideal approach is to integrate these two aspects into an overall unified process-product experience that includes setting exciting worthwhile goals and faithfully executing and savoring all the preparation and sequence of ongoing steps that build up to attaining the desired goal or destination. And this leads us to a useful metaphor about taking a journey.

The way I've taken has been mostly smooth, safe, and interesting, with some significant periodic challenges, and I'm grateful for my good fortune, thanks in large part to loved ones, friends, students, and colleagues who have accompanied me. At this stage, I like to think of myself as a curious 72-year-old learner, enthusiastically continuing life's exciting journey with a spirit of exploration, and the goal of gaining a deeper understanding of what is traditionally referred to as the Big Three: the True (empiricism), the Good (morals), and the Beautiful (aesthetics). From the outset of beginning this book, the primary strategy of my one-way journey has been to consider life's many challenging aspects as objectively and critically as possible, using a balanced approach that relies on the highest human faculties of reason and intuition, and supported by sufficient evidence (the known). My sustained hope throughout the four-year research and writing process has been to gain some higher-level insights that might illuminate some of life's most profoundly challenging issues—and, finally, to share what I've learned with others.

As we continue our explorations, I encourage you to think about your life's journey, including your primary mission in life, your dreams, and your goals. Where are you now—physically, mentally, spiritually—and where do you wish to be in one year, five years, ten years—at life's end? Every journey or worthwhile activity begins with a first step. And though we may take time out along the way to rest or just to enjoy "being" in the moment, our challenge is to continue making steady progress toward our goal or final destination. I hope you'll join with me throughout the remainder of this book, as we explore some serious topics related to aging, dying, and death—and, most importantly, how to cope effectively, in positive, proactive ways.

2

Seeking Meaning and Happiness

The Generational Quest for Meaning

Like their prehistoric ancestors, modern humans struggle to find meaning and purpose in life. This is often portrayed as a *religious* quest, but the struggle to find meaning can be a *spiritual* quest which is not necessarily religious. According to opinion polls, approximately 75 percent of Americans believe in God. Although there are significant differences among the generations, a religious outlook on life tends to prevail whether one is a member of the World War II generation or one of several post-World War II generations. And so, although the themes apply to subsequent generations as well, in this book we'll concern ourselves with the values and religious-spiritual quest of three generations we know the best: the World War II Generation, the Silent Generation, and the Baby Boomers.

Values of the World War II Generation

The oldest segment of the age 50-plus group—the so-called World War II or G.I. generation (who came of age in the 1920s-1930s)—remains the most religious, at least in traditional terms. Life for most persons in this generation is grounded predominantly in traditional religious communities and in traditional religious doctrines. The World War II generation built the America that for decades was respected internationally as a beacon of freedom and opportunity. Many men and women served loyally in the armed forces during World War II, while numerous civilians also did their part in serving the war effort. More than any other generation, approximately 427,000 service personnel gave their lives so that subsequent generations could live in freedom, peace, and comfort.

The World War II generation is "the greatest generation" profiled by newsman Tom Brokaw in his book by that name. All of us owe the World War II generation our undying gratitude. They grew up during the Great Depression, and they experienced a drastically different America from that of subsequent generations, as they endured deprivations, challenges, and hardships the rest of us cannot imagine. And these deprivations, challenges, and hardships prepared the World War II generation for a life attuned to simple pleasures, sacrifice, and careful stewardship of resources. Their legacy included core values of self-sacrifice, hard work, frugality, respect for authority, patience, duty before pleasure, and adherence to rules.

Values of the Silent Generation

The so-called "Silent Generation", who came of age in the 1930s-1940s, were a bridge between the World War II generation and the baby boomers who followed. These are approximately 50 million Americans, including me, who were born between 1925 and 1942. We were labeled "silent" because we enjoyed the benefits of victory during World War II without the sacrifice of involvement, and we managed to behave properly and obediently during the Eisenhower years and the early years of the 1960s. With the exception of those who volunteered to serve in the Korean War, we spent our teenage and college-age days in peaceful and relatively conformist pursuits.

The more adventurous members of this generation formed a small artistic population generally referred to as the Beat Generation. The "beatniks" were the vanguard group that paved the way for the "hippies" of the 60s. Thus, we were somewhat of a "blended generation" when defined in terms of ideology, religion, and spirituality, located somewhere in the middle of the American spectrum, with the inherited values of the World War II generation holding us tight during our childhood and youth. As with the preceding generation, our sense of meaning was largely nourished by traditional faith-based communities, together with a post-war consumerism boom and increasing scientific progress in technological areas. The Cold War cast a damper on life, with threats of nuclear war, and the McCarthy witch-hunts proved to be a disgraceful legacy. We were primarily a religious bunch grounded in traditional, conventional values, although many of us were also influenced by baby-boomers' values.

Values of the Boomer Generation

The most analyzed and dissected American generation has been the Baby Boomer Generation who came of age in the mid-1960s through the early 1980s. These are the 76 million post-World War II American children born between 1945 and 1964, comprising nearly 28 percent of the adult U.S. population. It is a huge generational group, making up the biggest wave of the "senior tsunami" which after 2005 (when the first of them turned 65) just started to "crash ashore."

Baby boomers have always had a distinctly privileged, affluent, some would say pampered, existence. Some of the technological and cultural developments during this era had a profound impact on American society, in both negative and positive ways, including: the proliferation of television sets and radio stations, which gave ascendancy to rock music by way of inexpensive vinyl recordings; the anger and activism unleashed by the civil rights and women's movements; and most of all, the onset of the extremely unpopular Vietnam War, which stirred up strong emotions "for" and "against", a youth-based counter-culture that broke away from such traditional values in religion, sex and marriage. Authority, traditions, practices, and behaviors were questioned and tested by the baby boom generation, with the result being more freedom of expression, more tolerance of diversity, more relaxed standards, and less connection to traditions of the World War II generation.

The baby boom religious scene also became more varied, as numbers of mainline Catholics and Protestants switched to more conservative evangelical denominations. Along with an expanded evangelical base came an influx of non-western religions, and a rapidly developing New Age spirituality that was influenced by the 60s youth movement, in conjunction with supernaturalism, paganism, and other isms.

For many boomers, life has been an inward-looking, self-fulfilling adventure, and it's likely the second half of life will be similar. Projections indicate that boomers will choose to work longer and stay physically active, remain technically savvy, and take better care of their health—as long as they overcome the growing obesity epidemic. The boomer's core values include optimism, team orientation, personal gratification, health and wellness, personal growth, volunteerism, and active political involvement. These values are considered a part of the postconventional (postmodern) perspective, and may also be thought of as "green", pluralistic values.

The Search for Meaning

Angeles Arien makes a case for the second half of life as a spiritual adventure that expands, deepens, and strengthens our basic nature. Arien's book—*The Second Half of Life: Opening the Eight Gates of Wisdom* (2005)—is based on myths and spiritual traditions from around the world. Arien likens these eight gates to *archetypal passageways* that deepen our experience and provide a map for the second half of life grounded in elder-honoring traditions. Each of these eight gates offers lessons that prepare and initiate us into elder-hood status. In brief, they are:

- *Silver Gate*—challenges us to welcome new experiences.

- *White Picket Gate*—asks us to reflect on our earlier life roles, and learn how to assume our new role as elders.

- *Clay Gate*—urges us to enjoy and care for our bodies, as well as accepting their limitations.

- *Black and White Gate*—encourages us to deepen our relationships in more intimate and mature ways.

- *Rustic Gate*—compels us to creatively enhance our lives, contribute to our communities, and leave a lasting, worthwhile legacy.

- *Bone Gate*—helps us find the courage to be our authentic selves as world citizens.

- *Natural Gate*—calls us to replenish our souls in silence and in nature, and to take time for reflection.

- *Gold Gate*—actively engage in nonattachment practices and prepare for our exit from this world.

It's frightening and bewildering to consider that our lives can go in so many directions in our senior years, and that it's totally up to us to make the most of what arises. The good news is that even under adverse conditions, we still have the inner capacity to seek new paths and find novel solutions to perplexing problems.

The noted psychiatrist and philosopher, Viktor Frankl (1905-1997), spent years in a Nazi death camp. He later wrote passionately about the importance of exercising our freedom, no matter how difficult our circumstances:

We are more than psyche; we are more than reactors to the environment; we are more than adaptors! We can open another dimension wherein lies our freedom of will, the human dimension.

With respect to his Nazi camp experience, Frankl declared that a person becomes a prisoner because of an inner choice rather than merely because he or she is locked up. Even in a death camp, a person can maintain a vestige of freedom and independence. A starving man in Dachau, for example, can give his last crust of bread to another man. Indeed, the one thing that cannot be completely taken away from an individual is his or her freedom to choose how to behave in any life situation or set of circumstances.

Frankl also spoke of an inner void (existential vacuum) that many people experience, having no purpose in living and a bleak outlook. He felt that any person who does not have a vibrant reason to go on living is doomed to confusion and misery. As we go through the second half of life, fear may come to dominate our mind. That's when inner resources must be called upon, and these include values, goals and challenges to give our lives meaning, direction and purpose.

Joseph Campbell also believed the only meaning in life is what we bring to it, whatever we ascribe it to be, and being alive *is* the basis of meaning. He taught that we have the choice to live in *rapture,* an ideal state in which we are filled with happiness or delight. To achieve rapture, a complete shift in consciousness is needed, from "out there" (future) to "here", in the eternal present. Rather than focusing on external worldly concerns, such as attaining fame, going somewhere, having lots of things, or needing someone, we gain happiness from our internal spiritual world. In religious terms, rapture is realizing that "the Kingdom of God is within us", a sacred space where our inner spirit or essence is free to explore the infinite.

The ancient Greek philosopher Heraclitus (ca. 500 B.C.E.) lived in a world of turmoil and change, and the new religion of Buddhism seems to have influenced him. For instance, he taught that "things love to conceal their true nature", that one must go beyond surface appearances to see reality's true structure and meaning ("It is wise to understand the purpose which steers all things through all things"). Most important, he taught that gaining self-awareness requires introspection and self-exploration ("I searched unto myself"), and one's instincts or inner resources are the path to enlightenment.

Heraclitus has many sayings worth pondering. Roger von Oech's book, *Expect the Unexpected* (2001) suggests using the following epigrams as meditation exercises. (Brief explanations are included in parentheses.)

- *Expect the unexpected, or you won't find it.* (Don't rely on your assumptions, be willing to explore options, prepare for all consequences, and pay attention to details.)

- *Everything flows.* (Observe changes in nature and appreciate turbulence.)

- *You can't step into the same river twice.* (Nothing remains the same, so be open to change.)

- *Lovers of wisdom must open their minds to very many things.* (Cultivate curiosity and see things in fresh ways.)

- *Knowing many things doesn't teach insight.* (Forget old assumptions and interpretations, and be creative with all available information.)

- *Many fail to grasp what's right in the palm of their hand.* (Become aware of obvious things, the many wonders of life.)

- *The most beautiful order is a heap of sweepings piled up at random.* (Look for meaning in random ideas, and beauty in the mundane.)

- *Those who approach life like a child playing a game, moving and pushing pieces, possess the power of kings.* (Assume a playful attitude in solving problems.)

- *While we're awake, we share one universe, but in sleep we turn away to a world of our own.* (Give attention to your dreams and visions.)

- *Dogs bark at what they don't understand.* (Be careful of criticizing things you don't understand.)

- *Donkeys prefer garbage to gold.* (Recognize that people value different things, that significant projects require work, and that things change their value.)

- *Every walking animal is driven to its purpose with a whack.* (Embrace failure and lack of success as a way of gaining insight and wisdom.)

- *There is a greater need to extinguish arrogance than a blazing fire.* (Have self-confidence, but don't overwhelm others with your ego.)

- *Your character is your destiny.* (Set worthwhile goals you believe in, and work hard to achieve them.)

- *The sun is new each day.* (Welcome fresh opportunities to forget and forgive past mistakes, and move forward creatively.)

The sum of ideas expressed by Frankl, Campbell, and Heraclitus is this: It's up to us to fill our lives with worthwhile meaning. Rather than expecting an outside force or deity to swoop in and take care of us, or blaming others for our pains and failures, we need to proactively seek self-improvement, engage in worthwhile activities, and create positive life experiences. This is the challenge for persons of all ages, and definitely for those over 50.

The state of happiness I'm referring to is not founded on materialism, such as owning a beautiful house with a swimming pool and tennis court next to a country club in Florida. Rather, developing a state of contentment requires striking a balance between satisfying essential material needs and developing life-enhancing, non-material qualities that help us reach our full human potential.

The Science of Happiness

> *Abraham Lincoln understood that happiness is essentially a way of looking at one's life. "Generally, people are as happy as they are willing to be," he said. His point: Happiness doesn't depend on what we have or what happens to us; it depends on what we think about what we have and what happens in us.* —Michael Josephson

Happiness is the focus of the World Database of Happiness in Rotterdam, which collects data on what makes people happy and why. Eric Weiner, author of *The Geography of Bliss* and a self-proclaimed unhappy person, used the Rotterdam database to seek out the happiest people in the world. Weiner found that the "happiest" nations, such as Iceland and Switzerland, are ethnically homogeneous, but ironically also have higher suicide rates. The "unhappiest" places are former Soviet republics, such as Moldova. We Americans seem to view happiness as an inalienable right, and unhappiness as a defect. Eric G. Wilson takes a contrarian view in his book, *Against Happiness: In Praise of Melancholy*, where he argues people need melancholy in order to be creative. Most people avoid suffering if given a choice, but writers and artists seem to use it creatively.

Scientists, psychologists, and sociologists give considerable attention to individual and group pathologies, but little attention to mentally happy people. Why are some people more resilient in handling life's crises than others? What motivates happy people, and what is it they desire in life? Martin E. P. Seligman, a University of Pennsylvania psychologist, in his book, *Authentic Happiness* (2002), says the time has come for science to undertake research into human emotion, to discover guideposts for the "good life", one of Aristotle's primary objectives.

In that vein, a 1996 University of Minnesota study of 732 pairs of twins found a strong genetic component responsible for mood and temperament. It seems our life's circumstances don't have much effect on the level of satisfaction we experience. Wealth, health, physical appearance, and socio-economic status have minimal effect on our "subjective well-being". People subjected to extreme poverty tend to be less happy than people who live above the poverty line, but once life's basic needs have been met, increased wealth doesn't seem to enrich life or make people happier. It appears humans may not be genetically predisposed to live a life of ease that great wealth promises. In short, we may gain more benefit from improving our "quality of living" than improving our "standard of living".

Seligman proposes that, rather than depending upon science to alter our moods through better body chemistry, that is, developing feel-good medication, a more sane, low-tech approach might be to work at developing "learned optimism" through cognitive therapy. Seligman argues that individuals can learn to inhibit the upper levels of their emotional set-point range by self-examining negative assumptions, savoring positive experiences, and managing the natural desire to acquire more. The goal is not simply to enjoy a range of pleasant emotions, but rather to develop a productive and meaningful life. Beyond pleasure, for instance, one might seek to develop long-term gratification, an enduring sense of fulfillment that results from maximizing one's strengths in worthwhile activities.

Tiger Woods, after winning the U.S. Open, British Open, and PGA Championship in 2000, and the 2001 Masters, became the reigning champion of golf. Although he didn't win a major tournament until the Masters in 2005, he wasn't worried about it, claiming: "I woke up one day and realized I don't need to be perfect." Compared to the typical perfectionist who is frozen by mistakes, Woods is a proactive learner, refusing to equate greatness with winning. Rather, his main concern is in his overall quality of performance, knowing that by focusing on performance the victories will come, and they did. Woods credits his family and charitable activities for providing balance in his life. His life's focus now centers on the work of his foundation, which includes a 35,000 square-foot Tiger Woods Learning Center in Anaheim, California.

Seligman offers no shortcuts to happiness, but he does offer three guidelines for meeting the challenges of love, work, and family:

• *Keep your illusions.* Bear in mind that perceptions change over time, and being positive may be more important than being realistic; the larger the romantic illusion, the better. Unfortunately, as we age the natural tendency is to relinquish or diminish our illusions or dreams, as the reality of aging ("I'm on a down-hill slide!") hits home. In general I agree with this "illusion concept", but I don't think illusions should override the truth, which can be discovered primarily through critical thinking and mindful self-observation.

• *Support others.* As a mature adult, demonstrate an interest in nurturing others, particularly children and grandchildren, who need positive guidance and reinforcement in their adjustment to the world about them. It seems that people who think of others in positive terms are prone to overlook and forgive minor trans-gressions, and thus will try harder to please them. Love and tender loving care, not indiscriminate praise, go a long way toward creating independent, self-motivated young adults and world citizens.

• *Turn work and life into play.* Seek a work and life orien-tation based on a passionate commitment to serve oth-ers, rather than as an opportunity to earn money, or as a career that requires a deeper investment in work to gain money, power, and prestige. Everyone has heard of people in mundane jobs who manage to enjoy ful-filling simple tasks, thereby making the most of any opportunity to improve life for self and others. Retir-ees, in particular, need to find worthwhile service-ori-ented activities to replace work careers.

Using a personal finance metaphorical approach to liv-ing well by spending our valuable hours wisely, one finan-cial planner (Levin 2005) offers five keys to earning a satis-factory return on life:

• Learn who you are and what you want out of life.

• Diversify among the types of worthwhile activities that give you the best chance of fulfilling your long-term life goals, and commit the amount of time and effort needed to aid you in reaching them.

• Rebalance periodically, at least quarterly, based on what is most important, including urgent needs, yet in accord with long-term aspirations.

• Pay attention to your life account; frequently review and evaluate what you're doing to attain all goals.

• Enjoy all that you have, including health, posses-sions, loved ones, freedom, and opportunities for self-expression.

To all these admonitions, I suggest four more. First, avoid seeking happiness in potentially harmful substances, such as alcohol, recreational drugs, or medications intended to calm or dull or heighten one's senses; but *do* seek happiness through pleasant physical activity and meditative disciplines. Second, take to heart Henry David Thoreau's pithy dictum for happiness—"Our life is frittered away by detail . . . simplify, simplify." Third, heed the wise words of J.K. Rowling's erudite character, Professor Dumbledore (*Harry Potter and the Chamber of Secrets*): "It's not our abilities that define us; it's our choices." And, fourth, rather than spending excess money on material things, spend it on worthwhile experiences: learning new skills, pursuing hobbies, taking exciting trips, or contributing to worthwhile charities. Quoting the great teacher/coach John Wooden:

> *We seek happiness in the wrong places and in the wrong form. The primary cause of unhappiness is simply wanting too much, overemphasizing the material things. Happiness begins where selfishness ends.*

In sum, by making appropriate choices and simplifying our lives, we are more able to focus on the goals that truly matter, and to effectively negotiate the complex issues associated with any worthwhile endeavor.

Downshifting and Enjoying Leisure Activities

The concept of down-shifting in retirement years could be compared to downward gear-shifting technique used in slowing down a car's forward momentum. Taking the gear metaphor a bit further, a steady freeway "cruising speed" that is both safe and economical, allowing occupants to relax and enjoy the passing scenery, could be thought of as the ideal condition for driving and riding. The breakneck speed of most Americans may be compared to more reckless, fast-driving habits of harried multi-task drivers, who tend to a variety of personal tasks while driving in busy traffic, including using their cell phones. To the other extreme, drivers going too slow on a freeway can also create hazardous traffic conditions.

Likewise, we have choices as to how we live our lives, at the extremes of very fast or very slow, or at an overall more moderate and balanced pace. The suggestion to "slow down and enjoy the scenery" needs to be heeded as we get older, not only because our reflexes slow down but because we've earned the right to savor each moment. Fear of boredom may also be a factor. Edward Hallowell, M.D., psychiatrist and author of the book, *Crazy Busy* (2006) says, "If you think of boredom as the prelude to creativity, and loneliness as the prelude to engagement of the imagination, then they are good things . . . They are doorways to something better, as opposed to something to be abhorred and eradicated immediately." I've discovered this to be a valid observation, in that some of my most creative moments have been when driving long trips (on freeways using cruise control) and allowing the mind to wander, or flying in an airplane and gazing out the window at a spacious scene of cloud formations and far-distant landscapes, or pausing when reading or writing to ponder an idea, as occurred when writing this statement.

On a larger scale, slowing down one's life pace might mean changing to a less stressful and interesting job, or sharing jobs (to reduce overall work time), or reducing the number of days worked weekly, or refusing a job promotion that might create greater stress, in effect negating worthwhile life goals. Getting off the treadmill of an overtaxed lifestyle isn't easy, but it can be achieved, provided one is willing to undertake an honest self-evaluation that includes drawing up a list of worthwhile goals, developing a workable plan, and making the necessary changes at a pace that's comfortable and effective.

Attacking the time-crunch problem also involves decisions about how we choose to spend our leisure hours. It's highly possible many Americans are squandering their leisure time, principally by watching TV, the one activity that has markedly increased since the mid 1960s. Indeed, Americans spend more than 15 hours weekly, which I'm embarrassed to confess matches my personal TV viewing time. Meanwhile, my wife increases brainpower by playing challenging games on the computer. In defense of my personal viewing habits, I select mostly interesting movies, newscasts, and educational programs, in addition to viewing an occasional sitcom or a special program. While watching TV, I often read magazines much of the time, especially during commercials, which are often muted. In addition to evening TV, I must confess that we've become hooked on viewing a long-running soap opera during our noon-time meal. I hasten to add that we use the commercial breaks to bus dishes or straighten up the kitchen, or read news magazines, so only 10-15 minutes are spent viewing.

Multitasking, however, may be overrated. Researchers at the University of Michigan discovered that for a variety of tasks, subjects lost time when switching from one task to another, and the amount of time increased according to the complexity of the tasks. Researchers also found that it took significantly longer to switch between more complex tasks. In short, on a superficial level multitasking may seem efficient, but studies indicate it actually takes more time, and the danger is that avid multi-taskers may lose the ability to concentrate on any single complex task.

The Satisfaction of Work

Work can be interpreted as either drudgery or play, depending largely on an individual's attitude. For persons locked into long-term employment positions that are either stressful or boring, retirement might look very appetizing—if affordable. If one is nearing retirement age, and needs to retain a position for a certain number of years in order to collect a pension and benefits, then the major option is to find a way to make work fun. In other words, an attitude shift is needed.

In accord with Seligman's recommendation, Joseph Campbell says that work begins when you don't like what you're doing, and I certainly agree. I've always enjoyed most aspects of my performing-teaching career—its challenges and its psycho-emotional rewards—so it's difficult to empathize with people who don't enjoy their work. I've known plenty of people in a variety of occupations, and I'm always impressed with those who are truly enthusiastic about their work, who look forward to going to work every day, and who take great pride in what they do.

One such person I recall was a long-term head custodian at Plymouth Congregational Church in Minneapolis. Clint was always upbeat, a genuine "can-do" person who greeted and treated everyone as though they were special, in addition to fulfilling his duties promptly and efficiently. He continued to work as long as his health allowed, and then volunteered his services as needed.

The highly respected organist/choirmaster of the same church, Philip Brunelle, also deserves to be singled out as one of the most proficient, positive minded, and content musicians I've ever known. In his mid-60s, indefatigable Philip exudes great enthusiasm and energy as he moves nonstop from one major music project to another, including frequent trips to conduct nationally and internationally. His goal is to continue in his church position until he dies, so he'll probably never fully retire, unless incapacitated in some way.

So, for those who enjoy meaningful careers, work is usually experienced as a form of play, especially as expertise is gained. At the prime of his life in Vienna, Sigmund Freud is said to have loved his work, compulsively living by the clock and the to-do list, as most accomplished achievers do. According to Swami Vivekananda:

> *Work like a master and not as a slave; work incessantly, but do not do slave's work. Ninety-nine percent of humans work like slaves, and the result is misery; it is all selfish work. Work through freedom. Work through love!*

Some people prefer working alone, while others choose a more social work environment. Most people seem to prefer a balance, with some time to work alone, and some time to collaborate with others. As a university professor, I've enjoyed a balanced work environment, from working solo at home researching, writing, and tending to administrative matters, to collaborating with colleagues and students in meetings, classes, and performances. Currently, as a professor emeritus, I spend most of my time at home, which allows more opportunity to pursue special projects. Regarding the loneliness experienced by writers, Don Hall says, "One disease of working alone—the way most writers work—is dependence on mood. Mood is no measure and flips from highest to lowest in a millisecond".

As a writer, I find that the term "work" can be interpreted broadly to cover a variety of activities. For instance, I consider my writing as a combination of work and play. While writing is a productive goal-based activity, I also think of it as a creative act, less so than writing a novel perhaps; but when I'm through "playing" at writing, I have something to show for the time and effort spent. So writing for me is a hobby, an educational tool, and a challenging form of play, somewhat similar to the enjoyment people get when playing challenging games. When involved in writing projects, I normally spend an average of 10-20 hours weekly at writing, so enjoying the process is essential, especially when the final product—a book—takes months or years to complete.

Learning To Learn

Since knowledge is power, our *capacity* for learning is the measure of our power to respond to life's challenges and opportunities. Even though we've always heard that "the best things in life are free", the pursuit of material goods is what primarily drives most people through their pre-retirement years. The challenge becomes *learning for its own sake*, and not merely as a tool for making a living. A burning curiosity is like a lantern in the dark, as it spurs discovery of new patterns and pathways.

Learning is the surest way we have to enrich our lives by expanding our horizons and deepening our perspectives in dealing with practical questions as well as fundamental questions, such as: "What is the meaning of my life?" and "Who am I and what kind of person do I wish to be?" Once the basics of life are secure, anyone should be able to take advantage of the many opportunities available for learning, especially in the U.S., where most people have access to such resources as schools, libraries, historical societies, art museums, and zoos, in addition to internet educational information, books, educational TV, and the like. The accumulation of knowledge can occupy a lifetime, and it is never too late to get started down that path.

Ironically, support for public education, from K-12 through higher education, has slipped over time, leading to program cuts that, while appearing necessary for budgetary reasons, often appear excessive. A parallel trend is the practice of colleges and universities to emphasize professional and vocational education, to fill jobs offered in the commercial sector. This re-tooling, while good for the economy in the short term, neglects intellectual tools for the long haul. These include critical thinking skills—the ability to analyze and evaluate a variety of conflicting pieces of information from a variety of sources using a variety of problem-solving strategies and tools, both independently and in collaboration with others. From my experience, the most effective path to developing critical thinking and creativity is a well-rounded, liberal arts education, which provides a basis for an expansive and inclusive world view, one that embraces all countries, cultures, and ideologies.

One unusual phenomenon of the job market in the past few decades has been the increasing numbers of highly educated citizens who appear content to work in less than glamorous, prestigious occupations. Two of our three sons illustrate this trend. Our second son completed a bachelor's degree in independent studies, and elected to join his wife in a move to a lovely farm located in Wisconsin. His wife, a physician assistant, serves as the primary breadwinner for their family, while he pursues home, farm, and community projects, including constructing and maintaining farm buildings, homes, and presiding over the local food cooperative. Another son spent four years post bachelor's degree, supporting himself since college days as a general loader at UPS, with the goal of retiring in a few years. Meanwhile, he's working part-time with a local charity in preparation for a new career.

I mention these two because both sons are well educated and articulate, well-read, sensitive, responsible, contributing members of society. Their stories illustrate that material success does not define self-worth, and that general education, not employment aimed at putting bread on the table, is the key to finding meaning and happiness in the long haul. What is true in the first half of life is doubly true in the second half.

3

Accepting the Reality

Aging: Some Not-So-Good News

An aging citizen in America today is the collective outcome of several developments over the past few decades: our traditionally independent spirit; wide-ranging mobility; increased prosperity; improved medical care; easy access to media-generated information; and our fascination with youth and beauty, along with other factors. Our independent spirit has encouraged us to follow our dreams—fulfilling all material wants, remaining healthier, having easy access to news and information, and pursuing the career of our choice, no matter where it may take us.

Our proclivity to follow our individual dreams has caused Americans to become uprooted from family and community. With the exception of recent influxes of family-oriented immigrant groups from Eastern Europe, Asia, and Africa, the formerly close-knit American family, neighborhood, and community continues to wane. Hence, if seniors are isolated and lonely in their old age, it might be because they've elected to separate themselves from their children and old-time friends, as evidenced by northern "snow birds" who elect to retire in warmer climes, far distant from their roots and surrounded by other old folks in attractive, gated communities. (It should be noted that there is a growing trend of transplanted snowbirds returning to their native home areas upon reaching old age, when they can no longer enjoy the charms of their adopted retirement communities and are in need of special care.)

Though youth is an admirable stage of life, our national penchant for everything youthful, fresh, new, beautiful, glamorous, and exciting undercuts our ability to age with dignity and grace. Recently this trend has gradually reversed, thanks to such senior icons as Clint Eastwood, Katharine Hepburn, Paul Newman, Sir John Gielgud, and others who have starred in leading movie roles as senior characters. On television, several elders have played supporting roles in TV sitcoms and shows, and some shows have even featured seniors, such as Angela Lansbury in her mystery series. On the other hand, with the baby boomers reaching retirement age, senior populations are expected to increase dramatically, so perhaps the media will create more movies and TV programs targeted to seniors featuring seniors in leading roles.

While seniors may feel their bodies deteriorating, along with declining libido and drive, the inner child or young person they once were is always present, though possibly squelched. In Anna Quindlen's poignant book, *Blessings*, 80-year-old Lydia ruminates on lost possibilities and stagnation of her shadow-like existence:

> *She could feel the girl and the younger woman, and she wanted them suddenly, terribly, as she had not wanted them before. It was as though all the people she had once been were contained inside her failing flesh . . . The curse of having young people around the house was that they were always so redolent of possibility . . . She had filled her days mourning that shadow life, and it had no more meaning than the chattering of monkeys.*

Visual Symptoms of Aging

For persons averse to discussing declining body functions, and easily discouraged over the concept of growing old, it might be preferable to skip this section. On the other hand, based on the rationale that having more knowledge can motivate us to take better care of ourselves, it seems that learning as much as possible about the aging process might help us forestall the long-term effects of aging.

The noticeable effects of aging are obvious. In general, our bodies tend to take on rounded or sagging shapes that are increasingly out of balance with the trimmer proportions of our former youthful selves. Typically, with the exception of back-rounding due to spinal curvature caused by osteoporosis, curves are the result of enlarged body parts, beginning with the torso and spreading to limbs and neck. Though most body rounding is due to abnormal weight gain attributed to overeating and under-exercising, some weight gain is natural. In most cases, along with weight gain, which is usually due to an increase in fat cells, comes loss of muscle tone, strength, and stamina. But, fortunately, the amount of muscle loss can be somewhat moderated through exercise of all muscle groups.

A telltale sign of aging is the condition of our skin, which is typically more sagging, wrinkled, dry, and blemished, primarily due to too much unprotected sun exposure in youth, but also because of gravity, which also has a long-term effect on bones, muscles, ligaments, and tendons due to compression, stress, and aging.

A few years ago I participated in a photo shoot with two fellow performers in which the three of us were huddled together looking downward into the camera. When I first viewed the photo, I was struck with how my facial muscled drooped away from the face, causing grotesquely distorted features. In contrast, I've noticed that when lying on my back, the opposite happens, creating a natural face-lift effect. Therefore, lying on one's back produces the least amount of facial sagging. Unfortunately, older folks don't have the flexibility or incentive to look skyward all the time, nor can most afford the costs of a face-lift.

Other obvious visual symptoms include the loss of clarity and sparkle in the eyes, the likely result of age-related eye diseases, such as cataracts and glaucoma. And there's also the obvious quality and quantity of head hair. Unless we resort to hair coloring, the natural aging color tends toward shades of gray and white, or speckled. I think one's natural color is best, for nothing appears quite so superficial as hair that looks so much younger than the person sporting it. Actually, graying or white hair can look very distinguished, especially if one has lots of it. But, as any older person knows, not all hair is desirable, notably the wild sprigs of unruly facial hairs that suddenly appear in or on the ears, nose, and eyebrows, the latter turning kinky and bushy. Such body hair growth requires constant vigilance, as it seems new ones are always sprouting that, if left untouched, can grow to inordinate lengths.

Such visual aging symptoms are evidence of *entropy*, the tendency of orderly systems to become disorderly, as exemplified by a rusting automobile in a junkyard, or the natural deterioration of all living things. The consensus among medical experts is that, beginning around age thirty, the average human body starts to break down, progressing at a snail's pace of approximately one percent per year. Biological research into aging describes a complex process in which molecular, cellular, and organ changes cause a progressive decline in the body's ability to respond to disruptions in its natural homeostatic equilibrium. The process of aging is most likely due to a combination of factors, notably genetics, hormonal changes, and lifestyle.

Biomedical Aspects of Aging

As recently as the 1980s it was believed that cells were predestined to die at a predetermined biological time, according to DNA's programmed "biological clock" memory that controls aging in living creatures. Although all cells don't seem to have the same programming, it was believed that the morphological (formal and structural aspects of an organism) and behavioral consequences of aging were strikingly the same across a wide range of physiological systems. In opposition to this theory, Jay Olshansky, a biodemographer at the University of Illinois, agrees with his gerontologist colleague, Steve Austad, and other researchers that there aren't any physiological determinants of mortality, that is, no molecular switch, ticking chromosomal clock, or somatic schedule that signals death. These experts claim that there is plenty of evidence in nature that the rate of aging is very flexible, based on comparisons of species' life spans, for example, three weeks for a fruit fly, three years for a mouse, 200 years for a quahog clam, and 4,000 years for a bristlecone pine, all featuring the same cellular processes. Austad suggests that the advantages of our human social system, in addition to our ability to manipulate the environment, will eventually be encrypted into our DNA, so that nurture becomes nature, with culture influencing biological destiny (Wright 2003).

Perhaps the most sensible explanation of aging is the "wear and tear" theory, which pinpoints the progressive damage done to cells and organs by the lifelong normal process of carrying out their functions. Some of the characteristics of aging at the cellular level include *atrophy* (deterioration of cells), *dystrophy* (malfunctioning of cells), and *edema* (excessive accumulation of fluids in tissue), all of which are precursors of more important morphological changes, such as decreased elasticity and compliance, destruction of nerve fibers, and abnormal tissue growth. Regardless of a particular physiological system, the behavioral consequences of age-related structural changes can be profound, with aging biophysical organisms such as the respiratory system and musculature usually producing slower and less accurate responses because they are weaker, less stable, uncoordinated, and lack endurance.

For instance, maximum heart rate and oxygen consumption decline approximately 1 percent per year, meaning that any physical exertion gets progressively more difficult. Moreover, between the ages of 30 and 80 muscle mass decreases from 40-50 percent, thereby reducing strength and slowing metabolism, and by age 65 the average senior has lost 30-40 percent of his or her aerobic power.

Researchers are now concentrating attention on one specific part of the cell: *mitochondria*, the energy-generating organelles that control metabolism and supposedly help regulate length of life. Mutations may cause mitochondria to operate inefficiently, thereby producing waste products called *free radicals* (reactive molecules), which are known to damage and weaken cells. In alternative fashion, deteriorating mitochondria might cause cells to weaken. In a parallel finding, researchers are discovering the advantages of fast metabolisms in prolonging life, most likely due to more efficient mitochondria that ward off free radicals. As proof, mice with faster metabolisms have been shown to outlast others by a third (Smith 2004).

One molecular geneticist, Cynthia Kenyon, has had some success in extending the life of worms from an average lifespan of several days to six times their normal lifespan, by changing hormone levels and enhancing the effect of fewer than 100 targeted genes, all of which produce favorable substances. Some produce antioxidants, some make natural microbicides, some help transport fats throughout the body, and some keep the cells functioning well. The one thing all have in common is their effect on aging. In general, the more active these particular genes, the longer an organism will probably live (Carmichael & Ozols 2005). In another study, a few gene-activating compounds (STACS) were discovered that reportedly help repair damaged DNA, and the most potent compound was *resveratrol*, a molecule produced in plants, such as red-wine grapes. Tests on several living species, including mice and fish, indicate an increase in vitality and longevity, with fish increasing 59 percent (Sinclair & Komaroff 2006).

The aging process is inextricably bound to *hormones*, a group of substances of variable composition produced in most living systems and transmitted by the circulation of various body fluids. Produced by the endocrine glands, hormones serve to regulate metabolism, growth, and reproduction by controlling specific chemical processes, and by coordinating the function of various groups of internal organs. Endocrinology is the medical specialty that deals with hormones, and an endocrinologist is the specialist to consult regarding hormonal related disorders. Hormone therapy consists of the administering of endocrine drugs, excluding anabolic steroids that can be dangerous when used excessively and indiscriminately, as we are learning from reports of athletes who suffer from a variety of negative health symptoms.

The growth hormone, a pituitary protein that drives our physical development, is only one of several that declines with increasing age, and the sex hormones—*estrogen* and *testosterone*—follow a similar pattern. For instance, the testosterone level in men drops about 10 percent each decade beginning around the age of 40, in turn affecting libido (sexual drive), muscle strength, and even spatial thinking. Replacing hormones can rejuvenate skin, bone, and muscle, but since the other purpose of sex hormones is to enhance fertility, there are some lifestyle tradeoffs. It seems that the price we pay for being sexual beings can result in diseased sexual organs, such as prostate cancer for men, and breast and ovarian cancer for women. Surprisingly, research studies indicate that longevity is higher for childless women and eunuchs. For example, during the 1940 and '50s, anatomist James Hamilton studied a group of handicapped men who had been castrated at a Kansas state institution. Though the average life span was 56 in this institution, the neutered men lived to the average age of 69, a 23 percent advantage, and what's more, none of them went bald. The effects of taking excessive hormones are well documented, as demonstrated by athletes who abuse testosterone, and in turn suffer from a range of ailments, including hypertension and kidney failure (Cowley 2001).

Stress hormones, in particular, play a major role in the aging process. During periods of heightened arousal, a class of steroid hormone known as *glucocorticoids* are released by the adrenal glands, in turn activating the shift of metabolism from anabolic (synthesis of complex substances from simpler ones) to catabolic (turning complex substances into simpler ones), by breaking down glucogen in the liver. When *glucogen*, a form of stored energy used by the body in emergency situations, is used up, glucocorticoids start breaking up protein, which causes muscle loss. DHEA (*dehydroepiandrosterone*), a steroid secreted by the adrenal cortex, also appears to play a major role in the aging process. As a stress-hormone precursor to *adrenaline* and *cortisol*, youthful reservoirs of this important hormone are gradually depleted throughout our lifespan. If your head is swimming from trying to understand this complex process, relax. The gist is this: stress hormones wreak havoc with our bodies.

Several studies of the effects of stress on aging have been undertaken, and the results are rather conclusive. According to Dr. Herbert Benson, president of the Mind/Body Institute at Harvard Medical School, chronic stress is linked to a higher risk of heart attack, high blood pressure, and insomnia, as well as more intense hot flashes for women, a lower threshold for pain, and increased anxiety, depression, excessive anger, and hostility.

In a University of California-San Francisco study, researchers found that chronic stress—even the perception of stress—had a significant effect on aging. Their study involved 58 women, 39 of whom cared for a chronically ill child. The women caring for sick children had lower levels of telomerase, an enzyme that restores the length of *telomeres*, the tiny structures on the tips of chromosomes that serve as a protection device, similar to the way tips of shoelaces function. Under stressful conditions they shrivel up faster than normal, and when they become too short, cells can no longer divide. As more cells die, aging effects become apparent, such as dry, wrinkled skin, weakened muscles, and deteriorating senses. Another discovery of the research was that these women had greater oxidative stress, a measure of damage done to cells by destructive forms of oxygen. Other studies of persons caring for ailing spouses have found similar results in stress levels (Foreman 2004; Carmichael & Ozols 2005).

The aging process is associated with increasing illness and fatigue, but tolerance to either is a highly individual matter, and closely related to one's emotional, mental, and physical health. For this reason it is difficult to develop clear-cut guidelines that apply equitably to all persons. For example, extremely hardy persons may be capable of sustained physical activity in spite of organic ills or consistent mistreatment of their bodies. In contrast, many sensible individuals abide by all the appropriate health guidelines, but still experience physical difficulties. The fact is that each person has an individual constitution (genetics, character, lifestyle) that determines how he or she deals with mind-body stress. And, for reasons not completely understood, some people are able to cope more effectively than others, though the differences may well depend upon an individual's perceptions and attitudes when coping with stressful events and situations.

In short, we have the capability of compensating for both our natural and acquired limitations; first, by developing awareness of them, and second, by forming strategies to deal constructively with specific problems.

The Aging Brain: Drain and Gain

Not too long ago it was believed that we lose massive amounts of brain cells throughout the aging process, beginning around age 30. But recent research shows that actual loss of brain cells is minimal through the aging process. On the other hand, the brain does gradually shrink, losing 2 percent of its weight every decade after age 50, primarily due to water loss and shrinking dendrites, from an average of 3 pounds at age 50 to 2.6 pounds at age 65.

Along with brain shrinkage, overall mental performance declines, notably in the areas of recalling recent information and processing new information; for example, learning how to use new electronic equipment, multi-tasking, or juggling more than one activity at the same time. After age 60, the brain has accumulated so much information that it becomes overloaded, causing long-term memory to become less reliable. In other words, the aging brain simply processes information slower when experiencing something, remembering it, and acting on it, somewhat similar to how a computer's hard drive remains intact, while processing speed slows down. This mental decline is attributed to slower activity in the frontal lobes, where data is processed, sorted, and retrieved on demand. In addition, some brain cells are lost through shrinkage (about 20 percent between the ages of 50 and 90) in the deep hippocampus area of the brain, causing a decrease in the brain's ability to produce the chemical messengers acetylcholine, dopamine, and serotonin. Reportedly, the loss of serotonin is most likely the reason for disrupted sleeping habits in old age (Foreman 2001; Begley & Foote 2001).

More recent studies are revealing the role of "white matter" in brain development and function. Gray matter or the cortex area, serves as the "topsoil" of the brain, and is responsible for mental computation and storage of memories, among other essential functions. White matter, which lies beneath as the brain's bedrock, makes up nearly half of the brain capacity. It's filled with millions of communication cables known as axons (with synapses at the ends), and the sheath that coats them is a white, fatty substance called *myelin*. Neuroscientists now speculate that the quality of the myelin sheath plays an important role in insulating and protecting axons, in addition to increasing the speed of nerve impulses. So it now seems that white matter is just as critical as gray matter in explaining how we master mental and social skills, as well as why it's hard for old dogs (like me) to learn new tricks. Moreover, this discovery helps explain why it's crucial to develop certain complex skills—such as language or playing a musical instrument—at an early age, when challenging mind-body activities hasten and strengthen myelin production. Of course, old folks can still learn, but it takes a different type of learning that involves using the synapses directly (Fields 2008). Scientists may yet discover a way to strengthen myelination, perhaps in time to help some of us maintain and perhaps regain some brain functions.

To summarize, the decline of brainpower occurs on several fronts (Begley & Foote 2001):

• *Frontal lobes*, the seat of higher mental activity, shrink as much as 30 percent by age 90, causing a shortening of attention span and making it more difficult to multi-task.

• *Anterior cingulated gyrus*, the region responsible for impulse control and emotional regulation, loses D2 receptors that snare dopamine, a chemical associated with pleasant feelings, making it more difficult to enjoy former pleasant sights or memories, and decreasing the ability to hold one's tongue (I know the feeling).

• *Temporal lobes*, which control many activities, including speech and hearing, can shrink about 20 percent by age 90, though loss of hearing might actually be due to damage to the nerves that connect the ear with the brain.

• *Substantia nigra,* the part of the brain responsible for fine, highly coordinated motor activity (writing, sewing, playing piano), can shrink 30 percent by age 90.

• *Visual cortex,* the region that interprets and assembles messages sent from our eyes, has little connection to loss of eyesight or visual problems, which are actually caused by deterioration of the retina and the optical nerves.

• *Cerebellum,* the region responsible for balance and coordination, including controlling rote movements, such as bike riding, running, and walking, is more lasting, with no indication of age-related neuron loss (at last, some good news).

• *Hippocampus,* the region that forms and retrieves memories, can lose 20 percent of its neurons between the ages of 60 and 90, accompanied by a loss of acetylcholine, a chemical crucial in transmitting messages through the brain.

On the positive side, ample evidence suggests the typical human brain resists aging by growing new connections or *dendrites* as we age, especially for elders who remain mentally and physically active. The latest research shows that the aging brain is very flexible and capable of modifying itself through genesis and *neurogenesis* (creation of nerve cells), principally by growing new cells that divide and become healthy neurons. The happy outcome is the aging brain's ability to compensate in remarkable ways for losses in speed. For instance, whereas young brains may typically use one hemisphere for certain tasks, aging brains may recruit both brain hemispheres to help out in solving problems.

Also, the accumulated experiential knowledge gained over several decades, including the development of an extensive verbal vocabulary, helps older people cope more effectively in everyday life. This accumulated knowledge and experience lead to *wisdom*, which may be thought of as the ability to place things in context, and to make appropriate decisions based on limited information. Primarily for this reason, most persons occupying prestigious positions of responsibility and power tend to be over fifty years of age, as confirmed by the U.S. judicial system alone, in which nearly 40 percent of the 1,200 federal judges are over age 65.

In the brain department women seem to fare better than men, as male brain power fades more quickly with age, mostly due to shrinkage in the frontal cortex-lobe beginning in the 20s. Brain research at the University of Pennsylvania suggests that by age 50 the frontal lobes of men and women are of equal size, after which a male's brain size and overall mental acumen declines faster, including the ability to remember. One explanation for male brain diminution is attributed to genetic programming, which is affected by hormones, especially in the critical first 24 weeks following birth. Also, males tend to overwork certain thinking patterns to the exclusion of others, for example, maintaining typical male traits such as spatial reasoning but being unable to recognize emotional states in people (Dawson 1996). Here's substantial reason for males to work at developing yin-romantic and right-brain characteristics throughout life.

Of the five types of memory, at least three are affected by aging, the exceptions being semantic memory and implicit memory. The five types are (Smith 1995):

- *Semantic memory*, the ability to recall the meaning of words and symbols, is highly resilient throughout life.

- *Implicit memory*, the ability to reproduce conditioned responses, mastered skills, and a series of motions, usually lasts for a lifetime.

• *Remote memory*, or stored data, appears to diminish over time in normal people, though the problem might be more attributed to retrieval skills in sifting through a lifetime of accumulated information.

• *Working memory*, which is associated with extremely short-term tasks, seems to slow down between ages 40-50, especially when older people are placed in distracting environments.

• *Episodic memory*, which deals with recent experience, also dwindles slowly over time, beginning in the late 30s. An example of episodic memory would be having total and immediate recall of a particular poem learned long ago, but not being able to remember where you recently left your car keys.

There are four stages of mental dysfunction and decline, as listed below (Arnst 2001).

• *Age-associated memory impairment* (AAMI), as illustrated by occasional forgetfulness, primarily of new information, such as names of people recently met.

• *Mild cognitive impairment* (MCI) that includes severe or frequent memory lapses, such as repeatedly missing appointments, but no other mental impairment.

• *Dementia*, or severe cognitive decline, marked by large memory deficits caused by a number of diseases, such as stroke, substance abuse, head trauma, and Alzheimer's.

• *Alzheimer's*, a progressive brain disease associated with the apoE4 gene, that begins with mild memory loss and eventually destroys all cognitive functions, leading to death.

Dementia affects more than 40 percent of Americans over the age of 80, while Alzheimer's disease affects one person in four over the age of 85 (Restak 2002). There is little human dignity in this living form of death, which appears to be an arbitrary act of nature, though possible causes may range from genetics, trauma, and toxins to lifestyle choices. Sherwin Nuland (1995) says, "If there is wisdom to be found [in dealing with Alzheimer's], it must be in the knowledge that human beings are capable of love and loyalty that transcends not only the physical debasement but even the spiritual weariness of the years of sorrow." Fortunately, new medical research focusing on DNA and stem cells may yield some positive results for improving the outlook for Alzheimer's victims. As far as most old folks are concerned, the brain ages slower than the body, so most of us can rely on adequate brain functioning to keep us mentally active.

Interestingly, a person's age can be determined in at least three ways, according to chronological, biological, and psychological criteria. *Chronological age*, the simple number of years lived, does not automatically determine an individual's health status or performance ability. Longevity in life is largely determined by *biological age*, reflecting a person's overall health as measured by such factors as blood pressure, heart rate, and vital capacity. Perhaps of even greater influence, however, is *psychological age*, as determined by an individual's mental perceptions, overall attitude, and related behavior. Though we have little control over our chronological age, we have considerable control over factors influencing our biological age, and even more so regarding our psychological age.

Physical Symptoms of Aging

As we age, physical problems increasingly accost us, notably weakening of muscles and joint (tendon, ligament, and muscle) problems that affect movement and mobility, often the long-term result of inefficient biomechanics and repetitive-motion syndrome. Also, youthful injuries caused by accidents or playing sports can come back to haunt us with joint and limb problems. The important hinging joints, such as wrists, ankles, knees, hips, back, shoulders, and neck, are particular prone to wear and tear.

Though I escaped serious injuries in my youth, I managed to experience some in adulthood, including damage to both shoulder joints from over-strenuous exercising, and my lower back from lifting weights improperly. I also have a left knee that slips out from time to time, and has to be shaken back into alignment. The lower-back problem (two severely degenerated discs) is manageable through proper care and exercise, but stiffness in the back is more noticeable, and takes a while to loosen up. *Osteoarthritis*, a degenerative process affecting cartilage that can be set in motion by an injury or exacerbated by overuse, can develop into a crippling disease, drastically limiting mobility in old age. I'm hoping that my exercising routines will ameliorate my condition rather than aggravate it. Since I believe so strongly in the value of exercise, I may tend to overdo certain techniques, thinking that if a little exercise is good, perhaps more is better. Finding a proper balanced approach is the goal.

The senses are also on the front line of encroaching old age, with eyesight leading the way, followed by hearing, then the sense of smell and taste, and, finally, touch, though kinesthetic sense (balance, movement) may deteriorate earlier for deconditioned folk. With the long-term bombardment of various environmental noises, including loud rock music—especially when listened to for hours at high-volume through earphones—the younger generations, beginning with the rock-era boomers, will most likely experience hearing problems earlier than older pre-rock generations, possibly before experiencing visual problems. Bettye and I experience tinnitus (ear ringing), but so far we're still able to communicate fairly well, though we occasionally enjoy hearty laughter when one of us repeats what we think the other has said and the translation is completely nonsensical. According to experts, non-voiced consonant sounds are the first to not be heard clearly. As for eyesight, we've both worn corrective glasses, she since childhood and I since age 26. I'm told I have incipient cataracts, so they'll need to be removed eventually. I'm hoping that all the reading we do will strengthen our eyes rather than wearing them out. We read while using a treadmill, which can be challenging, especially when trying to decipher small print.

Another significant problem relates to quality of sleep, with deep sleep declining to half of what it was at age 20. High levels of the stress hormone cortisol can influence many aspects of brain function, including the biological rhythm that governs sleep. As we age, the length of sleep drops considerably and is more fitful, due to increased aches, bathroom trips, and disturbances that at one time would have been ignored. Long gone are the occasions of my sleeping 8 hours straight, without awakening for any reason. Following prostate surgery, my nighttime bathroom trips have been reduced to one, and occasionally two, but my normal sleeping time has ranged in the nightly six-hour range for several years, in addition to occasional snoozes during post-lunch reading hour and evening TV viewing.

Skin diseases are also prevalent among the elderly, especially so for those who have been—and perhaps still are—sun worshippers. I've had two basal cell skin cancers removed in recent years, so I'm diligent about scheduling annual skin examinations with my dermatologist. One thing for certain: Bettye and I now avoid long sun exposure, and when we do go outside we cover up as much as possible, including applying high-protection sunscreen.

The sun's long-term damaging effects can be easily discerned by comparing parts of one's body that typically have been covered during periods of sun exposure with sections that have not been covered. In my case, if the rest of my body were as clear and freckle-free as my swimsuit area, my overall skin condition would be excellent. Today, when I see older folks baking in the sun, typically with tanned but leathery, mottled, and wrinkled skin, I wonder if they're aware of the potential consequences. I'm particularly concerned about the young people today who are addicted to tanning booths. Who knows what problems they'll have when they reach their golden years?

Bone diseases such as osteoporosis are also a sign of aging, and can begin as early as the 30s. Women can lose up to 20 percent of total bone mass in the first 5-7 years following menopause. Bettye had a hysterectomy in 1979, followed by years of taking estrogen tablets. In recent years tests have revealed some noticeable decline in bone density, so she's been taking medication to retard the rate of loss. Most people have some degree of osteoporosis, and it seems the only recourse one has is to help prevent or postpone most diseases, primarily by eating nutritious food and vitamins (vitamin D, in particular), exercising regularly (weight-bearing balance training included), getting plenty of rest, developing relaxation skills for coping effectively with stress, and taking appropriate medications.

According to Sherwin Nuland (1995), the major illnesses among older persons are the so-called seven horsemen of death that hunt down and kill the elderly: atherosclerosis (artery disease); hypertension (heart disease); adult-onset diabetes; obesity; mental depressing states, such as Alzheimer's and other dementia; cancer; and decreased immune resistance due to infection (such as from AIDS).

Nuland says, "The very old do not succumb to disease—they implode their way into eternity". Though this is a grim scenario, it is the reality of what we face at the end. Viktor Frankl quotes Benedict Spinoza: "We cease to suffer when we have an adequate picture of our suffering." Nuland's image of the old "imploding their way into eternity" helps us face reality, and after we've accepted that picture of reality the end of life seems less threatening.

The Aging Voice: A Special Consideration

As a singer and voice teacher, I would be remiss if I failed to mention the physical symptoms of the aging voice, a subject rarely addressed in books about aging. The voice has been described as "the loudspeaker of the soul", the revealer of our mind-body state, and our primary instrument for communicating with others. We all know that when the voice isn't functioning well, we have difficulty expressing our thoughts and feelings with confidence and skill, which helps us maintain a sense of self worth and efficacy.

The following presents a general overview of an aging singer's voice (Remick, 1993):

A process of aging begins in every singer at, roughly, the age of thirty. The muscle tone of the abdomen begins to decrease. The lungs lose their elasticity. The thorax loses its distensibility. The neck bones become less flexible, and this affects the ability to raise and lower the larynx; the larynx loses bulk and muscle tone; the cartilage in the larynx becomes ossified. Joints on the back of the larynx can stiffen, and the result is increased breathiness. The vocal cords begin to thin out and bow; the surrounding connective tissue grows flaccid. Because the cords [vocal folds] do not close as easily as they once did, the singer overcompensates. He pushes. A still breathier tone results. Also, hearing becomes less acute. The singer's feedback system goes awry. One sign of age is that the pianissimo in the upper middle register loses its shimmer, and the nature and volume of the secretions in the throat change; hydration is more erratic; high notes become more of an adventure.

The symptoms of voice decline are very obvious to listeners. We're all familiar with the voices of older folk we've known, particularly the very old. Voice qualities can range widely, from weak and breathy to weak and scratchy, or perhaps somewhat strong, but rough, crackly, or growl-like. Think "Satchmo" (Louis Armstrong) for rough, and the mock witch-like voice for crackly. It's sad to observe the very old, such as those living in retirement and nursing homes, as they struggle to communicate with one another. With an inevitable loss of hearing, coupled with declining physical strength and voice, it's very difficult, if not impossible for communication to be effective. And the situation is exacerbated when seniors are gathered in groups, as happens in lunchrooms, where noise levels can be very high.

In closing this chapter, we end on an upbeat note. Regardless of all the negative aspects we've discussed thus far, I urge you not to lose hope or heart. In the next chapter we'll explore the positive sides of aging, including measures to take in maximizing our mind-body energy resources to get more out of life.

4

Maximizing Mind-Body Health

Prevention vs. Symptom Management

Our marvelous human bodies contain all the requisite substances and systems for effective functioning, and serve
as the sole vehicles for transporting us throughout our
uniquely adventurous and challenging life journeys. Even
so, reputable health experts consistently warn us that too
many citizens are not giving sufficient attention to developing and maintaining optimal mind-body health.

Scientific data showing the deplorable state of health
worldwide is consistently being publicized in the media,
generally indicating a steep increase in chronic health
problems, especially in relation to diabetes. Most of the
blame has been attributed to an increased consumption of
junk food and to such sedentary, time-sucking habits as
viewing TV and playing video games. We are also grossly
affected by an ongoing degrading of our natural environment, including polluted air and water, and toxic food
sources, in addition to ingesting harmful substances (recreational drugs, tobacco products, etc.), and undertaking
preventable, life-shortening behaviors that result in debilitating transmittable diseases, such as HIV/AIDS.

A highly talented former student died prematurely in
his early 40s, after a life plagued with obesity-related medical problems. In childhood and youth he had been seriously overweight, and the extra pounds discouraged physical activity. His diabetes began in his youth, and was controlled with insulin; unfortunately, proper diet and exercise was never part of his regime. When he began studying

with me at age 26 he was grossly overweight, and for the entire time I knew him he was unable to establish healthy eating habits and a regular exercise program. His poor body gradually succumbed to the diabetes in his final years, including declining vision, amputation of a leg below one knee and a toe on the other foot, stomach-stapling surgery, and, finally, a kidney transplant, which failed to function adequately. Within three months following the transplant he suffered a stroke and died, a tragedy that might have been avoided, or at least postponed for years, had he been more diligent with preventive measures.

For the past two decades I've considered mind-body health *the* number-one priority, and the rationale is clear: *only with good health and wellness can we function optimally in achieving our life's goals, and in the process create a general state of happiness.* It's a sad commentary that only a relatively small portion of the world's population achieves peak performance in all life activities, with the deliberate intention of preventing illness and maximizing energy from all psycho-emotional, physical, and spiritual resources. Another way of stating the obvious is to emphasize that a large segment of the world's population gives little attention to developing and maintaining optimal health and wellness, a do-nothing strategy I have difficulty in comprehending.

Developing Energy

Energy, which is the ability or power for accomplishing tasks, is essential in mind-body health and wellness. It's no secret that we gain energy from nutritional sources (food and drink), from environment (sun, air), and from a combination of sleep and rest. In recent decades we've learned the importance of regular exercise, even though only a relatively small portion of our population exercises sufficiently on a regular basis. In addition to physical sources, we also gain energy from cultivating supportive social relationships, maintaining a positive mental attitude, and behaving ethically and morally, areas to be discussed later.

Although everyone may not be capable of functioning at the superior level of Olympic-level athletes, each of us can make the most of our natural endowment and latent potential, no matter what our age or condition. For instance, at the ripe age of 72, I'm extremely grateful that my overall body-mind conditioning enables me to handle most of life's activities adequately, primarily because of my persistent attention to health issues.

Regardless of who we are or what we do, overall health and wellness improves when we adopt an active lifestyle, similar to athletes in training. Most athletes set specific short, medium, and long-range goals, aim for high standards in technique and performance, commit to regular self-disciplined effort and training. In their commitment to systematic and rigorous training regimens, athletes are able to produce a high level of mind-body energy for any given task.

As we age, motor units are gradually depleted; for instance, up to 20 percent of thigh muscles are lost between age 30 and 70. Although dormant muscle fibers inevitably atrophy (wither away), muscle growth can still occur with vigorous exercise and an intact neural system. We either "use it or lose it". We may not be qualified to participate in the Senior Olympics as viable contestants, but we can always increase our physical activity, if only by increasing the amount of regular walking, stretching, or lifting.

As with most mind-body functions, the role of opposites can be observed in muscle activity, such as the contrasting functions that occur between agonist and antagonist, fast-twitch and slow-twitch, tension and relaxation. How we learn to reconcile or integrate these opposites in a balanced manner determines how well our muscles function in assisting us with a multitude of tasks in fulfilling our life goals.

Exercise, Fitness, and Sunshine

Health professionals are increasingly placing exercise in a central position of importance in creating and maintaining good health. For losing weight and keeping it stabilized, exercise is sometimes placed higher than diet on the scale of recommended guidelines. Of the two types of exercising—*aerobic* (requiring oxygen, as in walking) and *anaerobic* (not requiring oxygen, as in lifting weights)—most experts claim aerobic is more important, though both types are highly recommended in creating a well-balanced exercise program. Aerobic exercise is particularly good for our brains, as it increases BDNF, a chemical that encourages neurons to form new synapses and strengthen existing ones.

Most people are able to walk, though some might need to use a walking stick for support, or walk slowly. The point is that any walking is better than sitting! Experts encourage novice walkers to begin slowly and gradually increase the pace, according to one's progressing capability. Running is out for many aging folks, but brisk walking may work well, with swinging arms. If not brisk, then at any pace that's practically achievable.

My favored option of aerobic exercise is run-walking, a balanced type that combines the beneficial qualities of both running and walking, creating a smooth-flowing hybrid form that resembles the speed of a slow run and the motion of fast walking. I use a treadmill set for an eleven-degree incline and a pace of 4.2 miles per hour for 30-45 minutes, for a total of 2-3 miles daily (16-18 miles weekly) and this seems to keep me in good condition.

Other low-impact aerobic activities include swimming or aquatic aerobics, skating, bicycling, stair climbing, and cross-country skiing. Of course, any type of outdoor activity should be undertaken with attention to previous physical conditioning, equipment needs, weather conditions, type of terrain, traffic density, and pollution levels. Stressful physical exercise, such as marathon running, is also known to depress the immune system by over-stressing the body and depleting energy reserves. Body parts can only take so much jarring and pounding, especially feet and leg joints, so running or jogging should be undertaken cautiously and limited in time and scope. Exercise gurus emphasize "fun exercise" as opposed to "punishment exercise." Of course, appropriate footwear is essential, along with clothing suitable for existing weather conditions.

With hindsight I regretfully recall the many hours I spent as a youth baking in the sun, hoping to achieve a glorious tan. In 2004 a dermatologist diagnosed two suspicious looking blemishes that turned out to be basal skin cancers, which happen not to be too dangerous. So I had them removed, and now must report annually to my dermatologist to have all suspicious looking skin blemishes examined. On the other hand, a controversy rages over exposure to sunlight. It's a fact that our skin manufactures vitamin D in response to ultraviolet (UV) light, and some scientists explain that the simple solution to the deficiency most people have is 5-10 minutes of unprotected UV exposure to the sun or tanning machines two or three times a week. However, other reputable scientists insist that the dangers for causing cancers are too great, and that it's better to get vitamin D from food sources. What's one to do? Strike a discretionary balance perhaps, with one day per week of sunlight exposure for 5-10 minutes, and the rest of the time depend on taking supplements.

Typically, young people naively think they'll live forever, so why worry about potential problems that sun worshipping might create when they're older. Alas, many sun-worshippers are habituated to frequenting tanning salons, which pose equally dangerous exposure to harmful rays as the sun. The real downside, of course, is the potential for developing skin cancer, especially melanoma, which strikes three times as many people today as three decades ago. Therefore, whenever possible it pays to avoid getting too much sun exposure; and when outdoors for long periods, all body surfaces should be covered, and exposed skin protected with a high-grade sun block.

In addition to various outdoor recreational activities, an overall exercise plan may also include typical outdoor tasks (for those who resist leaving their long-term homes for condos or townhomes), such as lawn-mowing, leaf raking, and snow shoveling. As a regular habit, aerobic exercise can be gained without spending much extra time, simply by taking stairways instead of elevators and escalators, and parking some distance away from an intended destination and walking. The overall objective is to adopt a physically active lifestyle.

Exercise options during inclement weather periods might include using a health club, walking in an enclosed shopping mall, or procuring some personal indoor exercise equipment. Special exercising equipment designed for walking, stair climbing, cross-country skiing and cycling work very well indoors, with the additional benefit of reading, watching TV, or listening to a radio while exercising. Aerobic dance provides a well-rounded workout that can be undertaken either at one's home or in a social situation; though it can be strenuous when led by overzealous young exercise trainers. And if music volume levels are set too high, hearing can be protected using earplugs.

Warming up and cooling down before and after physical workouts are highly recommended, with the goal of stretching and loosening muscles, increasing or decreasing blood flow, and increasing or lowering the heart rate. When the blood supply to muscles is increased and muscle temperature is raised, muscles become more flexible and less susceptible to strains and pulls. Depending on age, level and type of workout, and overall physical condition, stretching should take 5-10 minutes before and after exercising, and it should be done slowly and smoothly to avoid potential muscle injury, soreness, and sudden cardiovascular stress.

Muscle tone and strength can be improved through muscle conditioning exercises performed 2-3 times weekly for 10-20 minutes each. Exercises such as calisthenics (push-ups, sit-ups), isometrics, and moderate weightlifting require a more strenuous use of muscles, so they need to be exercised cautiously, especially when starting. Sit-ups work best when using a "crunched position," with knees bent, hands behind the head (to support the head, neck, and back), feet unhooked (not supported by a weight), and using slow up-and-down curling movements.

Increasingly, exercise experts are advocating weight-bearing workouts in conjunction with cardiovascular routines to ward off injuries, osteoporosis, and heart disease. Failing to strengthen muscles as we age leads to loss of muscle mass, flexibility, and balance. Beginning at around age 20, humans lose approximately one percent of muscle mass every year, which means that physical inactivity between ages 40 and 70 may result in a 30-plus percent loss of muscle, with an increase of fat and weight gain. Muscles are built and strengthened by workouts that create microscopic tears in muscle tissue. The body responds by repairing the tears with protein, which forms new filaments that increase muscle bulk and strength.

In practicing what I preach, I begin each day (seven days per week) with a two-hour exercise routine that includes a variety of exercises: (1) muscle stretching and strengthening (Qigong movements, yoga poses, and specific back muscle exercises, and moderate weightlifting); (2) aerobic workout (fast walking on a treadmill or outside); (3) cool down (Qigong and Tai chi); and (4) meditation.

Here's my typical weekly routine, which, admittedly, is more than the average person has time for or the inclination to pursue:

Monday, Wednesday, Thursday, and Saturday

• Basic body conditioning (30 minutes)—a combination of Qigong warm-ups, yoga poses, stretching and back-strengthening exercises.

• Aerobic routine (45 minutes)—fast walking using a treadmill set at 4.2 mph at an 11-percent incline to cover 3-plus miles; or an equivalent same-speed outdoor walk-run of equal distance.

• Cool down (12 minutes)—combination of Tai chi and Qigong exercises (self-massage).

• Meditation (30-plus minutes)

Tuesday, Friday, and Sunday

• Tuesday and Friday—same routine as other days, plus 20 minutes lifting light-to-moderate hand weights (5 lbs. pair and 15 lbs. pair for each hand), and a 30-minute fast-walking workout on the treadmill at 4.2 mph to cover 2 miles; or an outside walk-run equivalent.

• Sunday—same routine as other days, with exception of a 30-minute aerobic workout (instead of 45 minutes) using the treadmill, or occasionally substituting outdoor exercise lasting 30-60 minutes, such as biking, walking, or hiking.

In general, I try to temper my exercising by refraining from strenuous activities that might lead to excessive wear and tear of body parts, particularly any moves that might affect my lower back, which can be very sensitive to certain types of movements. Finding a balance between over-stressing and under-stressing body parts is the goal, the point at which one gets the greatest return for the amount of time and effort expended.

I realize that my exercise commitment is more than most people are willing to undertake, and this is understandable given the hectic pace of living, especially for anyone who isn't yet retired. But if good physical health is a priority in one's life, time will be found. I managed to begin a regular exercise routine for an hour or so daily three decades ago, at age 43, when I was heavily involved in professional activities. By sticking to a regular regimen for several months, daily exercising became a firmly engrained habit. So, if you're out of shape and low on energy, I beg you to consider getting off your duff and start exercising!

To summarize, here's a proposal for a weekly moderate-level exercise program:

• Daily muscle stretching and warm-up exercises, but especially before and after any strenuous exercise (5-10 minutes).

• Muscle-strengthening exercises, preferably 2-3 times per week (10-20 minutes).

• Aerobic exercise for a minimum of two or three sessions (20-60 minutes), depending on the type of exercise.

• Variety of physical activities (sports, household work, etc.).

• One day of rest and recuperation (no strenuous exercising).

Of course, before undertaking any type of exercise program, sedentary, out-of-shape persons are advised to have a thorough physical exam, including blood pressure monitoring and an electrocardiogram (EKG). A rule for exercise as well as singing: *Always listen to your body and it will tell you what you are able to handle at any given time.* I think most people will agree that getting the most out of life begins with a serious prioritized commitment to maintain a healthy mind and body and a state of wellness.

Efficient Body Alignment

One major objective of an exercise program is the development of efficient, graceful, and healthy body movement. For a variety of reasons, most people with misaligned body postures are simply unaware of their condition, and perhaps even ignorant regarding the importance of correct body alignment. As a singer and voice instructor, I've spent countless hours working with students' postures, not just for singing purposes, but also because proper body alignment contributes to good health and longevity.

As everyone knows, physical carriage or "body language"—including posture, movement, and hand and facial gestures—reveals much about who we are. People we admire usually have a certain bearing—a trait that is especially observable with classically trained singers, dancers, and actors. People who learn how to maintain an up-stretched body alignment through effective body mechanics and exercise may be better equipped in staving off old-age spinal problems, including curvature of the spine, scoliosis, and degenerating discs.

In my own case, it's conceivable that I might have avoided some of my lower back and neck ailments, including two degenerated lumbar discs and a slight case of scoliosis, had I addressed certain spinal issues earlier in my life; for instance, supporting my flat feet with the use of proper arch inserts in my shoes, using yoga and Pilates exercises to strengthen back muscles, learning efficient body movement techniques, and avoiding abusive behavior, like lifting heavy weights improperly. As it happens, training as a singer probably helped prevent an earlier onset of back ailments, as I've always tried to maintain an up-stretched and efficient body alignment. One of the most useful methods for body alignment and efficient biomechanics is the Alexander Technique, which is discussed in the next chapter.

Perhaps the most useful exercise for mind-body coordination and overall health is the practice of *yoga*, which originated with religious ascetics in India approximately 5,000 years ago. The term "yoga" is a Sanskrit word usually defined as "union", and generally refers to a combination of philosophy, physical exercises, chanting, and meditation. The generic term for the physical practice of yoga is *hatha*, a proven way of exercising to develop strength, balance, and mental focus. For people considering studying yoga, it pays to be aware of the different forms. Some of the principal styles taught in the U.S. include the following:

• *Ashtanga.* Sometimes associated with *power yoga*, an Americanized form, ashtanga is vigorously athletic, using a practiced series of linked postures in rapid succession, in addition to some chanting and meditation.

• *Bikram.* A fairly recent form that is franchised worldwide by Yogiraj Bikram Choudhury, a flamboyant guru in California, Bikram consists of a very strenuous set of postures and scripted information that's practiced in an overheated room (around 100 degrees).

• *Himalayan.* As a traditional, holistic approach, Himalayan teaches a yogic lifestyle that includes meditation, philosophy, nutrition, breathing exercises, and gentle physical practice.

• *Iyengar.* Most likely the best known and widely taught form, Iyengar yoga was created by B.K.S. Iyengar, an Indian yogi who emphasizes proper body alignment and a slow, steady progression in mastering a few poses that are held longer than other forms.

• *Kripalu.* Another gentle, moderate form, falling somewhere between ashtanga and Iyengar, kripalu concentrates on flow sequences along with longer holds and body alignment.

While young people may enjoy undertaking the strenuous approaches of ashtanga, power yoga, and Bikram, older folks are wisely more inclined to undertake the more moderate and gentle forms. I use some of the more gentle exercises and find them helpful, but I would never attempt some of the strenuous, body-contortion exercises used in the more aggressive yoga styles.

Establishing proper body alignment requires an efficient balancing between all body parts, from head to feet. Any out-of-alignment body part will cause muscles, ligaments, and skeletal framework to be placed under various stresses, with the potential of causing a series of problems as we age. Hence, efficient body alignment is essential for overall health—in addition to improving one's appearance and personality. The following suggestions should prove helpful in developing a flexible, dynamic posture.

• Back up against a wall, allowing as much body surface as possible to touch the wall, but not with the backside of the knees, which should remain unlocked. Shake your entire body and release any unnecessary muscle tensions. At waist level, place one hand behind (on lower spine, palm outward) and the other hand behind the head for a cushioning effect and better alignment.

• Maintaining this uplifted posture, move away from the wall and assume an athletic stance, as though ready for action, vital and balanced, with feet planted firmly on the floor. The ideal balanced state is a combination of both weightiness and buoyancy.

• To achieve a balanced stance, place feet apart 6-8 inches, one foot slightly in front of the other.

• Keep the knees flexible and unlocked (double-jointed people have problems with this position).

• To avoid swayback tendencies, tuck the posterior slightly to balance the pelvic area.

• The abdominal area should remain relaxed on inhalation and the lower abdominal area should firm up when intentionally exhaling while producing a vigorous hissing sound, by blowing air through closed mouth and teeth.

• Keep the chest comfortably high but not exaggerated, i. e., pushed out and upward in the manner of a soldier at attention. The rib cage should be slightly expanded outward, but not forced.

• Let the shoulders remain relaxed, loose, and straight (not pulled forward or pushed backward), with arms dangling at the sides.

• Maintain an up-stretched, flexible neck.

• Create a head position that's balanced on top of the spinal column so that it can roll easily in any direction, somewhat like a bowl inverted on the tip of a pencil.

If all the steps have been followed as suggested, you should feel taller, more uplifted, and buoyant, with a sense of expanding in all directions. In the next chapter we'll discuss breathing techniques that will help achieve a sensation of expansion—in all directions.

Diet and Nutrition

In retrospect, I wish I had known as a child, youth, and young adult what I now understand about the importance of healthy eating and regular exercising. Because information about proper eating habits and the need for exercise was not publicized widely prior to the 1970s-1980s, I had a belated start. Thankfully, in my childhood and youth, processed (junk) foods were not as common as today, and, of greater importance, portions of food servings were more sensible. I was also fortunate not to have abused my body by smoking tobacco, drinking alcoholic beverages, or using recreational drugs. At age 26 and tipping the scales at 185 pounds, I realized I was bordering on portliness, so I began paying more attention to my diet. Over the past three decades I've maintained weight in the range of 150-160 lbs., with occasions of dropping below 150 lbs. in recent years, possibly due to some bone and muscle loss.

Here the term *diet* refers to any nutrition program designed to provide energy for an active lifestyle. Weight control can be a fringe benefit of a healthy diet, but it should not be the main objective. Focusing primarily on weight loss rather than achieving good health is usually non-productive, since yo-yo patterns of gaining, losing, and regaining weight can be more harmful to health than not dieting at all. A more sensible option is to permanently change eating patterns, which in the long term improves overall quality of life and longevity. But, to begin with, it's important to set some priorities focused on achieving health and wellness, a crucial step requiring serious self-examination, as well as changes in attitudes and behaviors.

Weighty Issues

According to U. S government surveys, adult obesity has increased dramatically in recent years, and the U.S. Surgeon General has proclaimed a national obesity crisis. When studying published guidelines of acceptable weight ratios for persons of certain age, height, and gender, we learn that 65 percent of adult Americans are overweight, with a body-mass index of 25-29, or obese, with a body-mass index of 30 or more, percentages double that of 20 years ago. It's difficult to comprehend that approximately 44 million Americans are considered obese! Data from the National Health and Nutrition Examination Survey (NHANES) show that among adults aged 20-74 years the prevalence of obesity increased from 15.0 percent (in the 1976-1980 survey) to 32.9 percent (in the 2003-2004 survey). And in 2001 the U.S. Centers for Disease Control and Prevention estimated that percentages of obesity ranged from a low of 14 percent of young adults in the 18-to-29-age group, to a high of 26 percent of mature adults in the 50-to-59-age group. Even worse, several reputable studies of large numbers of children reveal alarming health trends, including increasing cases of obesity and heart disease, that are thought to be caused by excess consumption of junk food and drink, overeating, and lack of exercise.

The important point is that age-associated weight-gain is normal, but because the amount of weight gain is greatly increasing among all age groups, obese adults are in greater danger than in previous generations. Though a few pounds of extra weight may not grossly affect one's performance, "morbid obesity" or weight more than two times ideal body weight creates a serious handicap. The National Institutes of Health conclude that being overweight has adverse effects on health and longevity, contributing to psychological stress, high blood pressure, high levels of cholesterol, sugar diabetes (type 2), heart disease, stroke, gallbladder disease, certain cancers (endometrial, breast, and colon), shorter life spans, respiratory problems, sleep apnea, and osteoarthritis. Not surprisingly, obesity is associated with low levels of physical activity, which further lessens overall fitness.

A recent study sponsored by the Kaiser Permanente Division of Research in Oakland, California has raised serious concerns about excessive body fat around the waistline. The long-term study involved more than 6,000 people in their early to mid-40s with large amounts of body fat in their gut zones. The findings suggest that excessive body-fat accumulation around one's mid section (big-belly syndrome) is a sure predictor of serious future health problems, including diabetes, heart disease, cancer, and dementia, including Alzheimer's Disease. It seems that fat's proximity to vital organs causes the release of noxious chemicals, which can stoke inflammation, and in turn constrict blood vessels and trigger other processes that might eventually damage brain cells. Apparently, the longer one maintains excessive body fat around the waistline, the greater the chances for deteriorating health in later life. So, if you're carrying excess fat baggage in this area, take heed and lose weight, but only in a sensible manner.

In direct contrast to obesity is the excessively thin or emaciated body type that is glorified by the media, fashion, and entertainment industries. The misinformed notion that "one can't be too thin" partly accounts for the alarming rise in such life-threatening eating disorders as *bulimia* and *anorexia nervosa*, both of which result in such practices as self-starvation and compulsive exercising. Obviously, controlling weight by means of fasting, laxatives, and self-induced vomiting are neither permanent nor healthy solutions to weight control.

Unhealthy Nutrition

Excluding psychological issues, the chief causes of obesity and related illnesses may be attributed largely to the typical American diet, which is alarmingly high in fat, cholesterol, sodium, and refined sugar, but only moderately sound in terms of healthy ingredients, such as fiber and complex carbohydrates. Regarding the latter, most people fail to distinguish between bad and good carbohydrates. "Bad" carbohydrates—high calorie, processed foods, such as white bread, pastries, doughnuts, and the like—contribute to obesity and such diseases as adult-onset diabetes.

However, "good" complex carbohydrates, such as most fruits, vegetables, and whole grain breads should be a part of any balanced nutritional diet. I fear that the low-carbohydrate diet craze promoted in recent years may ultimately prove dangerous to the long-term health of many people.

So-called "junk food" is also very high in nutrition-empty calories, such as refined oils, trans fats, and sugars. Studies show that soft drinks alone provide 1.5 pounds of sugar per week to the impoverished diet of the average 15 to 19-year-old American student, who guzzles 24 ounces of soda daily. More recently, soft drinks have come under a heavier barrage regarding the damage they precipitate in so many people's overall health. Thankfully, some schools are voluntarily replacing soft drinks with fruit drinks in their dispensing machines, a positive move that's also duplicated with the food services in some schools that aim to provide both nutritious and tasty options. This news is well and good for the future of younger generations, but we also need to continue addressing all nutritional concerns in the greater public arena, including the type of products marketed in grocery stores and restaurants.

Contrary to popular fad diets that advocate low-carbohydrate, high-fat food and drink, such as the waning Atkins Diet, the majority of nutritionists claim the chief culprit in the American diet is increased fat consumption. With proportions of fat in diets continuing to increase, the typical citizen now consumes an average of 35-45 percent of calories (units of heat energy) as fat. Of course, it's important to distinguish between *monounsaturated fats* (olive oil, nuts, etc.) and *polyunsaturated fats* (corn, soybean, fish, etc.), both of which lower *low-density lipoprotein* (LDL, the "bad" cholesterol) and raise *high-density lipoprotein* (HDL, the "good" cholesterol). In addition, one should consume minimal amounts of *saturated fats* (whole milk, butter, etc.) and *trans fats* (margarines, deep-fried foods, etc.), both of which raise LDL (bad cholesterol).

Cholesterol becomes an even more complicated subject with the more recent discoveries of "small LDL", bad cholesterol known as LDL Pattern B, which increases the possibility of increased risk for heart disease. Its good counterpart is HDL2B, super-efficient cholesterol that helps clear blocked arteries. Though scientists are still researching the cholesterol issue, we can rest assured that it's not just the *amount*, but the *type* of food we eat that creates weight and health problems, some of which are related to the amounts and types of cholesterol our bodies produce, with trans fats (partially hydrogenated oils) and saturated fats (typically found in meats and coconut and palm oils) presenting a serious threat. The positive news is that many fast-food franchises are finally banning trans fats, and some large cities are going one step further by passing laws that ban them. Perhaps these actions portend the beginning of healthier eating in the fast-food realm.

The negative effects of yo-yo dieting can be explained by *homeostasis*, an evolutionary adaptation that seeks to regulate and maintain the body's equilibrium, similar to a thermostat. For instance, when we get overheated, we cool down by sweating. In like fashion, when we lose weight, the body tries to regain it. Fat cells grow larger when overeating, and continued overeating in childhood and youth results in newly formed fat cells that take up permanent residence in the body. This equalizing function is yet more proof that we need to seek a balanced approach in our consumption of food and drink.

Metabolism, a significant aspect of homeostasis, refers to bodily chemical processes that build and destroy tissue, and release heat-producing energy. When the amount of food intake is reduced, the metabolic "set point" tends to lower, causing calories to burn more slowly and a plateau of weight loss to occur, with a likelihood of even greater weight gain when the caloric restriction is lifted. Each time a new dieting regimen is undertaken, the body's metabolic rate moves even lower. Moreover, the basal, at-rest metabolic rate (at-rest caloric expenditure) declines approximately two percent per decade starting around age 20, the main reason why older persons must reduce caloric intake to maintain constant body weight.

According to the Centers for Disease Control and Prevention, the average U.S. male consumes approximately 2,475 calories per day, roughly 500 more than needed. The average woman consumes 1,833 calories, but actually requires about 1600 calories to maintain a healthy weight level. One guideline suggests that men take in 500 calories for both breakfast and lunch, while women ingest 300 for each meal. Both men and women can then enjoy an evening meal consisting of 1,000 calories. Of course, the larger meal might be better put to use at midday instead of evening (Nakazawa 2006). As we age, we need fewer calories, so the amounts listed need to be adjusted downward—or else! So far, I think Bettye and I stay within the average limits suggested. But, were I to stop exercising, it would be necessary to reduce the amount of calories ingested by at least 500-plus calories daily, since that's approximately the amount I burn exercising.

"Fad diets," such as high-protein/low-carbohydrate diets that focus on one or two specific food sources, should be avoided. Dieters often experience a loss of essential vitamins and muscle tissue when undertaking harmful crash-diets. All that's needed is a well-balanced diet that includes all major food groups to fulfill normal nutritional needs. This means feeding from the variety of the major groups: vegetables, fruits, grains, legumes and limited amounts of low-fat meat. Although vegetables and fruits are generally thought to be nutritionally superior when fresh, frozen or canned foods are acceptable options, especially when can-packed in natural juices (or water) and free of excessive preservatives. A general guideline for nutrition is to seek out the natural state of any food source when possible, for instance, fresh apples rather than apple sauce. When and if possible, organic food and drink are highly recommended, especially if available from reputable local sources that are available at food cooperatives.

While concentrating on healthy foods, one should totally avoid the racks of high-fat snacks and high-sugar candies, soft drinks, and chewing gums available in most grocery stores. In addition to having loads of preservatives, fat, sugar and salt, most junk foods also feature high caloric content. Better alternatives include home-filtered drinking water (safer than most bottled water, and more ecological) and fruit juices, and fresh or dried fruit for sweet snacks. Plain popcorn is an excellent high-fiber, no-fat snack food, minus butter and salt of course. I have a not-so-bad-but-not-ideal habit of eating a large bowl of unembellished popcorn most evenings after supper, when watching TV and reading. It's a very filling snack, low in calories, provides ample fiber, and takes 20 to 30 minutes to eat.

Healthy Nutrition

If the truism "We are what we eat" has validity, then what should we eat? Dr. Michael Roizen, author of The RealAge Diet is opposed to the popular high-protein diets, claiming that persons who follow such diets over the long term can lose 4.7 years of their lives. He agrees with the recommendation by dieticians to reduce bad carbohydrates, such as refined flour and sugar, as found in junk-foods and white bread, but the complex carbohydrates found in fruits, vegetables and whole grains are essential. In sum, Roizen recommends the following foods as aids in the fight against biological aging (Roizen & La Puma 2001):

  • Vegetables—five or more servings per day, especially the most intensely colored vegetables. Deduct two years from your real age.

• Nuts—five ounces per week of good LDL fats, protein, and minerals. Deduct 1.5 years.

• Fish—three or more portions per week to gain a great source of protein and essential omega-3 fatty acids. Deduct 1.5 years.

• Whole-grain fiber—five servings weekly. Deduct 1 year.

Other excellent nutritional sources are the *Life Choice Diet* (2001) by Dean Ornish, M.D., and Walter C. Willett, M.D., author of *Eat, Drink, and Be Healthy: The Harvard Medical School Guide to Healthy Eating* (2001). Both experts propose sensible, moderate diets, but Willett's "Healthy Eating Pyramid" is perhaps the more balanced approach. His pyramid begins with an emphasis on physical activity and weight control, followed by a diet based on whole-grain, high fiber carbohydrates and healthy fats, such as liquid vegetable oils and foods made from avocados and nuts, in addition to an abundant variety of fruits and vegetables. For vegetarians, in particular, he recommends nuts and legumes as sources of protein, and everyone can benefit from adding fish (caution: mercury levels can be high in some types of fish) and moderate amounts of poultry and eggs. In 2005 the U.S. government published a food pyramid that reflects a similar program to that of Willett's, so it seems that progress is being made in a national campaign against obesity and bad health.

Willett writes that studies in cancer research have shown that there are essential antioxidant foods everyone should ingest: carrots, green vegetables, tomatoes, and crucifers, such as broccoli and cabbage. Also, possible life-extending properties are being investigated regarding the substances found in blueberries, red wine, and spinach. We eat most of these foods regularly, and though I recently experimented for a few weeks with drinking a glass of red wine daily (purely for medicinal purposes, of course), I decided to lay off when I read a health report suggesting that if one does not have a habit of imbibing, it's probably best not to begin. So until I have more concrete data regarding wine consumption, I'll remain an occasional imbiber, mostly on social occasions.

Yet another nutritional plan that seems to make good sense is *The Volumetrics Eating Plan* by Dr. Barbara Rolls, a professor of nutritional sciences at the Pennsylvania State University. The basic idea behind the plan is to manage weight by selecting foods that are low in caloric content or "energy density" (ED), the type that make you feel full or satiated. Some recommended selections include soups, fresh fruits and vegetables (salads), pasta, and low-fat, skin-less meats. A good choice for a cereal, for instance, might be Cheerios with skim milk, instead of granola or other sugary cereals. (I usually compromise by mixing in a little granola with a non-sugary cereal and skim milk.) High-calorie foods are not forbidden on the volumetrics diet plan, but they should be consumed only occasionally and in small portions. The book also contains many recipes. Although there is not extensive research following up on people taking the diet, a one-year diet involving 97 women showed that the group of women consuming the low density foods were able to eat more and lose more weight, up to 20 lbs. each. Many nutritionists have responded positively, by adopting the principles of volumetrics in their nutrition programs.

Thankfully, the list of healthy foods is very long, so listing every vegetable, fruit, grain, and meat isn't necessary. Yet, as we've learned thus far, certain types of antioxidants seem to stand out, including leafy greens (kale or spinach), tomatoes in various forms, berries (cranberries, blueberries, and blackberries), nuts (almonds and walnuts), flaxseed, and spirulina, a high-protein, blue-green algae that was a mainstay of the ancient Aztecs (Nakazawa 2006). Whole grains are also essential to a healthy diet, along with moderate portions of poultry and fish, especially wild salmon and tuna—but, again, be aware of mercury warnings.

To sum up, an adult healthy eater's daily guide might include the following portions of caloric intake, by food groups:

- Carbohydrates (45 to 65 percent), with an emphasis on complex carbohydrates, such as fruits, vegetables, whole grains, legumes, and soy products.

- Fat (20 to 35 percent), with an emphasis on omega-3, which is found in fatty fish, like salmon.

- Protein (10 to 35 percent), with an emphasis on plant-based proteins.

- Added sugars (around 25 percent), with emphases on the unrefined, natural sugars found in fruit.

Everyone needs life-essential *vitamins*, the organic substances needed for cell regulation and function. Vitamins promote good vision, create strong bones and teeth, form normal blood cells, and ensure proper functioning of the heart and nervous system. Contrary to advertising claims, no energy is provided by vitamins, but they do help in converting foods into energy. The 13 vitamins fall into two categories: *fat-soluble* (A and its precursor beta carotene, D, E, and K); and *water-soluble* (the B vitamins and C). This is an important distinction because fat-soluble vitamins are stored in the liver and fatty tissue for relatively long periods of several months, but water-soluble vitamins are stored for only a brief time, perhaps up to a few weeks. Because the body is incapable of manufacturing vitamins, they must be ingested. That said, the body does naturally synthesize some vitamins, such as K, D, and B12, and converts beta-carotene into A. Generally speaking, it's best to consume vitamins through a well-balanced diet rather than through supplementation, because of the synergy that develops between nutrients, including minerals and vitamins.

A study of vitamin effect on prison populations is currently being led by John Stein, a professor of neuroscience at Oxford University in England. Based on positive results of previous studies, including one managed by Natural Justice, a British charity, Dr. Stein believes that proper functioning of nerve-cell membranes requires adequate supplies of vitamins, minerals, and fatty acids. The nine-month Natural Justice study revealed positive results for prisoners who took the official daily requirement of vitamins and minerals, with the number of violent offenses reduced by 37 percent and minor offenses by 26.3 percent.

Several *minerals* are needed for maintaining healthy whole-body functioning, especially as we age and our bodies are slow in absorbing certain nutrients. Some of the more essential minerals include: *calcium* for preventing osteoporosis (best taken in conjunction with vitamin D to assist absorption); *fish oil* (omega-3 fatty acids) to assist with heart, memory, and learning functions; *selenium*, an antioxidant that protects against heart disease, arthritis, and various forms of cancer; *magnesium*, which assists in over 300 different body functions, including steadying heart rate, maintaining normal muscle and nerve functioning, and metabolizing food into energy; and *zinc,* which stimulates the activity of approximately 100 enzymes to strengthen immunity, heal wounds, and prevent infection.

Vitamin D, which is thought to be important in prolonging life by protecting the body against serious diseases, is especially relevant to aging persons. Perhaps best known as an essential ingredient for calcium uptake, vitamin D deficiency has been associated with osteoporosis, rheumatoid arthritis, certain cancers (breast, ovarian, prostate), and auto-immune diseases (multiple sclerosis) especially among people living in northern climes and for dark-skinned persons.

Vitamin D also appears to improve mood and may relieve symptoms of depression. A dosage of 1000 international units per day, or five times the RDA, is recommended by Toronto biochemist, Reinhold Viet. Vitamin D occurs naturally in some food, such as fish, but is most efficiently produced in the body by exposure to sunlight, so some medical scientists recommend 5-15 minutes of daily exposure to skin, especially in winter. Others recommend that persons with sensitive skin avoid sunlight altogether. A reasonable compromise might be to get at least one day of 10-15 minutes of sun exposure during winter months.

Research is still ongoing regarding the need for vitamin and mineral supplementation, but a growing body of scientific evidence supports taking certain supplements. Due to such factors as irregular eating habits, age, sex (hormones), and the state of the food industry, most people need some extra nutritional aid, particularly older folks. In the typical U.S. citizen's diet several factors contribute to vitamin deficiencies—skipping meals, eating at fast-food outlets, food processing practices, lengthy shipping and storage periods, and chemical toxicity. Hence, there is a strong likelihood that most Americans are vitamin and mineral deficient. Nevertheless, research varies considerably regarding various supplements, so the wise course of action is moderation in taking any specific supplement, in addition to staying abreast of the latest findings.

Bettye and I probably err on the side of taking more daily supplements, including a multi-vitamin, and moderate dosages of vitamins C, B, E, and D, minerals such as calcium, and zinc (once or twice weekly), and garlic and fish oil tablets. We try to stay abreast of the latest published recommendations and follow them faithfully, but one never knows for certain which scientific studies are valid, and which ones will be proven false later on. The advantages, disadvantages, and uses of vitamins and minerals are under constant re-evaluation by scientists, so it always pays to keep up to date and well informed.

Finally, eating and drinking healthfully can be very challenging in this age of plenty, but it is possible. To begin with, it pays to eat at home as much as possible, simply because it's easier to control what you eat. Because most restaurants serve tasty foods aimed at the general public, ordering healthy food can prove challenging. As long as you remain informed, cautious, and committed to nutritious food and drink, it should be possible to find healthy options on most menus, or by special request. And of course it helps greatly to have an overall plan to help guide your selection of food and drink on any occasion.

Liquid Intake

So far we've not mentioned the importance of taking in sufficient quantities of liquids as a vital part of a healthy diet. Since the typical body comprises more than two-thirds water, it stands to reason that to counteract an average loss of one liter per day we need to replenish an equal amount. Naturally, the amount for each individual varies depending on age, weight, activity level, diet, and temperature. The recommended levels are from six to ten 8-ounce glasses per day of liquid, which can be in the form of water or other beverages. Alcohol is the only drink that has a strong diuretic effect, though caffeinated drinks may cause a loss of up to a third of liquid contained in a cup of caffeinated tea or coffee. Also, the amount of liquid contained in foods, especially some high-water content fruits, vegetables, and soups, counts as part of total liquid intake.

Having mentioned alcohol, I would be negligent in failing to mention the mild controversy concerning the pros and cons of moderate drinking. Although the final verdict is out, scientific studies to date suggest that taking a glass or two of red wine daily is actually good medicine, and, for that matter, so is beer, schnapps, whisky, or a satisfying aperitif. Red wine, in particular, is loaded with the antioxidant *resveratrol*, which naturally stimulates genes that clean up free radicals, stabilize blood glucose levels, and make healthier cells. The primary benefit of alcohol seems to be the antioxidant's ability to raise levels of HDL, the good cholesterol that helps clear arteries of plaque. Measured dosages of alcohol make blood less sticky, and less likely to form blood clots that trigger heart attacks and strokes. Another benefit is that it appears to have anti-inflammatory effects, in addition to enhancing insulin sensitivity, which may explain how moderate consumption of alcohol is associated with a lower incidence of type-2 diabetes. Of course, heavy drinking has many negative health effects, including high blood pressure, irregular heartbeat, congestive heart failure, liver damage, death of brain cells, and perhaps even cancer, such as tumors in the mouth, throat, esophagus, and colon. In sum, for abstainers, it might be best not to begin drinking, but for persons who drink in moderation, limited imbibing is generally thought to be beneficial (Underwood 2005).

Determining the amount of liquid each individual needs daily is an imprecise science. The best advice is to take in a moderate amount of liquids daily, including tea. Recent studies at the American Health Foundation point to green and black tea as a healthy drink, primarily because of antioxidants that fight cancer, prevent clogging of arteries, reduce inflammation (arthritis), and neutralize some germs. Some experts recommend six 8-ounce cups of tea daily, and they can be hot or iced, decaf or not, but stick to the regular kind sold in bags or as loose leaves. Even coffee is getting positive press, with recent studies showing that coffee might reduce the risk of such diseases as Parkinson's and Alzheimer's.

It can be terribly confusing trying to do right for our health. I can remember when caffeine (coffee), fats of any kind, wine, chocolate, and numbers of so-called "bad things" were strictly taboo, but in recent years have been pronounced "ok" if consumed in limited quantities. For instance, because dark chocolate contains potent antioxidants that clear free radicals and protect against inflammation, some reputable nutritionists are recommending individuals consume one square or 1.6 ounces daily. Of course, chocolate contains high calories, as do nuts, so reductions in other caloric intake or extra exercising may be needed in maintaining stable weight.

In contrast to the bad-turned-good nutrients, certain herbal remedies (Ginkgo, St. John's Wort, etc.), calcium, Vitamin E, and various medications (such as the all-purpose aspirin), all once touted as helpful, are now suspected to be good-turned-bad nutrients. What's a person to do? I suppose the best course is to keep eyes and ears open to all new developments and research findings, meanwhile adopting a moderate course in consuming any food supplement or medication.

Preserving and Maintaining Health

We tend to take our wonderful biological organs, systems, and senses for granted—until we lose them! Older people, in particular, readily share woes related to losses in vision and hearing, in addition to declining olfactory senses and even nerve damage, which may affect kinesthetic abilities, including touch and movement. Keeping our senses alert and functioning well for as long as possible will assure greater coping capacity throughout one's life, especially during old age.

In this chapter we've focused on measures for enhancing mind-body health, as related to exercise and fitness, and diet and nutrition. In the next chapter we'll focus on coping with stress, with rest and recreation playing a significant role. All of these measures provide some protection against disease and illness, but some preventive measures are also needed, as the following guidelines suggest:

• *Develop and maintain proper hygiene.* Avoid contracting infectious diseases by keeping a distance from ill persons, carefully avoiding potentially contaminated surfaces (public doorknobs, desks, faucet handles, sinks, water fountains, trashcans, etc.), observing caution when shaking hands, washing hands frequently and thoroughly (15 seconds), and avoiding hand contact with your eyes, mouth, and nose. Washing certain fresh foods before ingesting them is also a good idea. And don't forget to practice good dental hygiene, by brushing and flossing teeth regularly. Finally, to reduce the effects of upper respiratory infections and allergies, practice daily nasal irrigation, which requires using a neti pot or squeeze bottle filled with room-temperature water and a quarter-teaspoon of kosher salt to cleanse away pollutants, mucous, and airborne pollens and allergens.

• *Avoid exposure to harmful substances.* Remain vigilant in avoiding recreational drugs, excessive alcohol, tobacco smoke, toxic chemicals (household products included), junk food, and pollutants in air and water. Breaking habits of ingesting harmful recreational substances can be extremely difficult, but doing so can make a huge difference in terms of health and longevity. For instance, cessation of smoking has an immediate positive effect on one's heart condition, and after abstaining for 15 years one's overall health is similar to that of persons who never smoked. Harmful substances to be avoided in certain foods include PCBs, mercury, pesticides, and a host of other toxins. In homes and workplaces some major substances to avoid are asbestos and lead, both found in construction materials.

• *Protect ears and hearing from loud noises.* More than 28 million Americans have some degree of hearing loss, from mild to severe, and the numbers may soar to 78 million by 2030. Because of increased levels of high-decibel music and use of earphones, people are experiencing hearing problems at earlier ages than heretofore. The standing advice from experts is to avoid loud, sustained noises, especially sounds in excess of 90 decibels for extended periods, the types of loud noise produced by a jet engine, a jackhammer, or even a lawnmower. Though I have a moderate case of *tinnitus* (ringing in the ears), my hearing remains fairly secure, thanks to not having been exposed to inordinate amounts of loud noises throughout my lifetime. On the other hand, my hearing would probably be better had I always used protective hearing devices, as when using lawnmowers or vacuum cleaners. For the past decade or so I've tried to protect my hearing whenever necessary, by avoiding loud noises or wearing ear plugs.

• *Protect skin from sunlight.* Avoid extended exposure to direct sunlight, especially in the middle of the day, and wear a sunscreen with a high SPF rating when exposed to sunlight for more than 30 minutes. As mentioned earlier, this is one admonition many of us oldsters ignored in our youthful eagerness to develop attractive summer tans. The result for most of us was a number of painful sunburns, especially on the shoulders and back. At the time, sunscreens were unheard of, but suntan lotion, though providing minimal protection, was very popular. As a result, our skins display the ravages of sun exposure, with blemishes (freckles, moles, spots) that appear only on areas where sun exposure was intense. The body parts that were not exposed or underexposed are relatively healthy looking, such as the underside of arms and bathing suit areas.

• *Protect body parts from injury.* Avoid high-risk activities, as can occur when riding a bike or motorcycle (sans helmet), or excessive physical activities, as may occur in running a marathon. One always has to weigh the health risks involved with certain recreational activities, but for me it's the long-term concerns that govern my actions. For example, in my early 40s I experienced hip and Achilles Heel problems associated with running six miles several days per week, which was more than my middle-aged body could take. So I cut down to three miles for each run and the problems ceased. About a decade ago, I decided that fast, smooth-gliding run-walking provided a workout equal to jogging, which is known to stress body parts, especially knee and hip joints.

• *Seek preventive medical care.* Schedule an annual physical exam and follow all recommended guidelines for medical care, including vaccinations and specific exams according to age and gender. Though the need for regular medical checkups in maintaining overall health appears obvious, many people, notably men, neglect receiving medical assistance until a crisis occurs.

For another set of guidelines, two well-known medical doctors (Roizen & Oz 2007), co-authors of two best-selling books (*You: The Owner's Manual* and *You: On a Diet*), offer ten steps for maintaining good health:

• *Eat tomato sauce,* which contains lycopene, an antioxidant associated with reducing blood pressure, minimizing arterial plaque, and lowering cancer risks.

• *Floss your teeth* to prevent gingivitis and periodontal disease, which can cause inflammation in your body and aging of the immune and arterial systems.

• *Drink coffee in moderation*, up to two or three cups daily to combat risks associated with Parkinson's disease and Alzheimer's—if you don't experience negative effects, such as headaches and gastrointestinal upset, which can be aggravated by caffeine.

• *Increase your HDL*, the healthy cholesterol (above 50 in testing), to avoid clogged arteries, which can lead to heart disease, stroke, impotence, and memory loss. Daily consumption of healthy fats (olive oil and nuts), an alcoholic drink, plus niacin and vitamin B5 supplements, are recommended.

• *Avoid bad fats*, such as trans fats and saturated fats, because they trigger a gene that causes arterial inflammation. Limit these combined fats to 20 grams per day.

• *Wash your hands* (and food) as frequently as possible to prevent catching and spreading diseases. Use clean rags instead of sponges for cleaning purposes around food.

• *Get an annual flu shot* (especially persons over age 55), primarily to avoid catching various illnesses, but also to decrease inflammation that can damage arteries and precipitate heart attacks or strokes.

• *Reach out to friends*, a well-known socializing strategy for reducing overall stress levels, which can contribute to arterial and immune system weakness.

• *Work out regularly*, as described earlier, to maintain healthy cardiovascular and cognitive functioning.

As mentioned previously, be sure to have an annual medical checkup, especially prior to undertaking a strenuous exercise program. I've obeyed this advice faithfully, and it has paid off. In the summer of 2003, I had my regular exam, followed by some lab work, which included a

PSA (prostate specific antigen) blood test, which is recommended for all men over age 50. Unfortunately, this time the PSA test indicated the possibility of cancer, which a biopsy confirmed, indicating a small cancer in the beginning stage. Within two months I had surgery to remove the prostate, and I'm happy to report an excellent prognosis, with no signs of cancer five years later. The point is, had I not been diligent about having an annual physical exam—plus requesting an annual PSA test several years ago—the cancer might have gone undetected, and possibly developing to the point that more serious surgery and other treatments might have been required, with more devastating results. Fortunately, because my physical condition was excellent at age 66, I was a satisfactory risk for surgery, and the subsequent recovery went very well, with a gradual return to normal exercise routines within four weeks.

In sum, make it a priority to schedule an annual physical exam, in advance preparing a list of items (information, questions) to share with your doctor. In connection with this discussion about illness and healing, a later chapter will delve into this topic in greater depth.

Summary and Conclusion

We have learned that finding the correct balance in physical exercise and activities requires gaining awareness of one's body, including a program of activities that develop and sustain energy resources without causing long-term damage to body parts. Knowing how far to stretch one's physical abilities is primarily learned through practical experience, keeping in mind that moderation is the main objective, which means not overdoing any single exercise or activity. Any strenuous physical activity—competitive sports, in particular—can create future health problems, as many professional athletes can attest, with injuries that cause suffering for their entire lives. Although most are compensated monetarily and psycho-emotionally in their youth for a few years, one has to wonder if a painful life-time injury is worth such an enormous price.

And the same guidelines apply to diet and nutrition. Any extreme type of diet plan may be considered a fad, but a sensible, moderate diet will include all major food groups, as suggested by the proposal set forth with Walter C. Willet's "Healthy Eating Pyramid". Finding the appropriate balance is not easy, but striving to consume healthy food and drink is within the realm of possibility, as long as one is committed to fulfilling such a worthwhile goal.

Finally, developing a well-balanced lifestyle requires giving attention to one's living situation. Finding ways to increase physical activity, connect with others, and eat nutritiously are greatly facilitated by living in a community that encourages these positive self-development practices. If one's job and lifestyle require extensive auto commuting that helps create inordinate stress levels and threatens health and longevity, then perhaps it's time to take stock and make some necessary changes, the sooner the better.

5

Coping With Stress

Explaining and Identifying Stress

Stress is a natural and essential ingredient of life. It may be thought of as any mind-body strain, from mild to severe forms of anxiety, fatigue, disease, or bodily injury. Practically every human activity has the potential of triggering stress, with stress levels depending on genetic makeup, psycho-emotional disposition, and overall level of health. The stress response is commonly referred to as the *flight-or-fight syndrome*, which is triggered when we are confronted with a challenge, and we are forced to either run away or stay and fight.

For instance, if you're scheduled to give a speech to a large audience in one minute, do you leave the hall or courageously walk out on stage? If you're an experienced, well-prepared speaker, say a politician or teacher, it might be an easy, non-stressful assignment. But if you're a first-time speaker and ill prepared, you'll probably feel one of several possible stress symptoms—sweaty brow and hands, upset stomach, the shakes, dry mouth, and so on. Depending on your personality, you may react to stress in various ways, as risk-takers tend to respond more positively while risk-avoiders tend to be more vulnerable. For example, a skydiver, a hang-glider pilot, or a cliff climber may thrive on the thrill and challenge of undertaking high-risk physical ventures, but risk-adverse folk (such as me) may be terrified to venture forth so bravely—or foolishly, depending on one's perspective.

Why should persons over 50 years of age be concerned about stress? Aren't most of our major stress-inducing times behind us? Not really. We still have to deal with the effects of five or more decades of stress accumulation on our minds and bodies. When we are subjected to any great stress, the hormones cortisol and adrenaline are released instantaneously, causing increases in blood pressure and blood glucose, while chemical changes in the blood enhance clotting ability to aid wound healing. However—and this is important—in the absence of any physical wounds, these survival mechanisms, when sustained for many years, can damage blood vessels, partially by causing inflammation, which can lead to plaque buildup and heart disease. In sum, the result of too many stress activations creates a chronic condition that's harmful to the immune system, brain, and heart. Excessive cortisol levels are toxic to brain cells, potentially damaging cognitive ability and increasing fatigue, anger, and depression. Also, the immune system becomes less effective due to repeated suppression of the disease-fighting cells, ultimately weakening resistance to infection. So this is why we need to learn how to control our reactions to stressful situations and events—on a daily basis. We can't make up for all the damage caused heretofore, but there are some restorative and preventive measures that we can take.

It's very important to realize that stress levels are governed largely by our perceptions of any event or activity. For example, if we are unskilled in handling a certain stressful situation, our feeling of inadequacy will create deeper anxiety, but if we are skilled in handling a particular activity, stress levels will be lessened. Ironically, for some ambitious people it's the daily stresses of living and working with people that create high-anxiety problems. For instance, while I may be accustomed to managing minimal levels of stress as a vocal performer, I'm not prepared to get in an airplane with a parachute strapped to my back for a first-time jump, a feat that would no doubt produce very high stress levels. But the good news is that, regardless of what stressful situations we may encounter, there are techniques and strategies we can all use to minimize stress, even in fearful and threatening situations.

Cognitive Therapy

Cognitive therapy is one effective coping strategy that psychiatrists and psychologists use in assisting persons with confronting and challenging distorted thought processes that underlie certain disorders. Persons who effectively manage the negative aspects of stress maintain a combination of several behavioral characteristics:

• *Present orientation*—a tendency to focus on immediate issues rather than global ones, for example, helping a sick person get well or feel better rather than worrying about death.

• *Commitment*—an intense involvement in whatever activity is undertaken, and the desire to do one's best.

• *Control*—a belief that taking action makes a difference; and accepting responsibility for whatever action is taken, regardless of the outcome.

• *Optimistic style*—problems are interpreted as temporary rather than permanent.

• *Challenge*—the ability to see any activity as an opportunity to grow, improve, and succeed, with a sense of curiosity and a receptiveness to change.

People who cope successfully with stress, generally speaking, prefer permanent, long-term solutions rather than short-term, band-aid approaches. In addition to setting realistic goals and priorities, they learn and apply effective time-management skills that help them reach their goals without encountering undue stress.

In setting the foundation for reducing stress, we also need to know how to replenish our energy reserves along the way. So we'll now consider three principal ways to recharge our batteries, beginning with sleep and rest, then meditation and relaxation, and concluding with recreation.

Sleep and Rest

The latest data about Americans from the National Sleep Foundation indicates that more than half report sleeping problems, and two-thirds receive less than the eight hours of sleep recommended by the American Academy of Sleep Medicine. The inability to fall asleep readily is known as *onset insomnia,* and difficulty in remaining asleep is known as *sleep-maintenance insomnia,* which is more commonly experienced by older adults. Of course, sleeplessness or prolonged stress leads to fatigue and physical lethargy, which affects our behavior in a variety of ways. What, then, do we know about the nature and function of sleep?

Sleep is promoted in the absence of light, when large amounts of the hormone *melatonin* are released from the pineal gland. Two primary functions of sleep are conservation of biological energy and thermal regulation for the brain and other vital organs. There's also thought to be a link between sleep and brain plasticity, reorganization of synapses associated with learning, and formation of emotional memory. Of course, the restorative function of sleep is well known, for we typically feel better after a night of sleeping soundly. Our biological clocks are based on a *circadian rhythm,* which creates the highs and lows of a 24-hour physiological cycle. There are five distinct phases of sleep, including *rapid eye movement* (REM), plus four progressively deepening non-REM stages of sleep, each recognized by distinct and varied brain waveform patterns. Some experts believe the number of sleep cycles occurring during each sleep period may be more restorative than the total length of sleep.

The amount of sleep one gets is correlated more with personality type than amount of activity during the daytime. Short sleepers habitually sleep 6.5 hours or less per night, normal sleepers get 7-8 hours per night, and long sleepers obtain more than 9 hours. The early bird and night owl types may be biologically determined. Studies show that it takes an average of 8.25 hours of sleep to optimize biological systems, so the more regular and peaceful the sleeping period, the more revitalized the body becomes.

Because individual sleep requirements vary widely, each person must determine how much is needed for optimal functioning, and schedule it into a daily time-management program. Steps for establishing "sleep hygiene" include:

• *Establishing a fixed sleeping schedule* by going to bed and getting up at set times when the body clock is stabilized.

• *Controlling the sleeping environment* by regulating room temperature to a comfortable level, minimizing noise, keeping the room dark, and using a comfortable bed.

• *Accommodating sleep* by exercising regularly, eating lightly before bedtime, and avoiding caffeine, tobacco, alcohol, and recreational drugs.

• *Preparing for sleep before bedtime* by taking a warm bath, pursuing low-key pleasant activities, and using relaxation techniques to calm the mind.

• *Using beds for appropriate purposes* such as sleeping, sex, and brief pleasure reading prior to sleep.

Many sleepless people resort to sleeping aids, which in some cases may only aggravate the problem, as some popular drugs, especially barbiturates and benzodiazepines (Valium), can cause drowsiness and be habit-forming. Bettye and I have never taken any sleeping aids—with the exception of those administered during hospital stays for surgeries and illnesses—and we plan on abstaining as long as possible. The latest types are the non-benzodiazepine hypnotics, such as Ambien, Ambien CR (controlled release), and Lunesta, the types mentioned in the *Mayo Clinic Health Letter* (January 2008) as potential aids for most persons who have trouble staying asleep, with the caveat that drowsiness may linger the next day.

In sum, getting sufficient sleep as we age is increasingly difficult, due to all manner of physical problems, including minor aches and pains, limbs going to sleep, snoring, and trips to the restroom. I can barely remember sleeping for 7-8 solid hours, without awakening at some point. Bettye's sleep patterns are variable, and sometimes irregular. In recent years she's developed the habit of awakening after sleeping three to four hours, then lying awake and reading for an hour or so until eventually falling back to sleep, and awakening nine to ten hours after she first went to sleep (around 10:00 p.m.) On a positive note, she gets in a respectable amount of reading this way, helping to boost her reading list to 100 or more books annually. We both agree that as long as we can average of 6-7 hours sleep nightly, we'll rely on non-medicated sleeping measures, including regular exercise, not eating too close to bedtime, refraining from caffeinated drink, relaxing before bedtime, and so on.

Relaxation and Meditation

Everyone can benefit from learning stress-reduction techniques, to calm the mind, increase mental concentration, and attune the body for appropriate muscle responses. Though one's emotional state largely determines the severity of muscle tension, relaxation techniques often begin with giving attention to developing deep breathing and muscle relaxation techniques. There are several methods for achieving greater awareness of body tensions caused by such ailments as headaches, muscle spasms and general aches, including progressive relaxation, meditation, and guided fantasies.

To think clearly and positively requires emptying the mind of negative thoughts, beginning with calming body activity, especially muscles and internal organs. The *relaxation response*, which is the opposite of the stress response, results in a slower breathing rate, a slower heartbeat, lower blood pressure, less need for cellular oxygen, depletion of hormones from the blood stream, and brain production of alpha or theta waves, indicating deep mental rest.

One of the most common relaxation techniques is *meditation*, which may be described as an approach to living with greater awareness by emptying the mind of extraneous thoughts and concentrating on one thing in order to aid mind-body relaxation, contemplation, or spiritual development. A useful analogy is that of watching a train loaded with your thoughts going by, but all the while resisting the urge to jump on the train to go with your thoughts. In other words, meditation can aid in developing objectivity, whereby we learn to witness our thoughts and emotions, rather than being completely guided by egoistic drives.

So the main purpose is not only to learn how to meditate effectively but more so to become a more fully awake, conscious person, and more capable of experiencing reality, rather than entertaining delusional ways of thinking and acting. By delusional I mean the mistaken, false, imagined, misperceived versions of events and activities that we are conditioned into seeing. To see reality clearly and accurately is the goal, and this takes distancing ourselves from our egos, creating a psycho-emotional state of openness (emptiness) that allows the truth of a situation to shine through. The old adage voiced by some meditation gurus—"Don't just do something, sit there"—is a reminder of the need to release and let-go, in effect emptying the mind of extraneous thoughts in order to create a fully relaxed and receptive mind-body state.

Dean Ornish (1993) lists seven reasons for undertaking meditation:

- To increase powers of concentration.

- To increase awareness of one's environment.

- To increase awareness of what's going on inside oneself.

- To calm the mind and to experience inner sources of peace, joy, and nourishment.

- To get a clearer picture or perspective of oneself.

- To experience the present moment rather than dwelling on the past or worrying about the future.

- To give oneself the direct experience of transcendence, perhaps the most powerful way to heal isolation.

Ornish claims that many practitioners recommend meditating once or twice per day for at least 20-30 minutes each time, but the length of time is not as important as the regularity. A shorter daily period works better than an extended session once weekly. For reasons of brevity, the exercise listed later is geared for approximately 10 or more minutes, which most people can manage.

Jon Kabat-Zinn, PhD, a professor of medicine and prominent expert in stress-reduction, provides another view of meditation (Moyers 1993):

Meditation is a discipline for training the mind to develop greater calm and then to use that calm to bring penetrative insight into our own experience in the moment . . . Much of the time we run around so much on automatic pilot, and we have so much chatter going on, and we're so busy, we hardly know who's doing the doing. Meditation is a way of slowing down enough so that we get in touch with who we are, and then we can inform the doing with a greater level of awareness and consciousness.

One simple and effective way to achieve the relaxation response is to combine meditation with *progressive relaxation* techniques. While moving thoughts slowly and progressively throughout the entire body, practitioners concentrate on relaxing certain muscle groups. This exercise requires tightening muscles, followed by completely releasing all tension, all the while paying attention to all mind-body sensations. This low-tech exercise is less complicated and less expensive than *biofeedback* techniques which require high-tech laboratory equipment (such as electromyography), as well as expert medical supervision.

Preparation for a relaxation-meditation routine might begin with selecting a one-syllable focus word, such as "love," "one," "calm," or "om." Throughout all stages of the routine, one should maintain concentration on either relaxing tense muscles or on the breathing process, inhaling and exhaling slowly. When the mind wanders, bring it gently back to the focal point of muscle relaxation, breathing, or focus word. Like any worthwhile exercise, this exercise requires considerable practice to master the mental focus used in relaxing tense muscles and quieting the mind. Ideally, one should strive to practice 15-20 minutes of meditation in the morning before beginning the day's activities, and another 15-20 in the evening at the conclusion of a busy day. Of course, any time given to meditation will help calm one down, even a minute or two, especially when beginning to feel stressed.

A few years ago I began meditating 15-20 minutes in the morning, but recently I've begun using a series of CD recordings known as Holosync, which starts out with 30 minutes daily for two weeks, and notches up to an hour daily, and continues with several levels, with each adding new material, including recordings of one's own voice. This unique program uses sound and subliminal material to affect brain waves, automatically helping the listener/meditator to relax and absorb information. In 1989, Bill Harris, founder and head of Centerpointe (www.centerpointe.com), created this program using an innovative technology, with the promise that it will hasten meditative progress — if used regularly and according to instructions. I'm hoping to achieve positive results, as I would like to confidently recommend it to others. One drawback for many people is the cost of the entire program, which can be expensive, but the first level will probably suffice for most people.

There are many forms of meditation, each adaptable to individual needs and objectives. The most popular and fundamental form of meditation is aimed at achieving mind-body relaxation. The relaxation exercise routine below can be completed in a few minutes. If distracted by surrounding noise, use earplugs, white background noise, or recorded relaxation music. Wear comfortable loose-fitting clothes and close your eyes to shut out visual distractions. This exercise can be especially helpful in calming and centering oneself before engaging in a stressful activity.

- *Sitting position preparation.* Sit with an erect posture on the front edge of a comfortable straight-back chair, with hands placed in a comfortable lap position. Keep knees separated 8-12 inches and angled slightly more than 90 degrees, so that your legs and feet are slanted slightly forward. Relax abdominal muscles, elevate chest comfortably but not too high as to cause tension, square shoulders, and gently stretch head upward with a sense of lift at the back of the neck. A slumping posture may cause one to fall asleep.

• *Rag-doll.* From this sitting position, collapse over and downward like a loose rag-doll, with head forward, spine rounded, arms hanging loosely, and chest resting on the knees. In this relaxed position use autogenic phrases ("self-talk"), such as "I'm feeling calm; my arms, hands, and fingers are heavy," and so on through the entire body. After 20-30 seconds, while taking a slow, full, deep breath, straighten back up slowly to a sitting position. When full upright posture is attained, take a breath and exhale, using a deep, peaceful sigh.

• *Tension/release body scan.* In the sitting position, mentally scan (X-ray) the entire body from toes to head, tensing and relaxing muscles. Begin with feet muscles by flexing and contracting toes and arches. Then, move slowly to the calves, thighs, hips and pelvis, lower abdomen (briefly observe breathing), stomach, back, chest, shoulders, arms, neck, and face. Facial muscles can be tightly drawn toward the center of the face, and released, then expanded outward using a terrified expression, and relaxed. Instead of deliberately tensing muscles, another option is to mentally scan from toe to head slowly for existing muscle tensions, releasing tensions at will.

• *Breathing focus.* While seated, begin by taking one or two slow breaths, through your nose, if possible, and then holding for four counts, and then releasing slowly. Next, observe normal breathing patterns for a few moments. If the rate of breathing is fast, allow it to slow down, or if it is shallow and high, allow it to settle deeper. At this point it is possible to coordinate a "focus word", such as "om" or "one", with each exhalation of breath, somewhat like imagining ocean waves gently rising (inhalation) and falling (exhalation). Whenever the mind wanders, observe any thoughts objectively, let them flow away, and calmly return to focusing on breathing. Continue this final stage for at least 5 minutes or more, until time runs out or you feel refreshed.

A *guided fantasy* routine may also help induce a calming relaxation effect. This technique involves vividly imagining pleasant personal situations that help induce deeper relaxation. Begin by closing your eyes and imagining a peaceful scene, such as sitting on a sunny beach (with a covering and sunscreen applied), calmly viewing and listening to the surf, or enjoying a beautiful, temperate day sitting on a rock ledge and viewing a panoramic mountain vista. Recollections of memorable places and times in one's life can be retrieved at any time for meditative and relaxation purposes. The idea is to imagine actually being there, using all senses (hearing, seeing, feeling, smelling) in reproducing the event.

In tense moments when time is at a premium, a ten-second *calming exercise* might prove helpful. Begin by envisioning seeing someone or something you care deeply about. Then smile inwardly and think, "My body is calm." Next, inhale more deeply than normal, and upon exhaling allow the jaw, tongue, and shoulders to relax and drop a bit. This brief procedure can help restore composure when encountering a negative or frustrating situation.

The exercise routine listed below provides a systematic approach for developing awareness of relaxation and tension, with the goal of learning how to release excessive tensions that often block psycho-emotional and physical energies. When doing these exercises, it will help to use a full-length mirror or video equipment for self-observation.

• *Tension/release.* Stretch arms and hands straight out in front; tighten and release. Spread arms straight out to both sides; tighten and release. Pull shoulders up to ears; tighten and release. Make a distorted, tense facial expression and release.

• *Shoulder Rotation.* Rotate two full turns, first with shoulders forward (up and over), then backwards (down and under). Note how the rib cage expands and the chest elevates when shoulders rotate to a backward position, as another goal is to achieve an up-stretched body alignment.

• *Neck and Head Stretch.* While standing tall, look over each shoulder by turning the head gently and slowly to left, then right, holding each time in position for 5 slow one-second counts (one-thousand, two thousand, etc.). Move head back to facing straight ahead, tip the head first toward the left shoulder, then the right shoulder, and finally, forward, holding each position for 5 counts.

• *Jaw Drop and Stretch.* Affect a "dumb-jaw" feeling with absolutely no facial expression other than stupidity or disbelief. Just let it hang loosely, along with the tongue, which should be very relaxed. Yawn contentedly with the jaw comfortably stretched, and then chew slowly and with exaggeration. Check under the chin (chin to larynx) for muscle tension. Most people tend to carry a lot of tension in the articulating organs, especially the jaw, tongue, and lips.

Humor and Positive Thinking

Among the most accessible strategies for handling stress is to learn how to relax, and one of the most effective ways is to have a good sense of humor, and laugh as much as possible.

Some medical research suggests humor and laughing exercises the lungs and circulatory system and increases the amount of oxygen in the blood, thereby assisting the healthy function of blood vessels, with tissue in the blood vessels dilating, increasing blood flow, and potentially reducing the risk of arteriosclerosis (hardening of the arteries). Another explanation says that laughter increases a disease-fighting protein, B-cells, the source of a disease-destroying antibody, and T-cells which help cellular immune response. Medical studies also show that laughter boosts levels of endorphins, the body's natural painkillers, and suppresses levels of epinephrine, the stress hormone. In short, laughter is a tranquilizer that lacks harmful side effects.

Since we're on the subject of using humor to achieve good health, let's try a practice exercise. A friend sent via email the following excerpted reports in patients' hospital charts, as written by their doctors. Enjoy!

- She has no rigors or shaking chills, but her husband states she was very hot in bed last night.

- Patient has chest pain if she lies on her left side for over a year.

- On the second day the knee was better, and on the third day it disappeared.

- The patient is tearful and crying constantly. She also appears to be depressed.

- The patient refused autopsy.

- Between you and me, we ought to be able to get this lady pregnant.

- She is numb from her toes down.

- While in ER, she was examined, X-rated and sent home.

- The skin was moist and dry.

- She has occasional, constant, infrequent headaches.

- Patient was alert and unresponsive.

- Rectal examination revealed a normal size thyroid (uh, hemorrhoid?).

- Both breasts are equal and reactive to light and accommodation.

- Examination of genitalia reveals that he is circus sized.

- The lab test indicated abnormal lover function.

- The pelvic exam will be done later on the floor.

- Patient has two teenage children, but no other abnormalities.

Principal Mind-Body Strategies

Several mind-body strategies are worth exploring, especially for persons desiring to improve muscle flexibility and posture, or to reduce stressful muscle-tension habits.

Aerobic and Anaerobic Exercise. In the previous chapter we discussed the importance of exercise for overall health; here we add its role in reducing mind-body stress. Besides improving circulation, exercise causes an array of chemical changes in the brain, including: boosting mood-enhancing activity of neurotransmitters, such as dopamine and serotonin; increasing the production of the so-called *neurotrophic* factor, a brain-derived chemical that helps neurons multiply and form new connections; and triggering the release of endorphins, the morphine-like chemicals that subdue pain and assist relaxation. Even 10 minutes of vigorous exercise that produces a pulse rate of 100-120 beats per minute can raise endorphin levels for an hour or more, creating what is known as the "endorphin high". Most experts concur that a regular, well-rounded, vigorous program that includes both aerobic and anaerobic exercise routines offers the best overall mind-body strategy.

Alexander Technique. One of the most popular and successful body-mind methods is the *Alexander Technique,* named after Australian Frederick Matthias Alexander (1869-1955). As a young actor in Melbourne, Alexander experienced frequent bouts of debilitating hoarseness, forcing him to reexamine his vocal technique. Over several months of astute observation, he came to realize he had developed some bad habits, associated primarily with posture, breathing, and laryngeal manipulation. For the next ten years he observed himself using three-way mirrors, experimenting with his body positions and movement. As he gained expertise, he began working with his brother and eventually other actors. He came to the simple conclusion that he had to unlearn a lifetime of detrimental physical and vocal habits of misuse and abuse, and to discover better ways of using his body and voice. For a detailed account of his efforts the reader is directed to Alexander's book *The Use of the Self* (1932).

According to Jane R. Heirich (1993), there are five fundamental principles of the Alexander Technique:

• A human being is a working unity and must be treated as a whole, which means that excess muscular effort anywhere in the body interferes with the rest of the system.

• A great many of our problems are the direct result of *how* we do *what* we do, such as using slouching posture and clenching our jaw when tense.

• What is familiar feels "right," or put another way what is habitual feels familiar (try clasping your hands together, first in a familiar way and then the other, and notice the difference in feeling).

• The working of the human organism is guided by "primary control," Alexander's term for a certain balanced relationship of the head and the neck to each other, and of this head-neck position in relation to the entire torso.

• An Alexander lesson is a process of re-education that begins with mutual awareness of the given conditions and an assessment of what needs changing, with the student learning to bring unconscious habit to the level of conscious awareness, thereby learning what habits to avoid and promoting new habitual behavior.

The three basic "directions" of the Alexander Technique are: (1) let the neck be free (allow the tension in the neck muscles not to increase); (2) let the head go forward and up (allow it not to be pulled back or down); and (3) let the torso widen out and lengthen up (allow it not to be short-ended and narrowed by arching the spine). This single sensory experience is the *primary control* and is not passive relaxation but an active process accompanying the execution of any movement (Duarte 1980). For anyone interested in exploring this technique, there is much available information; and qualified Alexander teachers are located throughout the world, especially in the U.S.

Yoga. Essentially, yoga may be thought of as a group of Hindu disciplines that promote unity of the individual with a supreme being through a system of postures, breathing exercises, and rituals. Patanjali, an ancient sage, taught *raja-yoga*, a Hindu technique used for developing spiritual enlightenment, in its complete form around 150 B.C. The technique consists of eight stages, usually known as the "limbs of yoga". The first two, which deal with ethical training, consist of certain *restraints* (non-injury, truthfulness, non-stealing, continence, and non-possession) and *obser-vances* (cleanliness, contentment, penance, study of scrip-ture, and devotion to God). The third and fourth stages involve training in body posture and control of the breath-ing process, the two stages most Westerners adopt. The fifth stage is concerned with withdrawal of senses from their objects. And the final three stages constitute yoga proper, with a process of developing mind-control through con-centration, contemplation, and absorption. The main forms of yoga are discussed in the previous chapter.

Prominent health experts tout the positive benefits of yoga, including Dean Ornish, whose research and work with numerous patients shows increases in health and wellness through proper nutrition and exercise. Some of yoga's promoted health benefits include preventing and healing a variety of illnesses, such as arthritis, carpal tun-nel syndrome, coronary-artery disease, and asthma. Per-sons interested in participating in yoga training should prepare in advance by researching the various types of programs and instructors that are available.

Massage. One of the oldest strategies for relieving physi-cal and psycho-emotional stress, massage has increasingly become more common, especially in sports medicine. Skill-ful massage therapists, for example, can press lactic acid out of muscles after strenuous exercise to ease the pain experienced by marathon runners and tri-athletes. Also, by dispersing fluids in muscles, massage usually reduces inflammation caused by sprains and injuries—if used two days following the injury. Research shows that mas-sage can reduce blood pressure, boost the immune system, dampen harmful stress hormones and raise levels of *sero-tonin*, a mood-elevating hormone. Other benefits of mas-sage are indirect, as when stimulated nerves transport sig-nals from the skin and muscles to the brain, subsequently triggering changes throughout the body. Massage stimu-lates the brain's *vagus nerve*, which causes the secretion of food-absorption hormones, including insulin. It seems that all nerve cells in the body are somehow interconnected, and even brain waves may be altered through massage.

Massage therapies include light touch as well as "deep tissue" massage. "Trigger-point therapy" can help relieve certain types of pain by prodding and stretching out sensitive aching spots, as when properly applied finger pressure on upper shoulder muscles relieves neck tensions. While greater pressure is usually needed for injured muscles and joints, persons needing simply to relax may find relief with a Swedish massage, with its gentle, long strokes. For additional information, contact the American Massage Therapy Association, based in the Chicago area.

Pilates. Designed to stretch, strengthen, and balance the body—especially the torso—Pilates uses a systematic practice of specific exercises coupled with focused breathing patterns that apply very well to overall fitness training and various kinds of physical rehabilitation. The origin of the method helps explain current practices. Its founder, Joseph Pilates, was a performer and a boxer living in England at the outbreak of World War I (1914). Along with other German nationals, he was placed under forced internment in Lancaster, England, where he taught fellow internees the concepts and exercises developed over 20 years of self-study and apprenticeship in yoga, Zen, and ancient Greek and Roman physical regimens. At that time, he began devising a system of original exercises known today as "matwork" (floor exercises), a regimen he termed "Contrology." A few years later, Pilates was transferred to another camp, where he became a nurse and caretaker for many internees with wartime diseases and physical injuries. There he devised rehabilitation equipment for bedridden patients, ingeniously using bed springs for spring resistance training. Modern Pilates equipment resembles the original concept, including spring tension, and straps to hold feet or hands, supports for back, neck and shoulder. This type of equipment both challenges and supports the body as it learns to move more efficiently, and serves as a effective complement to the challenging "matwork" exercises.

With regular, long-term practice, Pilates is said to yield numerous benefits, including improvements in bone density and joints, and increased lung capacity and circulation through deep, healthy breathing, which is a primary focus. An effective Pilates program includes exercises for improving strength and flexibility, particularly of the abdomen and back muscles, mind-body coordination, posture, balance, and core strength. As practitioners learn to balance and control their bodies, many experience positive body awareness for the first time, a capacity that influences other areas of life.

Other Body-Mind Strategies

Six other body-mind strategies are worth exploring:

Hypnosis. Dr. David Spiegel, of Stanford School of Medicine, says hypnosis is an effective way of enhancing people's control over certain bodily functions and sensations. He thinks of hypnosis as a form of "highly focused attention"—an induced state of mind that enables individuals to alter the way they perceive and process reality. In guiding a patient into a state of receptive concentration, a qualified hypnotist normally suggests that he or she imagines a safe and comfortable place. Once the patient is in a hypnotized state, the practitioner makes specific suggestions, usually calculated to help with a specific problem. At a certain point, the practitioner terminates the patient's trance, and follows up with instructions regarding use of self-hypnosis to reactivate and maintain therapeutic effects. Many people are better able to relax, manage pain, and deal with personality problems through hypnosis. [My father-in-law was able to induce self-hypnosis when having serious dental work, an admirable achievement. In some ways, deep meditation might be considered a form of self-hypnosis.]

Trager Approach. Founded by Milton Trager, M.D., the Trager method concentrates on appropriate muscle and joint motion. The objective is to produce positive, pleasurable feelings that enter the central nervous system, causing many complex sensory-motor feedback loops between the mind and body to trigger body tissue changes. A basic principle of the method is: When a body *feels* lighter, it begins to respond as though it *were* lighter.

Feldenkreis Method. Dr. Mosche Feldenkreis observed infants exploring new ways of moving, and found that similar movements could be used with adults to increase self-awareness and ability to function in a more fluid, less tense manner during any activity. The Feldenkreis Method has two main facets. *Awareness through movement* is a technique for groups employing imagery and keen attention during movement to change the brain patterns that organize and control body functioning. Another facet is *functional integration*, an intensive, hands-on, one-on-one teaching approach using a practitioner's touch to communicate change in another person's body organization, thereby enhancing muscular efficiency, coordination, and ease.

T'ai Chi Ch'uan. This ancient method uses both a form of self-defense ("hard style") and a slow-motion exercise ("soft style") that purports to circulate the chi (vital force) through the body to achieve health and longevity. Practiced for more than twenty-three centuries, it became formulated approximately 700 years ago by Chang San Feng, a Taoist priest of the Sung dynasty. T'ai Chi is a system of rounded, fluid, balanced movements that its believers practice daily to promote health and peace of mind. The goal is to "move like the clouds, eternally transforming without the appearance of change," thereby connecting with nature through movement. In balancing body energy (chi), the method demands considerable physical strength and mental concentration. I learned a four-minute T'ai chi routine by observing two instructive video recordings for several hours, and I do it as a warm-down in conjunction with a five-minute Qigong routine.

Qigong (Chi-Kung). Another Chinese discipline, Qigong is closely associated with Tai Chi and is often taught by instructors proficient in both mind-body strategies. Both strategies concentrate on developing chi (vital force or energy) and using it for energizing, healing, and restoring mind-body health. My wife and I underwent an introductory course taught by a Chinese master, Jinan (Eijah) Zheng, and we found it helpful in inducing relaxation through the regular practice of deep breathing, gentle physical relaxation exercises, and mental imagery. However, I'm still skeptical regarding some spectacular healing claims made by experienced practitioners. I'd like to see some hard evidence of healings based on verified scientific studies of all similar energy-based disciplines, not only Qigong.

Rolfing. As a method of "structural integration", Rolfing is based on the belief that gravity is the prime sculptor of the human form. When serving as a biochemist and a research scientist at New York's Rockefeller Institute for Medical Research, 1917-1927, Ida Rolf developed a concept of the body as a collection of major segments—head, chest, hip area, legs—each stacked on top of the other like a pile of blocks. When all blocks are perfectly aligned, as though a plumb line runs from the head to the feet, a body is considered well aligned and balanced. Rolfing requires a more vigorous hands-on approach than either the Alexander Technique or the Feldenkreis Method, using such manipulations as pushing, prodding, kneading, and elbowing, with the objective of readjusting the *fascia*, the connective tissue that connects the muscle.

It should be clear from all the above that both relaxation (quiet time) and recreation (play time) are needed to gain a sense of wholeness and balance. Any pleasant activity that reduces or alleviates stress and sets the stage for regeneration is helpful. So, rather than running full steam until we are exhausted, we should schedule regular stress-free, energy-restoring breaks throughout the day, in addition to scheduling more extended daily and weekend recreational activities. As we age, we need to remain active, but the type of activities and the way we pursue them will need adjusting, particularly as we move toward old age. In all cases, it helps to remind ourselves that mind-body health is the number one priority, not the self-induced "important" activity we're undertaking that contributes to creating high stress levels. To summarize, the basic lesson is to set reasonable and achievable goals, keep activities manageable, make adequate preparations, allow plenty of time to accomplish tasks, make time for exercise, rest, and recreation, and, as the young suggest: "stay cool"!

Relaxed, Deep Breathing

At the heart of most relaxation techniques is an emphasis on efficient breathing, which can be a tremendous aid in counteracting the shallow, tense breathing habits that contribute to feelings of stress associated with such emotions as nervousness and fright. In teaching group voice for the past 25 years, and private lessons for more than 45 years, I've observed hundreds of persons' breathing habits. Though many people improved their overall breathing through the study of singing, one case sticks out in my mind. A woman in her late 40s wrote me a letter at the end of a voice-class term, enthusiastically reporting that by improving her breathing habits through voice study she had finally found some relief from the chronic pain she had experienced following an auto accident a decade earlier. This inspiring report, plus many other positive experiences working with singers, confirms in my mind the benefits of learning efficient breathing techniques.

Although several disciplines concentrate on breathing technique, yoga is highly recommended as an overall mind-body strategy for developing efficient breathing skills. As an introduction, the simple breathing exercises below, which expand on the meditative relaxation exercise mentioned earlier, will help get you started.

• Sit with an erect posture on the front edge of a comfortable straight-back chair. Keep knees separated 8-12 inches and angled slightly more than 90 degrees, so legs and feet are slanted slightly forward. Relax abdominal muscles, elevate chest comfortably, square shoulders, and gently stretch head upward with a sense of lift at the back of the neck.

• Place your right hand open on your lower abdominal area (gut) with the thumb tip located on your navel. Relaxation experts speak of "centering" oneself by concentrating on a point approximately 2 inches below the navel, which is approximately where the focus of breath expansion and energy should be felt when speaking or expelling air.

• Place your left hand flat on your upper abdominal area (stomach area below breast bone or sternum), with your little finger tip touching your navel and right thumb tip. In this position you will be able to experience the effects of deep breathing.

• Empty the lungs by blowing out as much air as possible. Hold this empty position for 5-10 seconds before letting air enter the lungs to gain a full, deep breath. Allow the rushing air intake to completely fill the torso in a downward-and-outward manner. If this exercise is performed correctly, your hands will move outward as a result of incoming air. It's important to relax the lower abdominal wall rather than holding it in.

• With relaxed jaw, closed teeth (not clenched), and slightly parted lips, suck the air in slowly for 4-5 counts, suspending it for 1-2 counts, and hiss it out slowly for 10-plus counts or until the lungs feel empty and a need for air is apparent. Then let the breath be sucked in, causing the lungs to fill with air.

• Observe that when exhaling or blowing out, the action of the abdominal muscles is inward and upward, the opposite of when inhaling. If everything is working correctly, you should be ready to explore the connection of vocal tone and breath.

Another useful exercise to check your breathing involves lying down in a supine position on a bed or the floor. Using a small pillow to cushion your head — and to take pressure off your lower back — bend the knees at a right angle and place feet flat on the floor. Place both hands on your lower to mid-abdominal area to feel what happens when inhaling and exhaling. Relax all over, imagine you're about to go to sleep, and breathe naturally and slowly. Observe the rising and lowering action: hands rising upon inhalation and lowering upon exhalation. Breathe as deeply as possible, all the while remaining relaxed and calm.

Any breathing exercises need to be practiced regularly, which means daily. When experiencing fatigue, frustration, or stress of any kind, just take time—as little as two or three minutes—to practice the above exercises and relaxation techniques. You might be surprised at how much more relaxed you feel afterwards.

The Need for Peace and Quiet

Silence, like a poultice, comes to heal the blows of sound.
—Oliver Wendell Holmes

Noise is an unrecognized cause of stress in modern times. As we age, the internal ear becomes more brittle, especially the tympanic membrane; we also become more sensitive to loud noises and high frequencies, which are the first to disappear when hearing loss occurs. At least 30 million Americans experience either partial or full hearing loss, and noise pollution is the primary culprit in one-third of the cases. According to the Centers for Disease Control and Prevention, hearing problems increased 26 percent from 1971 to 1990 among Americans ages 45-64.

Young persons can typically recover from a sound/noise barrage in excess of 110 decibels (dBA), which occurs at a concert or listening to a portable "boom box" for up to three hours. As we age, the resiliency of our hearing diminishes. After enduring years of loud, abusive noise, the ears begin to tire, beginning with the loss of cells that respond to high frequencies. The first sounds to go unheard are voiceless phonemes, such as "s" and "f". Tinnitus, a high-pitched, continuous ring, hiss, hum, or roar, is a hearing affliction of many older people, including me. Though high-pitched ear ringing is usually masked by other sounds or, in most cases, just ignored, it is always present. Thankfully, the rest of my hearing appears normal for my age.

There's no question that modern civilization is bombarded with higher noise levels than occurred prior to the advent of the industrial revolution in the 19th century. Living in a major downtown area or neighborhood (as in New York City) can be a very noisy experience, with a chaotic cacophony of sounds and noises during the daytime that are seldom relieved by periods of peaceful silence. Even the nighttime sleeping hours can be interrupted by periodic loud noises generated by the likes of celebrating party-goers, sirens from fire trucks and police cars, overhead jet planes and helicopters, and early morning garbage trucks or construction crews. Media sounds also are ever-present, with a constant barrage of talk, noise, and music emanating from television sets and sound systems in most public places, as well as in our homes. The tendency for TV commercials to be louder than the regular programming is an obnoxious reality, one many often control by muting the sound during commercials. The overall effect has been a diminishing of our collective attention span, to the point that we require constant, mindless stimulation.

In addition to sustained, high-decibel sounds causing hearing loss, constant noise levels also diminish the overall quality of life, by raising blood pressure and stress-related cortisol levels, increasing irritability and fatigue, and interfering with concentration in learning and performing certain tasks. Even the natural solitude of our nation's woodlands, canyon lands, deserts, and plains is increasingly experiencing disruptive noises, led chiefly by such motorized vehicles as all-terrain vehicles (ATVs), snowmobiles, and off-road machines. In addition to creating thousands of miles of rutted and eroding trails, "off-road" vehicles are intruding on the solitude sought by nature lovers, as well as disrupting the natural habitat of creatures that populate delicate eco-systems.

Jim Glaser, a Sierra Club member and woodworker who lives in northern Chippewa National Forest, states that noise is the largest concern he and his neighbors have about the intrusion of ATVs in his area, especially on weekends when a steady stream pour by his cabin home. He says, "When I notice the sound the most is when I'm outside carving. The ATV noise is constant, always in the background. You don't hear the birds, the crickets, or the squirrels running through the branches of the trees."

Even the family home is not impervious to noise infiltration. In the last fifty years sophisticated citizens have traded brooms for noisy vacuum cleaners, push mowers for power mowers, manual hedge clippers, weed trimmers, handsaws, and drills for motorized versions. Also, entertainment systems have increased from simple radios and stereo systems to large-screen TVs and powerful sound systems. The typical modern kitchen is stocked with a variety of work-reducing equipment, some of which can be very noisy. (Our newest dishwasher is a quiet model, but our former bread-maker generated a beat similar to a pile driver, the major reason we retired it.)

In sum, we're surrounded by a variety of sounds and noises, inside and outside the home, some pleasant and some offensive. As cities grow into major metropolitan areas, more people are subject to noise associated with freeways and fly-over airplanes. (Fortunately, our condo is located three miles from the nearest freeway and over twenty miles from the airport, so freeway traffic and low-flying jets are rarely the problem they can be for neighborhoods in closer proximity.) Studies of second graders in New York City show that those exposed to regular chronic bombarding of fly-over jet plane noise of 90 dB—the equivalent of a vacuum cleaner—scored about 20 percent lower on reading tests than children who were placed in quiet environments.

Nature's sounds can also occasionally overpower one's hearing. For instance, when the hundreds of frogs in our former marsh pond area began their courting dance in the spring, the resultant din could be overwhelming. When the windows were open, it was almost impossible to hear the TV without turning it up to uncomfortable decibel levels. Noise produced by other natural phenomena, such as thunder, high winds, volcanoes, and waterfalls can also affect one's hearing.

So, what are some measures individuals and society can undertake to reduce noise pollution in order to protect our precious sense of hearing and improve the overall quality of life? Here are some suggestions:

• Guard against hearing loss, first, by avoiding continuous loud noise (in excess of 85-90 decibels) whenever possible, and, second, by wearing either earplugs or acoustic earmuffs when loud noises can't be avoided, for example, when operating power lawn and garden equipment such as leafblowers or chainsaws.

• Educate others, especially young children, about the negative effects of excessive noise.

• Convince the designers and manufacturers of noisy products to produce quieter models.

• Purchase power equipment, vehicles, and indoor appliances that are rated at quiet levels. (Check with consumer groups, such as Consumer Reports—www. consumerReports.com—for ratings of all types of equipment, according to cost, safety, efficiency, durability, and noise levels.)

• Organize grass-roots groups for the purpose of increasing public awareness of noise pollution (See Vermont-based Noise Pollution Clearinghouse—www.nonoise. org—for news about various noise issues, links to other anti-noise groups, and examples of effective ordinances.)

• Become an advocate for government policies that address all aspects of environmental noise pollution, backed by legislation aimed at promoting and protecting peoples' hearing, as well as providing quietude for relaxation, concentration, learning, and reflection.

I am convinced that heavy bombardment of noise in modern society is not only a threat to our hearing and listening, but also has a negative impact on our psycho-emotional state. Simply put, we need to have periods of quiet in order to concentrate, meditate, and function optimally.

Summary and Conclusion

Moderate to heavy levels of stress can cause both emotional and physical pain, and in some cases long-term suffering.

In learning to cope effectively with stress, we also learn how to manage pain through healing processes.

People react in a variety of ways to stress, some craving it and others fearing it, depending on the nature of a particular activity, event, or situation. Coming to grips with our anxieties and fears requires a balancing of our emotions and expectations. For example, when placed in a given situation that requires some type of verbal response or action, it might be best to proceed with caution, rather than reacting with a knee-jerk response, or running away from what might provide a potentially good opportunity to achieve something worthwhile. In such instances, it usually works well to take some deep breaths, calm and focus the mind on the situation, and consider all options before taking action.

Finding an objective viewpoint in emotionally charged situations is very challenging, but with practice it can be done. In practical terms, when confronted by an irate person yelling accusations without provocation, our immediate response is one of either fight or flight. But the middle-path option involves a calm observation of the situation, focusing the mind on the problem, making a decision based on reason, tactfulness, and responsible behavior. This Zen-like approach is more easily expressed than accomplished, but with practice one can achieve a more detached, objective, yet empathetic state of awareness. Thus, when faced with an irate person in a potentially inflammatory situation, the goal is to use both rational (cognitive) and emotional (intuitive) means to resolve the conflict and lessen stress levels. In other words, calm down, objectively consider all relevant information, and try to empathize with the irate individual's point of view.

Bear in mind that any response we make—in any situation, no matter the source or provocation—is usually within our control. Of course, when attacked by someone whose intent is to inflict harm, our natural response calls for self-defense. But, generally speaking, it's extremely rare for someone to *make* us act in any particular way. Rather, we have only our subjective interpretations and knee-jerk responses to blame. This concept alone has done more to modify my thinking and behavior, as I continue working on and gaining more objective self-understanding.

In conclusion, learning how to manage stress is a matter of balancing and integrating opposite aspects in any activity. Finding the balanced tension for physical action that is neither too much nor too little is the goal of any proficient person. In managing life's many essential activities—no matter how mundane—it behooves us to learn the most efficient way to use our bodies, including how to sit, stand, walk, and use all body parts.

Likewise, we seek to balance our psycho-emotional lives regarding the way we think and feel about everything that happens. The goal of seeking mind-body integration and balance is a worthy pursuit, regardless of one's particular life situation or psycho-emotional characteristics. Mind-body stress is an inevitable component of living, and learning how to manage stress greatly influences our overall state of mind-body health, by lessening pain, promoting healing, and helping us achieve our life's goals.

6

Cultivating Social Connections

None of us are as smart as all of us. — *Japanese Proverb*

Though it's possible to live, laugh, and love alone, it's easier and more fulfilling when connected to others, especially for the loving part. Some leading scientists are suggesting that we are genetically hard-wired altruistically as social animals, through such healing qualities as love, intimacy, compassion, and forgiveness. Intuitively, we seem to realize that our personal self-interests are best served in the recognition and support we give others, a truism we often fail to fully appreciate. We also recognize our dependence on the generosity, kindness, and attention of persons we admire and appreciate, especially our closest companions—relatives, friends, a partner or spouse.

The types of connections we have with other people not only affect the quality of our lives, but also determine our longevity. More and more we are learning that love, affection, and intimacy are largely responsible for the state of our overall health. Numerous surveys have shown that lonely people suffer more accidents, illnesses, and deaths at earlier ages (Ornish, 2005), an observation that becomes more apparent as we age. Having a clear awareness of how important human relationships are for individual wellbeing should inspire us to give more attention to those we love and care about, and others as well.

Part of the good news about aging is that we gain new opportunity to slow down and spend more time not only with our family and friends, but with our wider community as well. It is something I certainly need to work on.

In this chapter we explore various types of social relationships, beginning with a consideration of the fundamental human relationship between males and females.

Gender: Male and Female Roles

> *Where male power dominates, you have separation. Where female power dominates, there's a non-dual, embracing quality.* —Joseph Campbell

I discovered just how varied opinions could be regarding male and female characteristics when the topic came up in my graduate pedagogy class last year. Being the only male among ten female students, I should have been more careful in presenting research associated with male and female singers, specifically information related to teaching male and female singers of all ages. Some of the material used was excerpted from this chapter, including the "Periodic Table of Elements" satire below, which did not go over well with the women, even though it pokes fun at both genders. It was soon very clear that several students held moderate to strong feminist perspectives, while the rest accepted the satire for what it was meant to convey: that gender differences do prevail. In any case I learned my lesson, and if I ever approach the subject again, I'll tread more lightly.

According to the Judeo-Christian Bible, "In the beginning, God created man"; and later, woman, from a single rib obtained from Adam. Along with most respected Bible scholars, I consider the story of Adam and Eve's creation as a mythical, premodern explanation of how humans—male and female—came into being. The primal boy-girl relationship has grown deeply ingrained in the public consciousness over thousands of years. Yet, most statistics show that approximately ten percent of all human beings are either bisexual or homosexual, a figure that appears to have remained constant throughout human history. That's why many would argue that the creation story could be modified to account for the creation of Adam and Evan, as well as Alma and Eva. I don't wish to take sides on this issue, but I think my position will become clear as we progress.

First, we need to distinguish male and female characteristics, which, not unexpectedly, closely parallel right-brain/left-brain and yin-yang characteristics covered earlier. In brief, it is generally thought that men tend to be more left-brain-oriented, while women tend to be more right-brain types. Of course, there are more similarities between males and females than differences, but based on common experience, some differences do create problems.

An article in *Discover* magazine (Shell 2005) sheds light on the brains of males and females, first explaining the role of the X chromosome, and then offering findings comparing brain differences. David Skuse, professor of behavioral and brain sciences at the Institute of Child Health in London, has shown how the X chromosome influences social skills. Skuse discovered that test subjects inheriting X chromosomes from their fathers had better social skills that those inheriting them from their mothers. In comparing the physical aspects of brains in both sexes, the average male brain weighs 49.5 ounces and is composed of 50.8 percent gray matter, while a female brain weighs 44.0 ounces and averages 55.4 percent gray matter. Areas of the male brain that are proportionally larger than corresponding female areas are the frontomedial cortex, the amygdala, and the hypothalamus; and the areas that are proportionally smaller are in sections bordering the front and middle of the limbic region. As males age from 6 to 17, their brains show a 45 percent increase in white matter, a 58.5 percent increase in the size of the corpus callosum, and a 19 percent decrease in gray matter. Unfortunately, aging males are susceptible to declining tissue mass and fluid increases, which contribute to changes in mental abilities.

In comparison, the female brain experiences approximately 15 percent more blood-flow than the male brain, a flow that's present in more centers of the brain at all times. In addition, the female brain has 12 percent more neurons in the temporal lobe (language oriented region) than the male cortex. As females age, from 6 to 17, their brains show a 17 percent increase in white matter, a 27.4 percent increase in the size of the corpus callosum, and a 4.7 decrease in gray matter. And the downside for female brains is a slight decline with age, causing them to become more prone to dementia, probably because they are more susceptible to losing neurons and their connections.

Hormones also play major roles in brain function, with notable differences between the sexes. Males have less serotonin in their brains, which may cause them to fidget more, and more testosterone hormones, which cause them to be more competitive in nature. In contrast, females have more oxytocin, a hormone linked to the bonding effect, which accounts for their ability to discuss and display feelings more easily than males.

In recent years, brain researchers have used MRI and PET technologies to gather information about how male and female brains develop and process information. Results show that females have more active frontal lobes, stronger connections between brain hemispheres, and language centers that mature earlier than similar-age males. Males also tend to be more visually oriented learners, while females are more aurally oriented, as my wife and I exemplify.

The stereotypes of male and female differences are widespread in all social groups, and though some may be based on genetics (nature), most are the result of culture (nurture). Nevertheless, we all enjoy humor that comes any where near expressing reality. I think you'll agree that there is some thread of truth in the following two additions to the periodic table of elements.

Two Additions to the Periodic Table

Element Name: WOMAN
Symbol: WO
Atomic Weight: (don't go there)

Physical Properties: Generally round in form. Boils at nothing and may freeze at any time. Melts whenever treated properly. Very bitter if mishandled.

Chemical Properties: Very active and highly unstable. Possesses strong affinity with gold, silver, platinum, and precious stones. Volatile when left alone. Able to absorb great amounts of exotic food. Turns slightly green when placed next to a shinier specimen.

Usage: Highly ornamental. An extremely good catalyst for dispersion of wealth. Probably the most powerful income-reducing agent known. CAUTION: HIGHLY EXPLOSIVE IN INEXPERIENCED HANDS.

Element Name: MAN
Symbol: XY
Atomic Weight: (180+/-50)

Physical Properties: Solid at room temperature but gets bent out of shape easily. Sometimes flaky and somewhat dense. Pure sample difficult to find. Due to rust, aging samples are unable to conduct electricity as easily as young samples.

Chemical Properties: Attempts to bond with WO any chance it can get. Also tends to form strong bonds with its self. Becomes explosive when mixed with KD (Element: Child) for a pro-longed period of time. Neutralize by saturating with alcohol.

Usage: None known. May be a good source of methane. Good specimens are able to produce large quantities on command. CAUTION: IN THE ABSENCE OF WO, THIS ELEMENT RAPIDLY DECOMPOSES AND BEGINS TO SMELL.

Now, without going into depth regarding the roles of men and women in society, it should suffice to remind ourselves that women have traditionally been dominated by men; and despite the progressive movements in expanding human rights worldwide, women continue to be dominated in fundamentalist societies, as observed in various religious groups, including Muslim and Christian. Some American fundamentalist Christian groups are particularly forthright in promoting subservient roles for women, for example, as practiced in some Mormon, Amish, and evangelical communities. Randall Balmer, an expert on evangelical Christianity, provides an explanation for this practice: "There's a sense [among fundamentalists] that the world is out of control and chaotic, and that if we can control our women, then the world will be a safer place. That's a real perception on the part of religious conservatives, notably among Muslims, Catholics, Mormons, and Protestant fundamentalists."

Of course, there are more similarities between the genders than differences, and, as mentioned previously, there are more similarities as we age. I agree with those who believe we become more complete persons by striving to integrate and balance characteristics common to both genders. Actually, the trend of integrating gender qualities has been accelerating over the past thirty or so years, and will most likely continue to grow as both males and females become more "liberated" from historically traditional expectations.

One area that reveals this liberation in the blending of male and female characteristics can be observed in some clothing styles, as evidenced by both genders wearing slacks, suits, and other similar articles of clothing, especially in recreational attire. Aging men and women, in particular, tend to wear certain clothing that's similar, especially comfortable sweaters, slacks, socks, and shoes. For certain, high heels are out.

Even male and female voices have modified somewhat in accommodating modern tastes and conventions, with a trend toward high-voiced male singers, such as Michael Jackson, Prince, and many others. And female pop singers' voices tend to concentrate on using low (chest), "belting" voice production, occasionally flipping into a light, underdeveloped flute-like production for high notes. So, generally speaking, both male and female voices are moving closer in vocal range and timbre than was the case several decades ago. Likewise, voice changes are quite predictable within the general aging population, especially for persons in their 80s and older, with women's voices tending to lower in average pitch range, and men's voices, particularly tenors, tending to rise. Also, aging lower voice types may become rough or gravelly, and others may grow weak, breathy, and crackly. Professional voice users who have not suffered voice damage from smoking, misuse, or overuse, may well maintain effective voice use throughout their entire lives.

One good example of the merging of gender roles is reflected in the evolving expectations of fathers, who increasingly are more involved in the birthing and rearing of children. Men of my generation rarely participated in programs offering instruction in pregnancy, birthing and child rearing, and fathers were never allowed in the delivery room. After the baby's arrival and throughout childhood, it was mom who was expected to handle most of the childcare responsibilities. And dad's primary function was to provide the financial means of family support, while offering minimal childcare assistance. In contrast to the old-fashioned father's role I experienced, consider our youngest son, who has been intentionally involved throughout the entire process of pregnancies, birthing, and rearing of his two wonderful children. I often envy his fervent parental commitment, and I wonder how we older men could have been so unenlightened. I know that, were I to be a parent again, I would assume more responsibility, especially during the early, formative childhood years. Of course, some of us seniors are fortunate in having opportunities for relating more personally with grandchildren.

Alternative Lifestyles

We oldsters hold varying outlooks regarding non-traditional gender roles, notably homosexuality and alternative lifestyles, which includes gay, lesbian, bisexual, and transgender individuals. Persons at the preconventional or egocentric level tend to denounce non-traditional gender roles, while persons at the conventional or ethnocentric level tend to reticently tolerate them. But, thankfully, persons at the postconventional or world-centric level will generally be more open and accepting of any marginalized citizens. As you read this material, I encourage you to identify the stage and level of development you think best applies to you, based on your honest opinions.

To begin with, the best scientific research indicates that both homosexuality and heterosexuality are primarily the result of genetic dispositions, and not the result of nurture or individual preferences. On the other hand, there is some evidence substantiating the possibility that an individual's sexual orientation may be partially reinforced by learned behavior. Almost every child or adolescent participates in some form of sexual experimentation, including with members of the same sex, albeit typically on short-term, superficial levels. My intent here is not to debate the rationale or morality associated with preferred sexual lifestyles, but rather to address our human need for relationships based on mutual intimacy, devotion, and commitment. After all, 10 percent or more of persons over age 50 may be included in this group, including readers of this book.

Reverend James Gertmenian, pastor of Plymouth Congregational Church in Minneapolis, Minnesota, eloquently spoke to this topic in a sermon. He quoted New Testament scholar, Walter Wink, who writes: There is no Biblical sex ethic . . . The Bible only knows a love ethic . . . This doesn't mean everything goes. It means that everything is to be critiqued by Jesus' commandment to love." Gertmenian follows this quote by saying that anyone who claims they wish to change gays and lesbians by loving them is at best disingenuous and at worst demonic:

> *This coercive love, this imperious love, this self-righteous love, this narrow love, this legalistic love, this frightened love—this is not the love of Jesus, nor is it worthy of his name. Nor is it the love celebrated by Paul.*

Gertmenian goes on to quote the Bible passage attributed to Paul (I Corinthians 13:4-7), with a follow-up emphasis on the "rejoices in the truth" conclusion, which he declares reflects the reality of any gay or lesbian person who makes the long, arduous journey of coming out and proclaiming their true identity.

> *Love is patient; love is kind; love is not envious or boastful or arrogant or rude. It does not insist on its own way; it is not irritable or resentful; it does not rejoice in wrongdoing, but rejoices in the truth.*

The disturbing aspect of some sexual behavior, whether it is as a heterosexual or homosexual, is any negative form it might take. For instance, when two persons use each other solely for sexual purposes, with little if any concern for each other's personal qualities, interests, or needs, the morality of the act becomes suspect. Promiscuity, or casual, indiscriminate sexual relations with many partners, whether practiced by heterosexuals, homosexuals, transgenders, or any other genders, is not only foolhardy, dangerous behavior, but also demeaning to individuals and humanity. On the other hand, when two persons share a sincere mutual interest and affection for one another, and their behavior toward one another is intentionally positive and principled, then their social right to have a relationship, sex included, should be condoned and respected by society.

I suppose what I'm getting around to advocating is the importance of establishing a monogamous relationship, wherein two persons commit to one another for a long-term arrangement. Over my lifetime I've known many monogamous gay couples, and most have remained closeted in order to maintain their social standing in a society that is not totally reconciled to acknowledging homosexual lifestyles as legitimate. These couples have always remained discreet in their sexual behavior, at least publicly, and from all outward appearances they have been respected and admired citizens. Most of the gay couples or single people I've known have been involved in education, music, and the arts, the types of communities that, in general, are more highly educated, open minded, creative, and empathetic. Yet, I understand that gay persons, most of whom are as committed in their life-partner relationships as heterosexual couples, are equally as well represented in most fields and areas of life.

This discussion is very relevant for everyone, including persons over age 50, as there are many persons of diverse sexual orientations in this population, including many gays who have yet to come out of the closet. Moreover, many older folk are still locked into preconventional and conventional modes of thinking, whereby they find fault with anyone different from the traditional 90-percent population norm. It's not too late for us as a nation to reexamine our thoughts and feelings about this issue, and settle some terms based on reason and hard evidence. In short, we need to become more tolerant, more understanding, and more loving in our relations with all people, regardless of their sexual or gender orientations.

Sexual Attraction and Common Interests

Many people in the second half of life have been married or lived with a "significant other". And some have divorced or lost spouses and partners, and perhaps remarried—more than once in some cases. The search for the most qualified mate or partner may occur at any age, even in nursing homes, so for those who have not found a life mate, there's hope yet. To make the search easier, there are some website organizations catering to older citizens that might provide some guidance, such as Senior People Meet and Senior Dates. But, of course, it pays to carefully investigate any match-up service before joining and getting involved.

The qualities one looks for in a mate may vary somewhat, but most people are looking for some universally recognized qualities. At the outset, to create an initial interest in pursuing a relationship with someone, most people will agree that physical attractiveness and health is a primary concern, including evidence of good physical conditioning and a firm commitment to maintaining health and wellness. (Yes, I believe looks do count, not the typical Hollywood ideals of beauty, but rather the girl/boy-next-door wholesome features.) More important qualities might include: a strong moral character, including a positive psycho-emotional disposition; behavior that is socially acceptable, constructive, and life-affirming; intellectual curiosity, with an ability to converse on a wide range of topics; personal habits of cleanliness and neatness; and some passionate interests, such as a vocation, reading, art, travel, and certain recreational activities or sports.

It's a known fact that the more interests held in common the more secure a relationship will be over the long term. Although age differences might not matter, depending on the individuals involved, most people tend to prefer partners who are close in age, within a decade or so. Being in the same generation helps, primarily because it's likely that a couple will share more commonalities, including special interests, life experiences, and personal tastes.

Though it's widely believed that opposites attract one another, the concept applies more to personality types than the kinds of activities people pursue. For example, two very outgoing, life-of-the-party personalities might conceivably develop a competitive nature in certain areas of their relationship, whereas a "doer" and a "thinker" couple might balance out and enhance each other's contrasting qualities. This type of union is akin to the "better half" idea, whereby each person respects and celebrates his or her mate's special attributes.

In my own case, I've been blessed with a 50-year marriage to Bettye, a very special woman who meets and in some cases surpasses all of the criteria mentioned earlier. Our interests are very similar, as we are both musicians, she a pianist and I a singer. (Thankfully, she's not a professional singer, as two in a partnership can be one too many.) In addition, we are both teachers, with my having served in university teaching positions for 43 years, and she as a private piano teacher with a home-based studio. As a singer I've been very fortunate having a live-in pianist and accompanist, a very convenient arrangement that allows our respective temperaments and talents to mesh, reinforce, and support one another. For example, we have collaborated in presenting concerts, producing recordings, and creating publications, including a popular voice text/song anthology that contains several songs for which I created lyrics and melody lines and she created the keyboard arrangements.

We also share some of the same recreational interests and hobbies, such as travel, hiking, biking, and reading. Bettye's passion for reading has had a major impact on my intellectual life, as she continues to recommend and pass along books by prominent authors on a wide range of subjects, both fiction and nonfiction. Finally, our personality types are complementary, with my being more outgoing and she being more reserved, providing a model of typical male-female characteristics.

Obviously, sexual attraction and healthy sexual relations are important in any intimate loving relationship. As far as sexual activity prior to a long-term commitment is concerned, I think it depends largely on the circumstances and conditions, including the age and mind-body health of a couple, and the length of the relationship. Any sexual activity depends on the psycho-emotional and physical maturity of the two persons involved and the depth of their commitment to one another. Of course, like most Americans I'm concerned over the amount of sexual experimentation that's promoted in the media, especially among young people, simply because they are not mature enough to understand and deal with all the associated emotional and health issues. It's demoralizing to learn that sexual activity is occurring at younger ages, especially in the age bracket 13 to 15, and that some schools are providing condoms for 11 year olds, but it's a reality that must be accepted and somehow managed.

Of course, the idea of couples living together prior to marriage was unheard of in the 1950s, but the practice really caught on in the hippie days of the 1960s. As long as two persons are mutually committed, and willing to treat one another respectfully, there may be some positive benefits for cohabitation prior to marriage, as some oldsters apparently believe—and practice.

The state of marriage in the U.S. is constantly being researched, and the statistics don't always tell what's really going on. A 2006 *New York Times* article reported on a study claiming that a majority of U.S. women are living without husbands. Whereas in 1950 35 percent of women lived without a spouse, by 2005 the percentage reached 51 percent (Effron 2007). However, in a previous 2004 article (*USA Today*) it was reported that approximately 59 percent of Americans were married (8 percent more than the 2005 data), though nine out of ten persons were expected to eventually marry by age thirty—65 percent of men and 71 percent of women. If these poll results are accurate, the state of traditional marriage is not particularly healthy these days. Over the past four decades, the institution of marriage has been increasingly severed, partially due to marrying later, co-habitating or having children out of wedlock, adultery, divorce, or deciding not to marry again following divorce or widowhood. It's also a sign of the times that individuals focused on other priorities more often postpone marriage. It's a sad commentary that, whereas divorce rates were very rare prior to the 1950s, as many as 50 percent of all marriages end in divorce today.

My opinion about divorce is not carte blanche disapproval, for there are valid reasons some couples elect to go their separate ways, which makes sense when they've made every effort to reconcile their differences. Increasingly, it seems that many young couples' marital commitments are made rather lightly, without sufficient counseling and guidance before and after tying the proverbial knot. In hearkening back to the "good ole days", the general expectation was that couples were expected to stay together for life, regardless of how painful and damaging it might be to individuals, as well as the entire family. Hence, the divorce rate, while higher than my parent's generation, did not approach the high rates of younger couples today. The generation of my parents rarely divorced, though there is ample evidence that many of them should have considered the option, including my parents. Though mom and dad were respectable individuals—especially when dealt with individually—they were incompatible personality types, and occasionally treated one another uncivilly.

Speaking of civility, M. Scott Peck, in his book, *A World Waiting to Be Born: Civility Rediscovered*, declares that the presence of civility is the main feature that distinguishes

a couple's healthy relationship from an unhealthy relationship. This is especially the case in intimate relationships such
as marriage, which Peck defines as an organization of two
persons strongly committed to maintaining that relationship. Civility infers a relationship between persons based
on politeness, honesty, and trust, the foundations of any
successful organization involving two or more persons.

Family Culture and Traditions

Though the traditional nuclear family of husband, wife, and
children remains the dominant arrangement, several other
family arrangements are evolving, including gay couples
rearing children. While the number of heterosexual couples electing to have children remains high, economic and
lifestyle factors have contributed to a decline in the number of children per couple over the past few decades, with
the resulting norm of one or two children per household.
For a variety of reasons, not all couples are able or willing to have children, particularly gay couples. Yet, increasingly, more gay couples are electing to adopt children, or
in the case of lesbian couples, give birth to children who
are related genetically through technological assistance,
including artificial insemination. Other than the physical
impossibility of two gay people of the same sex begetting
children, I can find no legitimate reason why gay couples
should be treated any differently than heterosexual couples when it comes to rearing children. The main concern
is that all domestic partners possess the requisite desire,
means, and character to rear children in a hospitable environment that promotes positive growth and development.

There's no doubt that the family unit plays a significant
role in educating individuals socially, culturally, and spiritually. Though the nuclear family consisting of parents and
children (siblings) is the primary influence, extended families are important secondary players, and in some cases

play primary roles. Extended families involve grandparents, uncles, aunts, cousins, nephews, nieces, and others (step-relations). Family cultures vary, from distinguished family dynasties such as the Vanderbilts, Rockefellers, and Kennedys to middle class Americans, such as mine and my wife's, and, finally, to families struggling with poverty.

There is much to be said about wealth and its effects on families, but suffice it to say here that I think the pendulum is swinging toward unhealthy, out-of-balance extremes. Too many families are mired in a web of poverty and ignorance due to a depressed socio-cultural environment, lack of work and educational opportunities, and minimal economic means. Fortunately, some individuals manage to break out and move away from the confines of negative family environments and move on to create a better life for themselves and their families. In fact, America is built on the collective contributions of individuals who managed to escape impoverished living conditions by leaving their extended families and seeking opportunities elsewhere. This trend continues, as illustrated by individuals and couples moving away from their hometowns to other geographical areas where they are free to establish a new life based on their personal goals and values. And seniors also exemplify this mobile shift, with many moving to warmer climes, as well as less expensive communities for their retirement years.

Some family cultures can be stifling and confining, especially those with strong traditional expectations related to gender roles, occupations, and religious affiliations. For instance, extended families that are racially, ethnically, and religiously homogenous—whether Jewish, Catholic, Muslim, Hindu, Amish, Buddhist, or other—tend to set certain standards and mores that all family members are expected to adopt and follow. Fortunately, more and more young people, feeling trapped between family interests and personal goals, are electing to seek their own life's path. In my own extended family, which is primarily British-American, Southern, and Protestant, one nephew of our most recent young adult generation has broken this tradition by marrying a Jewish woman from Boston, where the couple now live with their three male children as a Jewish family. Also, two of our sons have married women who were formerly Catholics, and the other son married a woman who was a Quaker. All of them have moved beyond their family religious affiliations, and we honor their decisions. This trend also applies to older generations, though on a lesser scale.

In sum, my advice to anyone—of any age—who is oppressed by a powerful family culture is this: Tactfully ignore family traditions, routines, or rituals that create adverse effects, and go your own way. As Joseph Campbell exhorts: "Follow your bliss!" Mutual affection, respect, civility, and support are needed in all extended families, but individuals should feel free to find their own way, and this goes for older folks as well as the young.

Relationships Within the Family

What kind of support is needed within the immediate family? Aside from providing the basic essentials—food, clothing, shelter, and so on—the main requisite is to create a wholesome learning and living environment for *all* family members. Supporting one another with positive psycho-emotional energy or nurturing attention is the number one priority, which includes providing opportunities for mind-body growth and development, creating an environment based on moral and ethical behavior, and supporting one another's goals. I'm sure most people agree that all adult family members—parents, grandparents, uncles and aunts—should assist children in pursuing their personal goals and objectives, as long as the goals are deemed honorable and positive.

Aside from providing children with moral and emotional support, I think financial support should be judiciously targeted, with a concentration on providing all essentials, such as housing, food, clothing, education, health care, transportation, and so on for children until they reach 18-19 years of age. Following high school, students who continue into higher education deserve some financial support, especially funds to cover tuition, but I don't think it's wise for parents (or others) to provide financial support for non-essentials, such as entertainment, booze, and the like. Spoon-feeding young adults—or anyone for that matter—by covering their entire expenses does them a disservice, and often causes them to take everything for granted. Learning to live self-sufficiently and independently is a very important lesson in life, and it needs to begin as early as possible. To paraphrase the old saw, "Spare personal responsibility (for one's behavior) and spoil the person."

As grandparents, it's normal for us to be concerned about our grandchildren's educational opportunities prior to and beyond high school, but we've tried to be discerning in how much financial support we provide, as we feel that responsibility lies primarily with our sons and their wives. Before we older persons dish out funds to cover any family member's expenses, or give large amounts to favored charities, we think it's imperative to first secure our long-term financial status, including projected adequate income sources up to retirement age, home mortgages paid off (or nearly paid off), health care and long-term care covered, and sufficient savings invested to sustain them through old-age. This approach may sound uncaring, but it's founded on our belief that everyone should strive to be self-sufficient. Hence, we are firmly convinced our primary responsibility to our children and grandchildren is to cover all our projected financial needs, the goal being to protect them from having inordinate demands placed on them at some future date.

In contrast to showing appreciation and respect for one another by offering positive supportive comments and help as needed, it's regrettable that some older members of families use subtle put-downs, teasing, and general negative comments in dealing with young people. Others may encourage a spirit of intense competition in various ways, both overtly and covertly. On my dad's side of my family, my grandfather and one uncle were regular teasers, but since their attitude didn't appear to be intentionally spiteful or mean, their behavior didn't create any lingering bad feelings on my part. Overall, I'm very grateful for having had a very supportive extended family. I'm sure you agree that such negative treatment of another is a sign of immaturity, no matter the age of the misbehaving person.

Keeping in touch with family members periodically by telephone, snail mail, or email is an easy modern-day way to maintain contact. We try to maintain connections with relatives via an annual holiday newsletter, in addition to family gatherings during the Christmas holidays in Mississippi. Every few years we have attended a large summer family reunion that used to involve more than a hundred relatives on my mother's side of the family, but as the last few aunts and uncles have died off, the attendance has fallen in recent years to around 50 or more relatives. Although I firmly believe that family roots are extremely important in building a sense of self and place, I also feel that some individuals might need to establish new family traditions somewhere else, especially when large family cultures discourage personal growth and expression.

Aging Adult Care

Although this is discussed more thoroughly later, a word is needed about caring for loved ones who are seriously ill or incapacitated in some way, as is frequently the case with aging parents. Most people in the over-50 generations are involved either as caregivers or recipients of care. The modern practice is to place chronically ill persons in the care of institutions, as when aging parents are placed in assisted-care or nursing home facilities, where they receive professional care. In most cases, this seems to be the most humane approach, particularly when a caregiver is geographically separated from the ill person by a long distance. Most people are incapable of handling severely incapacitated relatives, so finding good medical care may be the most rational solution.

My wife and I have lived 1,200 miles from our parents for the past 38 years, but we have been very fortunate in having had siblings who lived near them and cared for them. Thankfully, they have been very willing to take on such a major responsibility, though in my sister Kay's situation, it proved a difficult assignment, with her shepherding our cancer-ridden mother through a strenuous final four years that culminated in a one-year stay in a nursing home before she died in 2001. Kay and her very supportive husband, Conrad, continued looking after our father, who stubbornly remained alone in his deteriorating home until 2003, when a series of declining health problems forced him into a nursing home, where he died within a few weeks. My wife's parents have also received loving care, principally from one of her two brothers and his wife. We have been very fortunate to have such willing siblings as caregivers.

The reason I mention this scenario is to show how siblings can work together in caring for ill parents or other family members. In brief, our solution was for me to provide some "guilt money" annually to cover part of caregivers' time and expenses. Also, when we visited two or three times per year, I usually spent a few days helping clean my folk's home. And because my sister was executor of our parents' modest estate, we agreed beforehand that her portion of the estate would be 60 percent, while mine would be

40 percent. In addition, she received the proceeds from selling two run-down homes, a minimal reward payment for handling all the business associated with maintaining and selling them. We managed to keep an amicable relationship throughout the entire parental-care process, with much of the success credited to my sister's good nature, devotion to our parents, and, to a lesser extent, our mutual agreement regarding an equitable financial arrangement. Finding the best way to care for our parents involved a series of compromises. By balancing my sister's and brother-in-law's needs and desires with ours, we effectively created a win-win situation for all concerned parties.

Cultivating and Maintaining Friendships

Both inside and outside of family relationships, there's a deep need to cultivate friends. Friendship has several meanings, but the typical qualities that distinguish genuine friendship are mutual trust, honesty, affection, and both physical and psycho-emotional support. Ideally, one's mate, partner, or spouse fulfills a top-ranking friendship role, and in many relationships as number-one friend and confidant. I know that Bettye understands and appreciates my combined characteristics (positive and negative) more fully than any other person with whom I've ever been associated. We share practically everything that happens in our lives, and I imagine most intimate, long-term couples share a similar bonding.

Unfortunately, friendship may be in jeopardy. According to a new study (*Social Isolation in America*) conducted by sociologists at Duke University and the University of Arizona, the average American has only two close friends. Moreover, one of four persons has no one to confide in. These findings reveal a serious trend of declining intimate relationships, one that has doubled in the last two decades. This ominous trend actually was studied as far back as the 1950s, when David Riesman's seminal book (*The Lonely Crowd*) warned readers that long-standing community ties and social relationships were being eroded by a growing corporate model of conformity.

The reasons for the loneliness of millions of Americans are many, including: busy personal schedules filled with work and extracurricular schedules, allowing little time to cultivate intimacy; the growth of spreading suburbs, with isolated residential communities requiring extensive use of automobile commuting; and the increasing use of technology, with more people using cell phones and computers that encourage using email communication, internet searching, and entertainment. The flip side of technology, however, is that people are probably communicating more often and with more people. I know that in some ways my communication with others has skyrocketed because of email use. And I imagine avid cell phone users are also in constant contact with their friends. Moreover, it's possible that as more people work from their homes part-time or full-time, couples and families might have more quality time together. For certain, a majority of retired couples have plenty of time to be intimate, like Bettye and I enjoy. And, so far, she hasn't kicked me out of our condo for being home most of the time.

Many retirees and folks who live in retirement homes have more time and opportunities for cultivating and maintaining close friendships. Most men and women socialize with friends regularly, either one on one or in groups associated with church, service clubs, book clubs, coffee clubs, card clubs, and to participate in various sports, such as tennis, golf, and bowling.

Social Relationships Beyond Family and Friends

As people worldwide grow more economically interdependent, the ability to relate effectively with people of different ethnic backgrounds, political stances, and religious beliefs is increasingly a challenge. While some countries maintain a homogeneous ethnicity, particularly Asian nations, in America there are fewer communities where everyone is so similar to everyone else in race, ethnicity, and religion. My wife and I have observed, for instance, an increasing influx of various ethnic groups into our area of the Twin Cities, which in the early 1970s was essentially a Caucasian stronghold of mostly Western European and United Kingdom descendents. Today, however, it's quite common to experience a wide variety of socio-ethnic backgrounds within our larger community and neighborhood, noticeably folk of various Asian, Hispanic, Latino, and Black (African-Americans and Somalis) cultures. The growing pluralism Americans are experiencing, especially in metropolitan areas, requires a diligent effort in gaining greater understanding of one another as we strive to achieve more common ground, a goal that will eventually require relinquishing some tightly-held traditional beliefs and behaviors, in addition to using English as a common language.

Understanding human cultural differences is the first step toward cultivating better social relations. One of the unsolved mysteries related to the historical development of the major world civilizations is discovering a logical explanation as to why some civilizations have flourished, while others seemingly stagnated and maintained their status as third-world countries. Jared Diamond, author of a very informative 1997 book—*Germs, Guns, and Steel*—and a professor of geography at the University of California-Los Angeles, sheds considerable light on this subject, explaining that the historical forces largely responsible for determining how civilizations have fared and prospered are primarily related to geography, which is closely associated with annual weather patterns and available natural resources. His explanation also clarifies the apparent ease with which certain civilizations, among them the ancient Greeks, Romans, Egyptians, Chinese, Mongols, and later the Europeans, were able to conquer, subdue, and even annihilate some culturally advanced civilizations. Diamond's findings have helped me better appreciate the adverse situations some populations are facing today—and, in some cases, have dealt with for many generations. Gaining empathy is a first step in reaching out to those beyond our normal grasp, a powerful lesson I learned from my mother, who was genuinely capable of relating to almost anyone, especially the downtrodden or marginal members of society.

It's becoming ever clearer that every single one of the six-plus billion humans alive today evolved over a period beginning more than a hundred thousand years ago. Moreover, it's been proposed that everyone derived from the basic DNA produced by a few common female ancestors—in collaboration with the male species, of course. According to most authorities, including Bryan Sykes and Steve Olson, we are all related and therefore share many commonalities, regardless of observable differences, such as physical appearance, religious beliefs, cultural traditions, and personal tastes. Thus, while *nature* has created us in most physical, mental, and emotional respects alike—and equal—*nurture* has made us different from one another, in some cases vastly and strangely different.

The challenge we face as individuals is to overcome our culturally-derived religious, political, and cultural biases. This is especially the case with older Americans, whose beliefs and perspectives have been culturally shaped over generations, with ingrained beliefs and biases that may be hard to change. However, only when people everywhere agree to honor common values that promote full individual development will everyone be free to enjoy balanced and meaningful lifestyles.

7

Pursuing a Moderate Lifestyle

Creating a Life Plan Based on Values and Principles

If you were to draw up a plan—a life map, blueprint, or outline of your life up to this point—could you recall what you did or didn't do in creating the lifestyle you've experienced thus far? Are you living as you originally envisioned, or are there things you wish you'd done differently? We get energy if we tape the following sentence over our desk and repeat it outloud each and every day: "Today is the first day of the rest of my life."

So, beginning from this moment onward, how do we go about creating a new life map for the *rest* of our lives? Since deeply held beliefs form the bedrock of our lives, influencing all actions, the first step is to examine our overall philosophy of life, including the values and principles that guide us. If we are honest and sincere in identifying our values and principles, the lifestyle we choose will be a direct outgrowth of our beliefs and guiding ideals.

The first step in taking control of your life is to prepare a written mission statement, including a list of specific life goals, that reflect the values and principles you wish to adopt for your life—from this point onward, whatever your age. Next, writing them down in a prioritized order helps to clarify and outline the basic information needed. As you proceed, you may be surprised to discover the values you genuinely embrace. A variety of emotions may surface, from satisfaction and relief to disappointment and frustration. Regardless of the emotional responses, this self-reflection exercise provides an opportunity for discovering and developing a set of worthwhile values and principles. Should any of the listed values raise a red flag, at least you've been forewarned and given an opportunity to take ongoing remedial steps in rethinking your values.

The Necessities of Life

What does it take to lead a happy, productive, and fulfilling life? Each of us will answer this question in various ways, but deep inside us the need to love and be loved is core to our existence. Let's examine some of the basic needs that must be met in order to maximize our quality of life, based on collected guidelines proposed by several personal development experts.

• *Security and Comfort.* The basic needs of shelter, food, and clothing are often taken for granted, but at the base of our "needs pyramid" is a safe environment, a comfortable home with adequate furnishings, sufficient quantities of nutritious food, drink, rest, and the requisite tools, equipment, and resources to sustain life in a moderately comfortable style.

• *Good Physical Health and Wellness.* I cannot think of a more critical need than the endowment of a favorable genetic inheritance and good physical health, which makes it possible for us to fully enjoy and participate in life. Having good health presupposes having adequate use of all senses (sight, hearing, touch, smell) and all body parts (limbs, organs), in addition to moderately attractive physical features. Of course, persons experiencing loss of senses or body parts may still be able to function adequately with assistance.

• *Average Intelligence (IQ).* Though it isn't necessary to be a genius, life requires the ability to understand and apply a broad range of knowledge and skills for coping effectively, including appropriate social behavior.

• *Above-Average Emotional Intelligence.* According to Goleman (1995), success in life is determined more by high emotional intelligence than IQ, because effective social skills—the ability to empathize and relate well with people using tact, common sense, and goodwill in a cooperative, collaborative manner—creates a more well-rounded, balanced individual.

• *Spiritual Foundation.* Knowing oneself requires connecting with the core of one's inner being, a challenge that requires a desire for self-understanding, a willingness to change, an understanding of meditative or self-talk strategies, and the discipline to follow through with deepening spirituality.

• *Social Connections.* As social creatures, we have a need to love and be loved, which under favorable conditions is fulfilled by developing close family ties, lasting friendships, ongoing collaborations with current or former colleagues or co-workers, and interdependent associations with numerous acquaintances.

• *Freedom of Expression and Behavior.* Aside from the basic life-sustenance needs associated with a secure, comfortable lifestyle and amiable social connections, an essential psycho-emotional value includes personal freedom, particularly as related to expression in speech and positive behavior.

• *Meaningful Opportunities and Pursuits.* Whether associated with career work or special interests, the need to find a purpose in life is a highly cherished and challenging goal, that involves the freedom and commitment to explore, discover, and realize one's innate talents and potential, by gaining a broad range of knowledge and essential life skills, such as effective coping, creative self-expression, and altruistic service.

• *Mobility.* Though the mobility enjoyed by Americans and other first-world people may place strains on the world's energy resources, the ability to travel anywhere freely is highly valued.

Of course, you may think of other worthwhile values common to most people. If you do, I suggest you jot down your ideas as you read, saving notes for later reference.

Inventorying Your Possessions

It's humbling to compare the lifestyles of individuals and groups, particularly between the rich and poor. According to published data, we Americans are the most consumptive and wasteful humans on the planet. For an idea of how far we've come, consider the simple lifestyle of Native Americans at the time European settlers arrived on the east coast. The amount of resources they consumed was minimal, and almost everything consisted of natural, biodegradable materials. Their "energy footprints" were extremely small, even when compared to the ascetic Puritans. What's more, there were ample natural resources to accommodate the numbers of people living off the land. In comparing the 17th century American lifestyle with that of today, I'm not suggesting that it was better for people, only that it was better for the natural environment, which is crucial to human survival. As we continue, I encourage you to take a moment to consider how radically our modern lifestyle differs from that era, especially in terms of materials—natural and manmade—that are consumed and wasted.

Although I'm certainly not trying to build a case supporting an austere primitive lifestyle, I do want to raise our collective awareness of how excess possessions can affect the overall quality of our lives. Perhaps the best way to begin is by undertaking an inventory:

• *Shelter.* Describe your principal dwelling abode. Is it an apartment or a house? Do you rent or own your dwelling? How many rooms does it have and what are they (bedrooms, baths, etc.)? How many total square feet? Does it have air conditioning? What special features does it have that enhance its livability (vaulted ceilings, track lighting, etc.)? How many people share it with you? Do you consider it adequate for your needs? Do you own more than one dwelling, such as a vacation home? What is the estimated current monetary value of all real estate properties?

• *Land.* Identify any land you own, including the lot your dwelling is built on. What size is the property? Does it have trees and landscaping? What special features does it have that enhance its worth to you (privacy, a view)? What other land or property do you own? What is the total monetary value of the land you own?

• *Furnishings.* Identify your major home furnishings. What furniture is contained in each room, and what is its quality and monetary value? What appliances do you own or use, such as: a clothes washer and dryer; a kitchen equipped with a stove/oven, a refrigerator, a microwave, and requisite cooking and food-processing items; and other items—television set, computer, and artwork (paintings, sculpture, photos, etc.)? What other special furnishings do you have, such as a central vacuuming system, hot tubs, and the like? What furnishings do you have outside, such as patio or deck furniture, barbecue grills, and the like? What is the total estimated monetary value of all these items?

• *Special Items.* Think of the special items you cherish, such as silverware, china, jewelry, keepsakes, family photos, vacation mementos, books, hobby equipment, and the like. What collective monetary value would you place on all your special possessions?

• *Clothing.* Look through your clothes closets and dresser drawers to identify all clothing items. Estimate how many items of each article of clothing you own, including undergarments, socks, shirts, sweaters, pants, skirts, shoes, and so on, including their quality. What is the estimated total monetary value?

• *Tools and Recreational Equipment.* Everybody needs a certain amount of basic tools and equipment. What tools and equipment do you have on hand for home and car repair and maintenance (lawn mowers, garden tools, wrench sets, drills, etc.)? Do you have any special recreational equipment for camping, biking, skiing, boating, skating, and the like? What is the estimated total monetary value?

• *Transportation.* Almost every American has at least one transportation vehicle, even if it's a bicycle. Do you own an auto, or more than one? What about a bicycle, a motorcycle or motor scooter, a snowmobile, an ATV vehicle, or other vehicle? What is the estimated monetary value of all vehicles?

Possessions Based on Financial Status

In reviewing the above list of possessions, I doubt that you've actually taken time to account for everything you own, but I hope my point is well taken: each of us owns a lot of stuff, some of it essential, but much of it unessential to living a fulfilling, happy life. It should prove interesting to present a rough estimate of how much my wife and I have consumed since we married in 1958, when we set out to create a typical American family lifestyle. As background,

I think it's accurate to describe our financial status as average middle-class Americans, so our accumulation of possessions should parallel most couples of similar age and financial means.

In 1985, when we moved out of a home we'd occupied for 15 years and into a new home we occupied for 21 years, we became more cognizant of the inordinate amount of possessions we had accumulated. Then, when we moved in 2006 into our condo, we renewed our awareness of how many material possessions we had collected, including items added since the 1985 move. In both cases, what drove the material-possession reality home to us was our decision to do most of the packing and moving of smaller items that could be transported by auto. Luckily, we remained within a three-mile radius of all three dwellings, and multiple trips spread out over a few days were feasible.

So, in reflecting on our last two home moves we became even more aware of the physical resources we'd consumed along our joint life's journey. It's absolutely mind-boggling when adding up the amounts of items and energy required for maintaining a comfortable lifestyle for two people. When considering home heating, cooling, and electrical usage, plus the oil and gas needed to transport us via auto, the amount of water consumed for drinking, bathing, and washing, we have had a major impact on our environment. And this is only for two people! What about the incredible amounts of trash and garbage we've generated? Assuming my wife and I generate the average American's garbage of 4.3 lbs. per day, my disposal alone amounts to 78,475 lbs. (or 35.3 tons) of trash and garbage in the 50 years we've been married. Adding my wife's garbage totals 70-plus tons. Oh, and we also must add the twenty-plus years of having three sons living with us, plus the twenty years of our single lives. And what about the gallons of normal body wastes we've flushed down the toilet into area lakes and streams? Moreover, we've birthed and reared three sons, each with their wives and kids have accumulated similar amounts of things and will continue consuming an ordinary amount of natural resources for years to come. And we're just average consumers. What about the Big Consumers, those who buy and dispose at exorbitant levels?

Although the daily disposal of materials is very significant in terms of bulk, the big-ticket items we consume and dispose of throughout our lives add up. For example, we've owned five homes throughout our marriage, and the four previous ones are still being used, so that's a wash, except for the fact that four of our five homes were brand new when we moved in, and, of course, each home still requires ongoing maintenance and remodeling repairs. And what about the eighteen autos we've owned (excluding our teenage sons' autos), all of which have been driven for approximately 700,000-800,000 miles over the past 50 years? It's safe to say that all but the last five are either in junkyards or, hopefully, recycled into some useful form. Then there are the several washing machines, refrigerators, microwaves, television sets, radios, computers, mattresses, and other "must have" items that have been either tossed or recycled. Excluding previous houses, if it were possible to collect all the possessions the two of us have owned throughout our married lives, and place them on an average city lot, I wonder how much of the space would be filled. I imagine it would take every square inch of our average-sized former home lot to park the autos and organize everything efficiently in stacks. The bagged garbage and trash alone would probably fill up and overflow the entire interior of our former 2000 square-foot home.

And now compare our average accumulation of possessions with that of two similarly-aged married couples, one extremely poor and the other filthy rich. I daresay the indigent couple's possessions would take up far less space than ours, while the very wealthy couple might require multiple acreage and a large building to store their lifetime accumulation of possessions, which might include two or more current dwellings and their furnishings, numerous automobiles (upgraded every year or so), other vehicles (motorcycles, boats, ATVs, etc.), and various luxury items. While there's little question regarding the wealthy couple's contributions to our capitalistic system and economy over their lifetime, there is a nagging concern about the overall impact on the environment, plus the impact on their psycho-emotional health, which must be affected in some ways.

The thesis I'm building up to is my belief that both poor and rich extremes represent imbalanced lifestyles. Based on information gleaned from readings, movies, and personal observations, I readily concur that extreme poverty sets the stage for a life of misery and unfulfilled human potential. But on the opposite end of the social ladder, the chaotic lives of many rich celebrities demonstrate that extreme wealth is not always a panacea for life's ills. Proof is readily available, as the media regularly reports on the extravagant, ostentatious lifestyles of affluent celebrities. The media like to focus on current young celebrities and their friends, but it's apparent that spoiled rich kids generally have little understanding and appreciation of what poor or normal people experience, including the prospect of achieving genuine happiness.

Some examples of conspicuous consumption are the luxury spas that cater to wealthy patrons, offering a heavy dose of pampering at daily costs that exceed $1000. At one off-road spa in Pennsylvania, guests can live it up, driving Hummer vehicles through 20 miles of rugged terrain (muddy ponds, steep slopes, and other obstacles). Ostensibly, the motivation is to gain an authentic "roughing it" experience, which happens to be environmentally destructive and wasteful of natural resources.

Media organizations are happy to update the public on a daily basis regarding the foibles of the rich and famous, including the sordid details associated with their miserable lives. Unfortunately, what is not reported in the media are the numbers of highly successful people who manage to find true happiness and meaning in life while living modest lifestyles. Perhaps we need to move away from the concept of achieving a high *standard* of living to a more enlightened concept based on *quality* of living.

Charity: Sharing the Wealth

Having socked it to the filthy rich, perhaps it's time I give some due recognition to those who earn great wealth through honorable means, and share their good fortune in aiding worthy causes, such as fulfilling human needs and caring for our natural environment. While most philanthropists enjoy luxurious lifestyles, some choose to live moderately, all the while sharing the bulk of their fortune with others, assisting family members with specific needs, or donating to special-interest charities. In such cases, great wealth may be justified. Serving as a conscientious steward of one's resources is an attribute of a well-balanced individual who is free of psycho-emotional entanglements and superficial motives.

Some notable exemplars come to mind, including former president Jimmy Carter, who lives a rather moderate lifestyle despite his apparent wealth. In the business world there are numerous examples of Good Samaritans who place social consciousness above gaining material wealth. A *Business Week* article (December 2003) titled "The Secret Givers" featured five outstanding examples of wealthy businessmen who shun publicity in disguising their extremely generous contributions to charity organizations. Among them: George Keiser, an oil and gas, banking, and real estate magnate, who has given $287 million to antipoverty programs; Maurice "Chico" Sabbah, a reinsurance business executive, who has donated $100 million to the American Hebrew Academy; Fred Eychaner, a media mogul, who has contributed $73 million-plus to a variety of causes; A. Jerrold Perenchio, CEO of Univision, who donated $50 million-plus for a medical center at UCLA; and Charles F. Feeney, owner of Duty-Free Shoppers, a chain of airport shops, who gave $1.6 billion to Atlantic Philanthropies, which has since grown to $3.7 billion. All of these individuals live moderate lifestyles, avoid conspicuous consumption, and share an utter distaste for publicity regarding their charitable philanthropies. Keiser, for example, describes himself as "anti-materialistic" and "uncomfortable and guilty about receiving recognition".

Feeney, who is in his mid 70s and a native of New Jersey, exemplifies the consummate philanthropist who voluntarily chooses to live a simple, frugal lifestyle, all the while giving away the major portion of his wealth to benefit others. His philosophy: "Life is awfully unfair, and nobody is getting out of this world alive." Having given away a 39 percent stake of his company twenty years ago, Feeney lives on the proceeds of his $1.5 million estate. He owns no house, drives no car, and hails his own cabs. His explanation? "I just don't get my jollies by flaunting money." Admittedly, Mr. Feeney provides a radical example of a model wealthy citizen, which, in comparison, makes our moderate lifestyle appear extravagant. It's easy to greatly admire his high character, and to imagine that numbers of wealthy persons might be inspired to emulate his lifestyle and philosophy of wealth sharing.

The billionaire Warren Buffett is one of the richest men in the world, but he lives on an annual salary of $100,000 as chairman of Berkshire Hathaway Holdings. In June 2006, Buffett donated $46.5 billion to charity, with $36 billion directed to the Bill and Melinda Gates Foundation, the largest single charitable giving act in United States history. Despite his immense wealth, Buffett is famous for his unpretentious and frugal lifestyle. In 1989, when he spent

$9.7 million of Berkshire's funds on a corporate jet, he jokingly named it "The Indefensible" because of his past criticisms of CEOs for making such extravagant purchases. He continues to live in the same house in the central Dundee neighborhood of Omaha, Nebraska, which he bought in 1958 for $31,500. He also owned a more expensive home in Laguna Beach, California, but sold it in 2004.

In contrast, billionaires such as Bill Gates (Microsoft) and Ted Turner (Time Warner) give extraordinary amounts of money to charities, but they also enjoy worldly lifestyles. Ruth E. Lilly, heiress to the Eli Lilly pharmaceutical fortune enjoys an affluent lifestyle in her hometown of Indianapolis. Though she doesn't hide her philanthropy, neither does she flaunt it. At age 88 she is an old-fashioned hands-on benefactress, visiting favored charities and doling out $10 million dollars annually, half of her total annual income. She grew up a pampered and isolated child, and later developed severe depression, which was ameliorated by taking Prozac, a drug pioneered by her family's company. In her 70s she began making up for lost time, and has since contributed approximately $545 million to charities, mostly to arts organizations, including a $100 million donation to the magazine *Poetry* (Conlin & Hempel 2003).

All philanthropists profiled thus far are older than 50. What about the younger generation? Indeed, there are excellent models of idealistic young entrepreneurs who practice social consciousness in unique ways, but since this book is about the over-50 crowd, I'll forego listing them.

Ironically, a trend of charitable giving in the U.S. during the last half-century shows that increasing wealth has coincided with decreased giving. According to pollster George Barna: "Generally, the more money a person makes the less likely he is to tithe." Inexplicably, contribution levels were higher during the Great Depression of the 1930s, when incomes were at their lowest compared to today (*Generous Giving* website). The average American donates a relatively small portion of total income to charities, and the percentage is proportionately less with increased wealth.

During the past 40 years the rate of individual giving has hovered between 1.8 percent and 2.6 percent of disposable income. In 1998, for example, about 70 percent of American households gave contributions, and the average annual household contribution was $1,075. And where do the dollars go? According to *Money* Magazine, of total charitable contributions in 2003 ($241 billion), 35.9 percent went to religious organizations, 13.1 percent to education, 5.4 percent to arts, culture, and humanities, and 2.9 percent to environmental groups. The Brookings Institution confirms the public's doubts about how charitable contributions are spent, as nearly one out of three respondents doubt that their contributions are being used responsibly and wisely. Several high-profile scandals have borne out such fears, including the highly trusted American Red Cross's use of 9/11 funds for other purposes.

I believe my wife and I may be considered average givers, though we would like to be able to do more, and plan to in the next few years. Like many people, we believe charity begins at home, with a primary obligation to take care of personal needs—before making large donations to charities. Everyone needs to establish a stable living situation that provides adequate shelter, food, clothing, and transportation. Beginning at age 30-40, everyone needs to make long-term financial plans, including building a sufficient retirement nest egg, preparing for long-term health care needs, and assisting children and grandchildren with special needs. With the price of a college/university education escalating so rapidly, creating a sizeable educational fund becomes ever more of a necessity.

As for persons reaching their early 50s, the need to prepare financially for retirement becomes urgent—to avoid depending on a potentially diminished social security fund and meager personal savings. In an ideal world, every person would assume complete responsibility for his or her life, including developing financial independence. Unfortunately, for a multitude of reasons, both plausible and questionable, some people simply can't manage their own finances, so help is needed from good citizens who are willing and able to contribute more of their taxable income, in addition to donating extra charitable funds to alleviate the burdens of the less fortunate.

Before concluding this section on charitable giving, I feel compelled to say something about the deluge of solicitations the average person receives from all kinds of organizations, both commercial and charitable. Older citizens, such as those of us who have lived in one area for many years, are strategically positioned to receive a huge amount of solicitations. I don't know how many mailing lists we're on, but out of curiosity I counted snail-mail solicitations for four weeks beginning August 21, 2000, and the total amounted to more than a hundred. Of course this didn't include telephone and email solicitations.

Since moving in 2006 we've taken several measures to reduce the number of solicitations, and overall they were more manageable for the first year, but now the deluge has again reached overload levels. In fact, we frequently resort to recycling most charitable requests—without even opening the envelopes. Who has time to read all the pleas for contributions, much less respond by sending a donation? Besides, once you give, they keep coming back for more. When will charities learn not to be so pushy? I particularly dislike the political "surveys" that arrive, typically with pleas for contributions. What's really annoying is that survey results are rarely forthcoming, which indicates the survey is simply a ruse to raise money, by making donors feel that they're contributing something to the issue at stake.

Our first line of defense against telephone solicitations is to simply refrain from answering all telephone calls, preferring instead to take messages—unless we're available and willing to answer a particular call from someone we recognize. In using email, we find that software security programs are fairly effective in limiting the amount of advertisements that pop up on the monitor or enter via email attachments. Regarding snail mail, we do what we can to avoid being placed on mailing lists, but that's nigh to impossible to track down, hence our strategy of recycling most mail without opening it.

What's a person to do? Charities need to solicit, but do they really need to send several requests annually, some disguised as updates, or thank-you notices, or "membership renewals", or, as mentioned above, those questionable "surveys"? And why must some pleas be so lengthy? Who has time or the inclination to peruse several pages of material? All that paper and expense seems to be a waste of donors' funds. I suppose the truism that it takes money to make money applies in charities as well as in commercial enterprises, but it can be disconcerting to realize some charities use a large percentage of their total donations to cover administrative costs, including solicitations.

No one ever explained that continuing my education beyond high school would result in solicitations from each institution of higher learning for my entire life, along with requests for alumni membership dues and contributions to certain units, scholarship funds, and the like. And what about Greek fraternities, and other types (scholarship, professional)? For those of us who graduated from three educational institutions the lifelong mailings and telephone calls continue accumulating. Moreover, as a long-term teacher at the University of Minnesota, I receive regular requests from the School of Music, College of Liberal Arts, Graduate School, College of Education, Friends of the Libraries, and the University Foundation. My wife and I contribute to more than 50 organizations each year, with about 10 of them receiving sizable donations. We contribute to two or three scholarship or memorial funds each year, even though the charities often put our names on a mailing list, and that brings more solicitations. We now attach a note explaining that our donation is a one-time, and we politely request not to be contacted again.

So how does one strike a balance in managing charitable donations? As a couple, I think we're mostly satisfied that we're doing the best we can. Setting priorities and realizing we can't be all things to all people is a good starting point. This means determining the worthy causes that begin at home, and planning for them, but at the same time giving fair attention to charities deemed most important. For us, this means focusing on organizations that promote arts, environment, population limits, education, health, and our church. For someone else it may mean giving attention to supporting any number of worthwhile causes—indigent populations, youths' sports programs, the physically challenged, and so on. "To each his own", as the saying goes.

Joseph Campbell provides a view of good stewardship in his inspiring book, *Reflections on the Art of Living*: "Money experienced as life energy is indeed a meditation, and letting it flow out instead of hoarding it is a mode of participation in the lives of others."

Stewardship of Possessions and Resources

As alluded to earlier, stewardship of resources also means caring for possessions and extending their useful life as long as possible. The majority of Americans believe in our economic system of *capitalism*, which is driven by the profit motive and characterized by wage labor and private ownership of the means of production. Aside from its serviceable strengths, however, there are some weak points, including the concept of "planned obsolescence", resulting in innumerable tons of garbage added daily to the world's overloaded and growing landfills. Few will argue that we need to stem the rapid turnover of new-model technologies, for instance, in creating more efficient personal computers, but it seems we could continue searching for more efficient ways to reclaim outdated electronic equipment and other products. Though the recycling of homes, home furnishings, automobiles, clothing, and some types of appliances is increasing, an ideal goal would to recycle up to 90 percent of all hard goods, including the possibility of using some materials for generating energy.

Whenever possible, our family's acquisition of possessions frequently involves purchasing used items, using them as long as possible, and caring for them as best we can. For example, most of our autos in the past twenty years have been purchased as used vehicles and driven over 80,000 miles each for at least 8-10 years, and because they've been maintained well, our sons adopt and drive them a few more years. For four years, I drove a 1989 Chevy Blazer inherited from my mother in 2002, and passed on to our oldest son in 2006, when we decided we could function well with one auto. Though the SUV's gas mileage isn't good, neither is it the worst on the road, averaging 20 mpg on the highway. Besides, it's in excellent condition and has low mileage. I respect the views of anti-SUV protestors, but I couldn't justify selling the car to someone who might drive it more often and less wisely. Our single auto, a Hyundai XG300 averages 27-28 mpg highway driving, and still has several thousand miles remaining on its 100,000-mile, ten-year warranty, so it looks like it will continue serving us well. Most likely, the next vehicle we purchase will use less fuel and provide better gas mileage. In addition, we're also gearing up to use more bus and light-rail transportation within the metro area.

Our sons set better examples of auto ownership than we do, one son and daughter-in-law in particular. They have a knack for purchasing older economy-model vehicles, performing most of the maintenance and mechanical work themselves, and driving them over 150,000 miles. Living in a rural area of southwest Wisconsin and maintaining safe-driving records lowers their auto insurance premiums, and because they drive only economy vehicles, their fuel costs are lower than average. After they've squeezed many miles out of each vehicle, they usually end up selling them for a little less than they paid originally, making their per-mile operational costs at or near any low-cost records.

So the concept of simplicity—getting rid of the inessentials and making do with the essentials—might be a worthy guideline to follow. As Toinette Lippe (2002) puts it:

> *As I thought about it, I realized that the result of gathering about you only what you need and relinquishing everything else is self-sufficiency. This is another way of saying that it is wise to be satisfied with what you have . . . Don't try to change things on the outside—in the 'real' world. The work has to be done on the inside. It is a matter of interior housekeeping.*

Seeking a Balanced Lifestyle

With all that's been said thus far, it's obvious where my sympathies lie. I'm not adamantly opposed to having great wealth, as long as it's earned honorably and used for worthwhile causes, such as helping unfortunate people and creating a healthier environment. But I do question the motives and psycho-emotional stability of individuals who have great wealth and a greedy thirst for material possessions, political power, and fame, all poor substitutes for developing a rich interior life that's guided by good character founded on moral-based values. As Elaine St. James points out in her first book, *Simplify Your Life* (1994), we've lost track of the things that make us happy, including life's simple pleasures.

In reflecting on what it takes to live a balanced lifestyle, I feel obligated to offer specific guidelines. Our personal lifestyle may not be suitable for everyone, for we are empty nesters in a quasi-retirement mode. On the other hand, we live pretty much the same as when we had three young sons and busy professional lives. Our overriding guideline, which has never been completely realized, is to live a simple lifestyle based on moderation, with a minimum of clutter or "things" that require undue attention. We partially attained this goal with our move from a house to a condo, when we eliminated an estimated 10 to 20 percent of our material possessions, and we can still reduce more. Indeed, if we were to cut back 50 percent on our possessions, we could still manage to live comfortably and be happy.

Creating a Personal Mission Statement

Listing our values and principles as we did at the beginning of this chapter provides some basic material for writing a mission statement, which can take a variety of forms, from a simple, brief paragraph to a longer step-by-step document. Here is my own mission statement, which I wrote a few years ago after reading Stephen Covey's books, *Seven Habits of Highly Successful People* and *First Things First*, both highly recommended.

I wish to:

• Live morally, ethically, and purposefully, in accordance with universal principles, humanitarian values, and rational societal guidelines.

• Seek truth, goodness, and beauty in gaining a greater understanding and mastery of life through ongoing self-improvement initiatives, guided by reason, critical inquiry, and spiritual concerns.

• Maintain an ongoing program of mind-body health initiatives, including diet and nutrition, exercise and fitness, recreation and relaxation, and spiritual concerns (meditation).

• Live in harmony with the natural environment, by paying attention to the consumption, use, and recycling of natural resources, minimizing any negative impact on the planet, and taking political action in support of environmental causes.

• Cooperate and collaborate with fellow human beings in creating the kind of supportive environment and mind-body conditions that enable all beings to fulfill latent potentialities.

• Lead a simple yet quality lifestyle focused on prioritized values and supported by modest consumerism.

• Organize prioritized activities around well-defined goals, with specific plans for accomplishing desired results.

• Maintain a balanced relationship between work, rest, and recreation.

• Remain fully mindful, alert, and passionately involved in the present, rather than dwelling unduly on past or future events.

• Accept the paradoxes and challenges of life with patience, grace, and courage.

• Create a legacy of worthwhile accomplishments that benefit the earth and humanity.

After I wrote the above mission statement, I was struck by the fact that there was no mention of anything related directly to my professional career as a teacher-singer. Nor did I see any mention of personal needs or wants, such as desired possessions or family-related matters. At the time I was writing this statement, I was oblivious to these observations, but upon reflection, I realized that the values and principles I listed provide the fundamental guidelines for all my personal and professional objectives. One important lesson I learned from this exercise is that our working careers provide less information about our true nature than we tend to think. For instance, I never mentioned my ambition to achieve success as a singer, teacher, or writer. I suppose that when we identify what's truly important, our career work becomes a secondary consideration in our whole-life experience, which, ideally, is exemplified by the professed values and principles that guide our lives.

Obviously, the kind of person we are influences our life's mission. We can only wonder what kind of mission statements might be written by such diverse personalities as former president Jimmy Carter, television host Oprah Winfrey, *Playboy* founder Hugh Heffner, business entrepreneur Martha Stewart, singer-entertainer Michael Jackson, golf pro Tiger Woods, or the infamous Timothy McVeigh, the mass murderer convicted and executed for his role in the 1995 Oklahoma City Government Center bombing. Although most persons will produce mission statements similar to mine, many will hold values that cross over between idealistic and realistic values, including a slant toward materialism. In the extreme position, a significant minority of self-centered, mostly materialistic-oriented individuals might come up with a mission statement that lists goals associated with gaining prestige and power, as evidenced by owning luxurious homes, autos, adult toys, and furnishings. And the overriding principle is to achieve these goals through whatever means possible, apparently to satisfy greedy, narcissistic objectives. The alarming fact is that some people do think and feel this way, all the while entirely unaware of their off-centered stance.

In reviewing the two types of mission statements, constructive perspectives are associated with "givers", those who proactively work at improving themselves and the world, while other perspectives may be associated with "takers", who are more concerned with what they *get* out of life. Ironically, "givers" actually *receive* far more than they give, with rewards that are more of a non-material nature, in terms of gaining respect and appreciation, and achieving a high level of personal satisfaction and self-ful-fillment. I think it's fair to surmise that most people elect-ing to read this book are "givers", as most "takers" would simply not be interested enough to make the effort.

If you've never written a mission statement, I strongly encourage you to do so, followed by writing down spe-cific life goals that complement and implement your mis-sion statement. As discussed in chapter 4, goals provide a focus for planned action, which is best achieved by setting up an overall game plan consisting of short-term, medium-term, and long-term goals. Though it's important to follow through with all goals, it's also essential to allow some flex-ibility for revisiting and revising goals along the way, espe-cially when fresh opportunities for personal growth arise.

If you're wondering if it's too late to undertake this exercise, shame on you. I wrote mine in my mid 60s, and I review it periodically to see if I'm still on track, or have had any new insights to add. The first day of the rest of our lives begins anew each day, so there's always time to undertake self-reflection, and thinking about and writing your life's mission is an excellent way to begin.

Assuming you've heeded my advice—by writing a mis-sion statement and listing your prioritized goals—you'll want to create a game plan for implementing them. But before doing that, we need to consider some other practical issues to help you evaluate what you have done, are doing, and will do to reach your objectives. In the next chapter we'll look further at some practical lifestyle issues, includ-ing ways of dealing with our many possessions, that is, what we need and want, what we have, and how we care for everything. Also, a follow-up to this chapter appears later, concerning what it means to live the "good" life and achieve happiness, a topic we've touched upon briefly.

In closing, the following poem by the American Transcendentalist poet, William Ellery Channing (1780-1842), succinctly summarizes the concept of what is needed to experience a more simple and moderate lifestyle.

My Symphony

To live content with small means.
To seek elegance rather than luxury,
　　and refinement rather than fashion.
To be worthy, not respectable,
　　and wealthy, not rich.
To study hard, think quietly, talk gently,
　　act frankly, to listen to stars, birds, babes,
　　and sages with open heart, to bear all cheerfully,
　　do all bravely, await occasions, hurry never.
In a word, to let the spiritual,
　　unbidden and unconscious,
　　grow up through the common.
This is to be my symphony.

8

Managing Money and Resources

He that is of the opinion money will do everything may well be suspected of doing everything for money . . . Who is rich? He that is content. Who is that? Nobody.—Benjamin Franklin

According to experts, the number one problem most people have is managing their personal finances. We Americans, in particular, have the most serious imbalance between income and expenses. A survey of 21,000 persons in May 2005 by A. C. Nielson revealed that Americans are the most cash-strapped among consumers in 38 international markets. In fact, 28 percent of U.S. residents admit to having no spare cash after covering their monthly living expenses. What's worse, Americans are ranked 33rd out of the 38 developed countries in terms of savings. The economic downturn of 2008 has only exacerbated most people's concerns about money, and retirees or near-retirees are justifiably worried.

A survey by Brightwork Partners for Putnam Investments analyzed people who retired in the first years of the 21st century, and the findings are worth some attention, particularly persons in the near-retirement age category. Although the survey is not up to date, the data shows the following (Block 2004):

- The average annual income for new retirees in 2003, before taxes, was $36,000. Approximately 42 percent of retirees reported incomes of less than $25,000 a year, and 25 percent reported incomes under $15,000.

• More than half reported their standard of living had declined since retiring; 30 percent said they were living comfortably, though not as well as before retiring; and 21 percent said they were struggling to make ends meet.

• Savings accounted for only a small percentage of retirees' income. In 2003, annual income and withdrawals from investments made up 11 percent of their total income, while Social Security produced 41 percent, and payments from a traditional or cash-balance pension plan accounted for 24 percent. This information suggests that retirees most likely will need to rely more heavily on personal savings and investments for income, as many large corporations are reducing or eliminating traditional pensions.

• Retirement doesn't get easier, according to 67 percent of retirees who said the longer they're retired, the harder it gets.

• Money does buy some degree of happiness, at least for retirees with high-incomes and assets. Approximately half of retirees with household incomes of $75,000 or more described themselves as "very satisfied" with retirement, while only a third of those with household incomes of $50,000 or less were very satisfied. Of course, there are other factors influencing respondents' answers, including personal qualities, values, expectations, and assumptions.

In an attempt to address these sobering findings, we'll look at various aspects of money management.

Wanting And Having It All

The modern world seems patterned after the old adage, "To the victor belongs the spoils." The widening chasm between the "haves" and "have-nots"—whereby the rich get richer and the poor get poorer—is creating surging discontent worldwide among lower and middle-class peoples. The organization Population Connection estimates that approximately 80 percent of the world's population lives in conditions ranging from mild deprivation to severe deficiency, with the gap enlarging because most world-wide population growth occurs in poor countries. Africa, the most rapidly growing country, is also growing poorer, mainly due to the rampaging HIV/AIDS epidemic. Meanwhile, in comparison to the citizens of impoverished countries, the majority of Americans enjoy an overall high standard of living. Even so, the economic gap between rich and poor Americans continues to widen, with the highly privileged growing ever more wealthy.

Robert H. Frank and Phillip J. Cook addressed this issue in their book, *The Winner-Take-All Society* (1995), and the disparity has worsened considerably since then. Just consider: CEOs of major corporations earn many times per year what the average worker earns (up to 364 times in 2006); certain athletes earn more in a single game ($150,000 for some baseball stars) than the average person does in two or three years; or that star entertainers earn more making a single movie than a K-12 school teacher earns over an entire lifetime. If there's any single topic that kindles a sensible person's indignation, it's the disparities of income between the winner-take-alls and average workers.

Unfortunately, the winner-take-all phenomenon in high-profile occupations spills over to affect all institutions, including academia, where star professors, athletic coaches, research scientists, and administrators are wooed with attractive salaries and fringe benefits. Star professors, for example, may be given full reign to pursue their research interests, and allowed to give minimal attention to teaching or service responsibilities within the institution. Meanwhile, dependable "drone professors" are expected to do most of the housekeeping functions that keep the institution on course and stable, including the essential roles of teaching, committee work, and minor administrative duties. True to the winner-take-all philosophy, these loyal servants receive meager to moderate salaries and go largely unrecognized for their valuable service and teaching. And the main reason can be attributed to the fact that research is more highly prized and rewarded, especially in the large public and private universities widely identified as research institutions.

Having spent my entire professional life in academia, I can well attest to the disparities in salaries and benefits that existed within my unit (School of Music), which is managed within the College of Liberal Arts. Yet, even though my salary was at the lower end of the university's salary scale—as is the situation nationwide in the arts— we've managed to live an abundant life, with sufficient funds accrued for retirement, thanks to long-term, consistent investing and frugal spending practices.

"Affluenza": Luxury Run Amok

Money magazine once featured a special report titled "The Affluent American", based on a survey conducted by the polling company Roper ASW. Questionnaires were sent to a nationally representative sample and 2,068 responses from financial decision makers who earn upwards of $75,000 annually were tabulated. The findings showed that affluent people in the survey earned a median income of $121,000 (the top 5 percent of income earners), had a median home value of $261,000, stashed away a median of $158,000 in savings and investments, and were saddled with $15,000 in debt. At least 54 percent of this group had a net worth of less than $500,000, while 24 percent had a net worth between $500,000 and $1 million, and 22 percent had a net worth over $1 million.

In light of the Roper Report, there's obviously some truth to the thesis discussed in the now-classic book, *The Millionaire Next Door* (Stanley & Danko 1996), the main difference being that more people have since been purchasing more luxury items than the frugal spenders highlighted in the book. But perhaps the economic downturn of 2007-2008 will serve to wring some excesses out of spending, with the possibility that economic moderation will return—at least for a while.

In the same *Money* article, the median net worth listed by age groups was $15,125 for those 25-34, $102,600 for those 35-44, $188,000 for those 45-54, $235,000 for those 55-64, and $173,000 for those over 65. These figures seem very low, showing further that most Americans are not saving enough for retirement, but more about this later.

Lavish consumption seems to have gripped increasing numbers of well-to-do people. Robert H. Frank, economics professor at Cornell University and co-author of *The Winner-Take-All Society*, has also produced another insightful book titled *Luxury Fever: Why Money Fails to Satisfy in an Era of Excess* (1999). The book's thesis focuses on the fact that two decades of income gains for people at the top of the economic ladder, with concomitant lavish spending on nonessential goods, have wasted national income, and have failed to make heavy spenders any happier. The author cites surveys that show money buys happiness only when people move from poverty levels to middle-income status. Beyond that, the average level of life satisfaction fails to correlate with greater accumulation of material goods.

Luxury items have been selling at increasingly higher levels in recent years. For example, luxury travel (defined at $350 per person per day) soared by 130 percent between 1990 and 1995, and continued higher until 2008. The reasons for the increase in luxury spending have been attributed to (1) necessities (food, clothing, etc.) taking less of buyers' income; (2) less expensive manufactured goods, especially such luxury items as computers, cell phones, cameras, TVs, and other electronic gadgets; and (3) more educated, savvy consumers. Items that used to be considered luxuries are now common. Is there anyone who doesn't own a television set or a cell phone? I wouldn't be surprised to see street people with cell phones in the near future. And even my wife and I are now using our basic "old folk's" (Jitterbug) cell phone for special situations, including emergency calls. If and when wireless phones eventually replace standard landline telephones, we'll probably join up with everyone else.

The most obvious sign of extravagant consumption is typically associated with home ownership, and nowhere is "affluenza fever" more apparent than when considering the homes of the rich and famous, particularly homes owned by CEOs of major corporations. But the unexpected lesson here is that the larger the homes and the income of the CEOs, the more their companies lagged behind other CEOs of S&P 500 companies who lived in smaller houses, by 7 percent on average! This discovery was reported by two finance professors—David Yermack of New York University and Crocker Liu of Arizona State University—who used addresses of 432 CEOs of S&P 500 companies to investigate the relationship between stock performance and the size of a CEO's home. Results showed that 12 percent of CEOs lived in homes of at least 10,000 square feet, or on a minimum of 10 acres, and the performances of their companies as a whole were below average (Sasseen 2007). But the nagging question is: Does anyone of sound mind and character really need so much room and ostentatious display to be happy and satisfied with their lifestyle?

Of course, people could make better use of extra money if it were used for personal worthwhile things, such as living less stressful lives, creating educational opportunities and experiences, or finding more time to exercise or enjoy recreational activities. Another positive way to use excess income is to contribute more to public efforts aimed at improving the environment, including measures to maintain clean air and water, provide safe streets and neighborhoods, promote recreational facilities in public parks and lands, and reduce overcrowding of roadways and cities.

In his 2002 book, *Open Christianity,* Jim Burklo, a progressive Protestant pastor and university chaplain, devotes a chapter titled "A Theology of Enough" to explaining what *enough* means. Burklo believes *enough* doesn't have much validity in the current global consumer economy, because it is a moving target, contextually associated with a particular time, place, thing, or person. For instance, when an individual has fulfilled the most basic needs, what is *enough* becomes a highly individual matter. For highly materialistic persons, *enough* is like an empty hole that can't be filled. But for those who are satisfied with a simple lifestyle and having minimal possessions, *enough* may be interpreted as a psycho-emotional state marked by profound calmness, satisfaction, and happiness, in other words, a life measured by *what we have* rather than by *what we don't have.*

The Age of Entitlement

A corollary to the surge in consumerism is the lamentable *attitude of entitlement* that affects a large segment of U.S. society, especially boomer and younger generations. Of course, most retirees depend on receiving regular social security checks and rely on Medicare benefits for medical needs, so no generation is immune to expecting entitlements.

It seems a truism that the more access we have to anything we desire, and the easier it is to obtain—without earning it through investing personal time and energy—the less appreciative and grateful we are. For instance, the experiences I've had in constructing, repairing, and maintaining a multitude of various possessions, including homes and autos, have helped me appreciate expert craftsmen who do similar work. Also, having enjoyed some tent camping vacations with our family in various state and national parks has given us an appreciation of "roughing" it on a minor scale. We used modern equipment, which made the outdoor camping adventure somewhat more comfortable, but we never owned a lot of expensive equipment and gadgets. The need for people to "camp" using all the latest gismos—loaded RVs included—might partially explain why fewer Americans are flocking to the great outdoors, ostensibly because of increasingly softer lifestyles, with kids preferring to stay indoors to watch TV or play computer games. It seems that in order to enjoy an outdoor "camping" experience increasing numbers of people feel they are entitled to take along all the toys and comforts of home. Otherwise, why would anyone want to rough it? Why? Because it helps build character!

Related to the weakening work ethic of Americans, especially wealthy citizens, is the ongoing illegal immigration controversy. How so? This may seem like a stretch, but consider that Karl Rove, one of President Bush's chief advisors, reportedly justified the administration's amnesty/ open border position because "I don't want my 17-year-old son to have to pick tomatoes or make beds in Las Vegas" (*National Review*). We've already addressed this issue—how many children of privileged backgrounds never learn the value of hard grunt work. Based on my youthful short-term work experiences in grocery stores (general flunky), mowing lawns, delivering newspapers (up at 4:30 a.m.), and, in later years, numerous house and lawn projects requiring physical labor, I and many other older guys have learned the benefits of performing humble jobs. In general, physical labor provides an excellent way to gain appreciation for the type of mundane, backbreaking work that poor immigrants willingly do, and for very low wages.

It seems reasonable to assume that the influx of low-skilled foreign immigrants is associated to some degree with a sharp decline in teenage employment in recent years. Meanwhile, wages of U.S. adult workers in manual and low-skill jobs are depressed by the unceasing flow of cheap foreign labor. But lest I digress too far in blaming immigration policy for contributing to Americans' sense of entitlement, I hasten to emphasize the point of this topic: American youth are not provided sufficient experiences with entry-level, grunt-work jobs, the type of hard work that helps instill qualities that build character. A contemptuous attitude toward people who perform honest labor certainly adds fuel to the controversy, as evidenced by Rove's inane comment.

The possible exception of the entitlement trend is the senior population, although almost everyone seems willing to let the government provide a comfortable and healthy retirement. The prevalent idea is that we've paid our dues in various ways, including service in the armed forces, or working for a lifetime and paying taxes, and in return we are guaranteed social security income and Medicare benefits. So it seems that no generation escapes the entitlement accusation. Even so, we oldsters, regardless of our means, somewhat escaped the growth of entitled materialism, whereby owning any item one desires is deemed necessary rather than merely desired. My generation's parents experienced the dark years of the late 1920s and 1930s, when the Great Depression affected the lives of all Americans, even the wealthy. We're thankful that our parents' frugal lifestyles rubbed off on us, and that we helped pass along thrifty habits to our three sons.

I should point out that our 1950s middle-class lifestyles would now be considered low-middle class. With the exception of the lowest classes, the lifestyles of middle-class Americans have generally been elevated, so that the middle-class of that era would be lower-middle class today. Evidence of this wealth inflation phenomenon is visible in the housing stock of larger cities, with large tracts of small homes built in the post-WWII years to accommodate a growing middle-class. Since then, tracts of new homes have gradually increased in size, from the 1,500 to 2,000 square-foot average to the considerably larger new homes of present day that range in the 3,500-plus square foot range.

When we examine U.S. society as a whole, it's impossible not to be aware of the attitude of entitlement that many people display. One of the signs of extravagant consumption is the trend of buying large homes that carry high mortgages. To furnish the home and keep up with the neighbors, owners tend to take on extra debt, and when faced with a financial catastrophe, such as a loss of employment or a mortgage rate increase, they may face bankruptcy proceedings, a trend made ever too clear beginning in 2006 with the national mortgage business melt-down. Even more disturbing is evidence that many high-spending Americans are diverting funds from savings, ignoring or avoiding preparation for old age and retirement. Saving for one's future is especially necessary given the precarious state of social security, with funds projected to run out in the next 20-30 years, and retirement age being pushed up to 70 rather than 65.

Everyone needs to combat the attitude of entitlement by reducing overall consumerism, and for us, this includes limiting gifts to children and grandchildren. I realize that if everyone reduced spending levels the economy might be adversely affected, but the pain might not be as long lasting as feared—once the excesses have been wrung out, and everyone has adjusted to a reasonable standard of living that also affords a higher quality of life. If everyone could adopt a simpler, more frugal lifestyle, corporations wouldn't need to be so bent out of shape with the idea of earning enormous profits—and continual growth.

One equitable solution for curbing consumerism, as proposed by Robert H. Frank and others, is to impose a sharply progressive consumption tax system to replace the

existing system, an approach aimed at penalizing ostentatious spenders and rebalancing income distribution. It's
comforting to know that reputable experts agree that making legislative reform and changes in health-care financing
might help control the inordinately high incomes of some
lawyers and doctors, in turn encouraging dedicated professionals more concerned with doing good than making
vast sums of money.

To Spend Or Save?

The proclivity for Americans to "have it all", and as soon
as possible, foregoing the notion of postponed gratification, has created a crisis in debt management, and along
with it, a lowering of the average savings rate. From 1998
to November 2004, consumer debt increased 35 percent,
while household income declined 4 percent, and the average credit card balance for U.S. consumers (those who
don't pay off their credit cards monthly) stood at $14,400,
an amount that nearly tripled in the past 10 years. Since
1998, it appears Americans were on a spending binge,
cashing out more than $500 billion from homes, spending
more than $50 billion in federal tax rebates, and adding
another $137 billion to their credit-card bills. The mortgage
debt also reached all-time highs, with homeowners owing
an average of nearly $96,000, a rise of 64 percent in five
years. Of course, the chief reason for the increased debt is
overspending, the dire consequence of which is a declining savings rate, averaging out to 0.2 percent in 2004, as
opposed to 11 percent 20 years ago (Reinan, 2004). And it's
getting worse. The savings rate has continued plummeting
since 2004—to minus 0.5 percent of income in early 2008,
the lowest since the Great Depression years of 1932-1933.

Knight Kiplinger, editor-in-chief of *Kiplinger's Personal
Finance Magazine*, has some insights regarding what he calls
the democratization of luxury. He claims that luxury fever

went mass market approximately when the stock market heated up in 1982. Prior to that time, the majority of middle-class consumers were willing to live more simply, presumably because they were more capable of distinguishing between needs and wants. As a result, the historic savings rate was considerably higher than the low rates of recent years. Of course, the 1970s were marked by economic woes that tended to slow spending, somewhat like we're experiencing in 2008.

Abiding by the time-honored tradition of "getting rich slow" by working hard, living frugally, and regularly saving and investing a portion of their incomes, a surprisingly large number of people accumulated respectable wealth. These are the people marketing professors Thomas Stanley and William Danko described in their 1996 captivating book, *The Millionaire Next Door*, in which it was suggested that, though conspicuous consumption may indicate a high income, it may not be a reliable indicator of net worth. As mentioned, one observation is that the young couples living in the new big homes, driving luxury cars, and living the good life might be living precariously on the financial edge, as the growing number of home foreclosures and bankrupt proceedings indicate.

In short, "pay yourself first" is the most sensible advice reputable financial advisors can offer. The importance of setting aside a portion of one's income for the future is an essential measure for building wealth.

Personal Finances: What We Did Right

Perhaps our personal financial history might be of interest in demonstrating the advantages of a long-term savings and investment program. First, let it be known that we don't consider ourselves financial geniuses, not by any stretch of anyone's imagination. On the other hand, neither may we be considered ignoramuses. True to our preferences, we probably fall somewhere in a comfortable middle position, which suits us just fine.

As a young couple, the main thing we did correctly was to curb our spending. We've never been in serious financial difficulty, and our debt load has always been limited to home mortgages and only two of our many automobiles, as we usually paid cash for slightly used vehicles. Carrying high charges on credit cards seems like an unwise practice, primarily because of high interest charges, so we systematically pay all monthly charges in full. I suppose the personal finance course we took together in college prepared us for some of the major issues, but it was our parents' modeling and our frugality that kept us solvent.

Because we both originally thought of the stock market as a benign form of gambling, our non-retirement savings during the 1960s were originally placed in traditional bank accounts, and in the early to middle 1970s we mostly utilized CDs for savings accounts, a plan that worked well enough, since the stock market was stalled for the entire decade. Fortunately, the University of Minnesota provided an excellent retirement program for faculty and staff, with several options left to the discretion of participants. Remaining true to my moderate-position philosophy, I opted for a 50/50 selection of Vanguard 500 Index Fund and Vanguard Corporate Bond Fund. About ten years later, I realized the stock fund was ahead of the bond fund by several thousand dollars, so I changed the mix to a 60/40 ratio, just in time to catch the long-term bull market that began in 1982.

In the late 1970s a Merrill-Lynch broker contacted us and convinced us to begin investing in stocks. Bettye's father was a long-time, successful stock investor, so by then we had grown more comfortable with the idea. Our broker also convinced us to place all our non-retirement funds in the Merrill-Lynch Cash Management Account, a full-service brokerage program that was a novelty at the time and offered a simple way of keeping tabs on most of our investments. For the next several years we bought and sold stocks, guided quite sensibly by our broker, and I actually developed an interest in tracking them. Overall, we came out ahead financially, but the vagaries of individual stocks and the time it took to keep up with them were proving to be too much trouble. At the peak of the high inflation era (circa 1980), our money market funds were earning up to 18 percent, while stocks were unpredictable.

In 1983, our financial lives changed drastically, partly due to a setback caused by my being turned down for promotion to rank of professor. At the same time, we became health nuts, dedicated to a diet and exercise program promoted by the Pritikin Longevity Center. As "born again" athletes, we were open to learning about any health-oriented products or programs. As luck would have it, some very personable Shaklee representatives contacted us, with a message of salvation. They offered us an opportunity to promote healthy products and earn huge sums of money in the process. Well, so much for the "making huge sums of money" spiel! There were some real down periods trying to "build the business", which included hounding relatives, friends, colleagues, acquaintances, and strangers, with exhortations to test our Shaklee products. There were some positive developments, including our growing awareness of health and environmental issues and products, entrepreneurial techniques, the value of setting goals, and developing greater communication skills. Financially, however, it was at best a break-even proposition when we stopped the business a year later. But there were some very positive outcomes, including the use of holistic health information in my three voice-teaching books (see bibliography). In addition, there has been a long-term financial benefit from ongoing book sales, with some royalty income that helps supplement our retirement funds.

So, spurred on by the hope of gaining moderate financial security by age 50, we determined to become savvy investors. By the mid 1980s we'd discovered Fidelity Investments, a discount brokerage company that has since become the largest discount fund company in the world. We switched from Merrill Lynch to Fidelity, with all financial holdings contained in a Fidelity Brokerage Account, which we highly recommend (other reputable companies offer similar accounts). Gradually, we began switching all stocks over to a combination of stock and bond funds. Our big winner for at least a decade was the celebrated Magellan Fund, which remained under the management of Peter Lynch, a prominent investment guru.

Around that same time I began contributing the maximum contributions allowed by law into a 403B account (equivalent of a corporate 401K account) through the university's payroll deduction program. This proved to be a very smart move, as my 403B account holdings eventually rivaled my longer-term, combined university/employee contributions in my basic retirement plan. We also took advantage of maximum IRA contributions for at least fifteen years, converting them both to Roth IRAs at the peak of the stock market in 2000, a move that, in retrospect, might not have been wise, since we ended up paying high taxes on funds that were reduced by 30-40 percent in the stock market retreat, but have since built back up. After maximizing all contributions as mentioned, we next contributed funds to annuities for each of us, the wisdom of which we're still debating.

Personal Finances: What We Did Wrong

To counterbalance our wise financial moves, allow me to confess some things we've done wrong. In the late 1970s we got carried away with the idea of owning a recreational lot in the north woods of Minnesota, so what did we do?

We bought *three* lots in *three* different campgrounds, all with the prospect fever of selling them at a profit, as real estate prices were climbing like crazy. Surprise! The market topped just as we'd bought our third lot, and over the ensuing years the high evaluations fell back down to earth.

Meanwhile, we bought a 35-foot 1966 Avion Travel Trailer, which was in top condition, and hauled it at various times to all three lots. But, for certain reasons—travel distance, lack of children's interest, inconveniences—the amount of time we spent using the lots and trailer was minimal. Actually, we spent more time repairing squirrel damage to the trailer than we did recreating and relaxing.

To shorten this sad tale, it took us over twenty years to finally unload these lots—at a financial loss, of course. The total expenses associated with owning the three lots—plus trailer—was approximately $25,000 to $28,000, including original costs, annual taxes, improvements, and maintenance fees. Subtracting the approximately $8000 we received for all the properties (average of $2000 each), we were in the hole about $20,000. And this doesn't include the lost investment opportunities had these funds been invested in stocks during the bull market of the late 1980s to mid 1990s, when all lots were finally sold. So we live and learn.

At the peak of our "get-rich period" in the mid 1980s, a former student who seemed to be an "expert" commodity speculator, was quite successful in buying and selling them on paper. Though he'd not tried using real money, he was ahead of the game in trading mock commodities, as he enthusiastically demonstrated to me on several occasions. Greedy with the idea of making great gains with the help of this knowledgeable genius, I agreed to put up a matching $5,000, which he played through a full-service broker. In short, we lost everything, which he simply couldn't understand, since he had done so well—on paper. Lesson Number Two: Don't get involved in risky financial ventures, especially with people with whom you are closely associated.

It would be reassuring to know these were our only financial mistakes, but there were more, namely, minor losses from two miserable penny stocks that were "hot tips" from a son's friend who was a broker, and a $1,000 loan to a former student who was starting up a landscaping business for which our youngest son served as a virtual slave one summer. The 20-percent return the owner promised on our "investment" failed to materialize, though by constantly nagging him, we eventually recouped our initial loan. Lesson Number three: Don't accept "hot tips" from anyone without carefully researching the proposed investment, and don't get involved in lending funds for risky financial ventures with people you know but aren't sure you can trust.

Money Management: Finding a Balanced Approach

In case you're wondering why I'm willing to admit our financial misfortunes, it's to point out how our naive financial expertise at that time resulted in an imbalanced money-management program. Prior to this period of self-examination, which included revisiting our goals and making future plans, we had been very conservative about most financial matters. Then, during the mid-1980s when we were actively seeking ways to increase our wealth, our actions tended toward the risky side of investing as we undertook what for us were some uncommonly risky initiatives. In good time, however, we reached a centrist position that became more comfortable because of its simplicity and balanced objectives. Specifically, we made the following financial moves:

• Concentrated a majority of financial holdings in a central account, which enabled us to easily view all securities at a glance on a secure website.

- Decided to use a single Visa credit card and pay off all monthly bills so as not to incur interest (we also have an American Express card, which we only use as a backup, and an Wells Fargo debit card used only for rare ATM cash withdrawals).

- Concentrated investments in two popular no-load fund families (Fidelity and Vanguard; now all Fidelity).

- Limited most of our investments to seventeen mutual funds, including one money market account (with checking and credit card privileges), seven stock funds (mixed objectives), two balanced funds, two real estate funds, and four bond funds (one municipal), with a portfolio that features a 60/40 (stocks/bonds) ratio that varies according to considerations associated with the financial markets and our ages.

- Paid off all loan debts, including our former home mortgage in 1993, our condo in 2006 (when we paid the cash difference between the home we sold and the condo), and a zero-percent interest auto loan on our car.

To be free of debt is a great feeling, and I highly recommend it as a goal, as long as it makes financial sense. In some cases it might not make sense, especially for young couples starting out with very few possessions and minimal cash on hand. But for retirees, I recommend a no-debt lifestyle, with the possible exception of investigating reverse mortgages for older folk who need more income.

In sum, we think we've finally developed an equitable balance in our investment portfolio. To be sure, we've had our financial bumps and bruises, such as the bear markets of 1987, 1990, and in this decade, which decimated the financial holdings of many Americans, including ours by up to 40 percent. Admittedly, we miss the boom times, when we gleefully observed our portfolio climbing beyond what we had envisioned possible in the mid 1980s. With the national economy once again in a down cycle, the prospects for recovery are not favorable for the next few years.

But regardless of how the economy performs in any single year or decade, we've appreciated the long-term financial benefits made possible by adopting three principal, time-proven investment strategies: *dollar-cost averaging* (making regular, systematic contributions to investment accounts); *diversification* of investment securities, and *buying and holding* a solid, well-rounded portfolio. Resorting to a market-timing strategy (selling and buying) is not recommended, no matter how dire the economic conditions, but occasional portfolio repositioning is a wise strategy. In any case, bear in mind that overreacting to market conditions by panicking and selling at the bottom, which inevitably corresponds with buying at the top, is the basic "no-no" of investing. "Buy low, sell high" is the overriding rule of intelligent investing.

Speaking of the stock market retreat following the long-term bull market from 1982-1999, *Newsweek* columnist Alan Sloan offers the following insight, which is very timely and applicable to the current slowdown (Sloan 2001):

> *You can't have boom all the time. Life just doesn't work that way. But don't go from irrational exuberance to irrational depression without at least a brief stay in the middle. The world isn't coming to an end. You shouldn't overreact to the negative news. Just as we old fuddy-duddies warned you not to overreact to the boom and expect it to go on forever. Just accept the fact that things are back to their natural order, with employers holding the whip in hand. The pendulum has swung back to a more stable, more healthy balance of power.*

The buy-and-hold philosophy requires much faith in the U.S. economic system, but history proves it works over the long haul. Of course, the system can collapse, though it's unlikely. We could theoretically have another major depression at some point, possibly with great financial losses. If so, we'll all be in the same boat, metaphorically speaking, and somehow we'll get by, just as our parents and their parents survived the Great Depression.

Perhaps some financial advice from a master investor is needed to bolster the strategy of remaining invested through thick-and-thin market conditions. Financial guru Warren Buffett wrote an insightful article for the *New York Times* (Oct. 16, 2008), in which he alerted the world that he was aggressively purchasing U.S. stocks, as their prices had been drastically reduced—and their value increased—with the plunge of all major stock markets, including the venerable Dow Jones Industrial Average, which had fallen from a high of 14,000 the previous year, to 8,500 during the second week of October. His words of financial wisdom bear witness to what many consider the primary principle of smart investing: "A simple rule dictates my buying: Be fearful when others are greedy, and be greedy when others are fearful". Of course, this is Buffett's way of expressing the formerly mentioned buy low, sell high dictum. Admittedly, this is easier said than acted upon.

Those who panic every time the stock market flounders, immediately reacting by selling good stocks or funds, will lose out on long-term growth of investments. I've known persons who have worked very hard accumulating extra money for their retirement years, yet their pattern has been to pull out of the market on major setbacks. I'm not aware if they managed to get back in before the 2003 market rallied, but I hope so. It's sad to realize that so many intelligent people—experts in their respective fields—remain blissfully ignorant regarding financial matters.

Seeking Financial Expertise

A viable option for many people is to seek professional guidance. Fortunately, we have an advisor assigned by Fidelity in conjunction with a "private client group" account. Our advisor is also a certified financial planner (CFP), the type of qualified professional we might otherwise consider hiring, as long as he or she is not affiliated with any particular brokerage house or insurance company and charges an hourly fee for services rendered. Trusting company-affiliated advisors to be impartial is extremely risky, because even though they may have the best of altruistic intentions, it is not in their best financial interest to be completely objective. This is one step that must be taken very deliberately, involving considerable research beforehand. We are very lucky to have such expertise available as we enjoy our retirement years, including managing the distribution of retirement funds plus tending to estate issues.

My most legitimate claim to any knowledge about investments is based on my ongoing reading of personal finance magazines, in addition to an advisement newsletter that focuses on Fidelity's network of funds. My experience tells me that no two professional financial advisors or advisement services will agree on any single financial advisement issue. As proof of this claim, I suggest reading any personal finance magazine and locating an article featuring several advisors giving their "educated opinions" about any specific financial topic, such as the direction of the stock market in the coming months, projected stock and bond returns, or recommendations regarding certain investments. The most revealing articles are those in which three or more experts offer specific recommendations for individuals or couples. In all cases the disparity of experts' recommendations demonstrates how difficult it is for an investor to know what to do.

In sum, I highly recommend that everyone assume personal responsibility for his or her financial health. Gaining knowledge about money matters isn't as difficult as it may seem, as there are many informative books, websites, and events that provide helpful basic information and guidance to investors. I've read a lot, and continue to stay abreast of what's happening with the investment climate, but I actually spend only a few hours annually tending to our investment portfolio. In addition to reviewing our monthly summary statements from Fidelity plus quarterly statements of retirement accounts, I reassess our portfolio every six months, and, if needed, we'll make some balancing adjustments once or twice annually. Of course, my wife and I always confer regarding any potential action just to be sure we're in agreement. We're never absolutely certain we've made the wisest move, but we'd rather be wrong than to pay someone else to make similar mistakes on our behalf. Of course, since we gained a professional advisor with Fidelity, we now check all of our decisions with him, as well as request his recommendations. Our decisions seem to have worked out well enough overall. We don't make the enormous gains that come from owning the hottest stocks or mutual funds, but the annual percentage of growth to date has kept up with the overall financial market indices. According to the overall recommendations of investment experts, aiming for a 6-8 percent annual gain is a reasonable objective. Expecting more is being delusional.

In this regard, most financial experts seem to agree that investors preferring a long-term, hands-off, moderate investment approach may find index funds a comfortable option. Because managers of index funds typically adhere to a buy-and-hold strategy rather than actively trading, index funds are also less expensive to own. There are many competing index funds for every conceivable security—stocks, bonds, real estate, etc.—so anyone can take advantage of the overall financial market's long-term growth using a balanced strategy that incorporates a variety of stock and bond funds. Both Vanguard and Fidelity are considered prominent index fund companies, and both feature low-cost management fees. Target funds are also a safe and sane way to invest for many hopeful retirees, as they guarantee a certain return that comes due on a specific date. Thus, for anyone retiring, say in 2012, a fund can be purchased for a given amount that will return a specific amount that year. Moreover, target funds can be purchased for each year thereafter.

Conscientious investors invest in companies and financial securities that have established reputations, with ethical track records. Though most companies provide worthwhile goods and services, some are not distinguished for promoting socially conscious and eco-friendly goals. Most folk have some strong preferences for specific causes. For instance, Bettye and I prefer to avoid companies associated with such harmful products (or services) as tobacco, junk foods, unhealthy drinks, gambling, or pornography. We also disfavor companies noted for unhealthy corporate cultures, indulging in unsavory business practices, using foreign sweatshop laborers, or damaging the environment. Regrettably, however, when dealing with mutual funds, it's very difficult to identify companies that suit a squeaky-clean profile. And, in honestly addressing investors' concerns about achieving favorable investment results, the truth is that overall returns of most socially conscious funds may not meet average market results.

The good news is that, according to an article in *Kiplinger's* financial magazine (Goldberg & Smith 2004), there are seven reputable funds that have been singled out for their overall respectable records: Ariel Fund, Ariel Appreciation, Capstone SERV Small Cap Equity A, Neuberger Berman SR Investors, Pax World Investors, Pax World Balanced, TIAA-CREF Social Choice Equity, and Vanguard Calvert Social index. As with all such ratings of funds, investors should always pay special attention to those that maintain a long-term "good company" record.

Developing a Sensible Money Management Strategy

Finding a balanced approach to money management begins with some careful thought and planning, based on realistic worthwhile values and goals. A simple, back-to-basics money management style affords a less stressful lifestyle. In the financial-help book, *Your Money or Your Life* (Dominguez and Robin, 1995), the point is made that for every item acquired, a slice of "life energy" is required from the owner. The couple recommends evaluating whether an item's expense is actually worth the time needed to pay for it (and maintain it). For instance, our former home's moderate-sized deck took far more hours per year in upkeep than the leisurely use for which it was originally intended. I'll venture our situation is similar to many other deck owners, especially those living in cooler climes. We're grateful that the small covered balcony deck we now have is much easier to maintain. I'm beginning to take to heart Ben Franklin's pithy statement: "He who lives sparingly [simply] need not be rich."

Here's a summary of ways to streamline money management:

• Develop a basic knowledge of financial management including investing; keep accurate records and stay informed.

• Distinguish between needs and wants, shop wisely, and reduce unnecessary spending.

• Place all financial holdings in a single discount brokerage account, preferably one that provides a checking account plus use of a credit card, and summarizes all holdings in a single monthly statement.

• Use a single checking account that allows recording expenses in specific categories, such as household, business, entertainment, etc.

• Use a single multi-purpose credit card, but have a back-up card for emergency situations; avoid specialty credit cards and frequent buyer clubs.

• Use automatic bill paying services connected with your checking account.

• Use one or two reputable low-cost investment fund firms that feature no-load or low-load funds, including index funds.

Planning for Retirement

Inexplicably, only a relatively small portion of the population prepares adequately for their eventual retirement years. According to General Accounting Office estimates, only about half of baby-boomers are saving and investing enough to maintain their current standard of living. Another survey, by Thrivent Financial, revealed that 36 percent of working adults confessed they hadn't begun saving for retirement, and only 16 percent reported they'd saved $10,000 or less. Obviously, non-savers can expect to have a lower standard of living—unless they commit themselves to an ongoing plan of saving and investing.

Compounding the retirement outlook for baby boomers and those that follow them is the age of eligibility for receiving social security, to age 67 for those born after 1960, a deadline that will automatically force more people to work longer. Estimates and pronouncements regarding the future of social security range from slightly positive to very negative, depending on various data sources. Personally, I like to think of social security as a back-up emergency reserve for retirement, as gravy income so to speak, with other financial resources providing the foundation for our retirement years. In short, though some form of social security will most likely remain in place, I heartily agree with the financial pundits who think it's wise to build supplementary funds, rather than rely on social security and Medicare to cover most living expenses.

Though American investors are fortunate in having enjoyed relatively stable financial markets over the past several decades, we have learned from experience that there will always be the inevitable ups and downs that affect overall investment portfolios performance. For example, the bear market that began in 2000 reduced most investors' portfolios by 20-40 percent within a three-year span, and only with the market's revival in 2003 did our personal investment portfolio finally approach its 2000 level (in January 2004). Of course, additional savings during that time also contributed to the increase. Unfortunately, with the current economic downturn, practically all investment portfolios have lost ground, and no one knows how soon it will recover. It helps to bear in mind that most financial advisors forecast a 6-8 percent long-term average growth for moderate-risk, balanced portfolios (mixture of stocks, bonds, etc.). It's possible to beat the average, but it requires taking risks and still being able to sleep well at night.

Some of the emotional blocks to acquiring the requisite funds for a comfortable retirement can be summarized according to the following factors (Quinn 2004):

- *Denial.* We fear what we don't understand, so the path of least resistance is to simply ignore the problem, similar to what happens with the concept of an ostrich hiding its head in the sand to avoid any unpleasantness. Denying there's a problem and putting any positive action off to a future date can prove disastrous.

- *Greed.* Not having a comprehensive understanding of financial matters and making unwise investment choices based on unrealistic, greedy objectives usually causes people to lose precious assets, in turn discouraging them and making it difficult to act wisely. We learned some valuable lessons through many trials and errors, but fortunately we were middle aged and had time to learn from our mistakes and recover some losses.

• *Fear.* Though it's natural to be concerned about accumulating sufficient retirement funds, some people worry too much, overestimating their ability to get by on less that the one-million dollars (in 2005) recommended by most financial managers. Realistically speaking, as long as one doesn't have extravagant tastes and materialistic expectations, it's possible to have a fulfilling existence living more simply and frugally, as many retired teachers and average-earning workers demonstrate.

The cure to overcoming these emotional blocks is to focus on what can be done today to create a more comfortable retirement fund. Regardless of one's age, a responsible financial plan will most likely require spending less and purchasing wisely. By cutting back on spending, it should be easier to save more by paying yourself first, at least ten percent of total income. Although there are some exceptions, most people benefit from paying off all debt as soon as possible, especially high-interest possessions. Finally, it may be necessary to continue working after reaching the official retirement age, perhaps on a part-time basis. Many retirees find part-time work very manageable and enjoyable, especially if it is interesting and service oriented.

Here's a summary of recommendations by financial experts for building a secure financial future:

• Calculate a realistic amount of money you'll need to live a comfortable retirement.

• Pay yourself first, by making sure a portion of every paycheck is pegged toward savings, preferably using an automated savings plan.

• Prepare for emergencies by setting aside at least three months of income in an emergency fund.

• Take advantage of any "extra money" offered by many companies, such as matching funds associated with 401(k) plans.

• Increase your savings rate a notch or two, especially when pay raises are forthcoming or expenses decrease.

• To create extra savings, find ways to cut and/or reduce certain expenses (life, car, and home insurance, loans, etc).

From 2002 to 2007 I thoroughly enjoyed a quarter-time teaching load in conjunction with a negotiated five-year phase-out retirement program, which allowed me to postpone drawing on retirement funds until age 70 and a half. During the same period, Bettye gradually reduced her teaching load to approximately half of her former teaching commitment. It's comforting to know we can continue teaching in some capacity for as long as we have the energy and the desire, and not because we need the income, but simply because we enjoy teaching and wish to remain productive citizens.

Creating a Financial Legacy

In the end—literally speaking—what happens to the financial assets one accumulates over a lifetime? Some senior citizens proudly sport amusing car bumper stickers stating, "We're spending our children's inheritance." Many seniors do spend down their retirement funds, but usually not in financing pleasurable pursuits. More typically, they exhaust their retirement funds on personal health and long-term care needs, including the possibility of spending time in nursing homes, sometimes for extended periods.

On the other hand, upon death many well-heeled people leave sizeable estates, in most cases willed to heirs and favored charities. Assuming one does have sizeable assets to pass along to either heirs or charities, how does one begin to allocate them? This is a question that needs everyone's attention at some point in their lives, usually beginning when one reaches the late 20s to early 30s, but certainly no later than mid 40s. After reading and researching this topic for several years, Bettye and I upgraded our simple wills to living marital trust wills, as it is more suitable for persons with assets that can be passed along to heirs or charities, thereby avoiding being taxed to death (pun intended). This is not the time and place to discuss the details related to various forms of wills, but I highly recommend everyone having one drawn up by an attorney who's proficient in estate and tax law. If you're in your 50s or older, and have not tended to this important matter, please do so soon!

We like the general concept of making a gift to a specific charity, whereby donors receive a pre-agreed monthly payment (annuity) for life, based on interest earned from the gift's principal. Upon death of the donors, the principal is then transferred to the charity. For example, assuming one donates $100,000 to a charity, the annuity payout could provide a monthly income for life or a designated period, say ten years. Thus, if the guaranteed rate were pegged at 5 percent, the payout would be $5,000 annually. Of course, a variable payback could be more or less, fluctuating according to the overall financial markets' estimated long-term returns. As expected, the age of the donor is a major consideration, with the payback adjusted according to the type of annuity selected, and whether a beneficiary is named. In thinking ahead, we are interested in considering such a plan, as a way of providing a steady source of income, as well as giving to a worthy cause we both believe in and wish to have supported in future years. This type of program provides a win-win option for both donor and recipient.

There are also charitable gift funds of a slightly different ilk, such as the Fidelity Charitable Gift Fund, which we initiated as the Ware Family Charitable Gift Fund in 2006 with a $5,000 donation, the minimum initial amount to set up an account. The main advantages of this form of giving are its simplicity, flexibility and convenience, in addition to tax deductions. Funds contributed in a given year may be carried over and allowed to accumulate for future designated charities. This particular fund allows contributors to send gifts to any approved charities using a website for this purpose. Charitable Fund personnel check the status of designated charities and, if approved, send checks to the amount of $100 or more. There is no minimum annual contribution, and there is no limit to how much can be contributed, but a balance of $5,000 must remain in the account. Several investment companies are offering similar charitable-gift funds, and they are rapidly gaining in popularity. We are satisfied that it serves our needs very well, and it's comforting to know that upon our deaths, our sons will assume control and be able to continue making contributions.

In addition to leaving our heirs and favorite charities portions of our estate, we are also concerned that all matters related to our legacy are addressed prior to any physical or mental incapacity we may experience in our final years. Such topics as living wills and arrangements for disposing of possessions are addressed later.

It seems appropriate to close this section and chapter with Jim Burklo's perceptive, concise, and liberal description of charity: "Charity is not just a percentage of one's wealth that one gives to others. It's a way of life that takes others into account, 100 percent."

9

Caring for Possessions

By the time most Americans reach college age, the quantity of their possessions has mounted to sizeable portions, at least enough to fill a car or small truck upon leaving for college or upon taking a new job away from home. The habit of collecting things begins early in life, as we are inundated from early childhood by well-meaning Santa Clauses who do not want us to go without, and who inculcate in us the desirability of owning lots of things, presumably to satisfy an unconscious need to build our self-esteem or to show off to others that we have "made it".

Too Many Things, Too Many Options

In my own childhood I also received many items as Christmas presents, a tradition my wife and I continued with our children. The number of toys we received was astounding, especially considering my parents' modest means. Almost every American we know has received an abundance of gifts, many of which are seldom used, if at all. Some of those well-intended gifts may remain in good condition, and in turn be passed along as gifts to other persons until being donated to a charity for recycling. Children's enthusiasm for most toys can be especially short-lived, as they focus great attention on this or that toy for a short while, until it breaks or the batteries run down, at which time it is relegated to a storage container until the garbage truck picks it up.

In sum, an attic or garage full of broken toys, once-used equipment, and unused gifts is a fairly typical situation in most of America's households. Though my wife and I make annual attempts to get rid of unused items, the number of items retained and rarely or never used is appalling—even after moving from a home into a condo and either throwing away or recycling numerous boxes and bags filled with useful items. For instance, though we've donated lots of clothes to charities, my wife and I retain certain clothes that are rarely worn, if ever, and others that we wear more often because we prefer them. Yet, we hold on to more than we really need. Why, I'm not sure, but we continue debating this minor problem. Surely it's better to give away unused articles so others can use them instead of hoarding them at home, where they gather dust, take up space, go out of fashion, and require some attention.

Of course, one of the major problems shoppers in the U.S. and other developed countries face is the opportunity (or curse) to selectively purchase possessions from among an increasingly wide range of options. This modern dilemma has been addressed by Barry Schwartz in his book, *The Paradox of Choice: Why More is Less*, in which he describes numerous cases of people who say they enjoy having lots of options, but actually are overwhelmed when the time comes to buy, especially when it comes to expensive, long-term items.

Those of us old enough to recall shopping for items in the 1950s can attest to the enormous increase in products vying for our attention today. Take breakfast cereal, for example. The typical hot cereals in the 50s were oatmeal, grits, and Cream of Wheat. The cold cereals were Corn Flakes, Raisin Bran, Wheaties, Shredded Wheat, and Grape Nuts. Today supermarkets showcase many variants of the old-time cereals (regular, fast cooking, instant, fortified, etc.), in addition to dozens of new cereals, including high-sugar, vitamin-fortified, multi-colored cereals aimed at children. When traveling on hiking trips, we have a difficult time deciding which type or brand of granola to buy—

one with various fruits and nuts, or unsweetened, or with more oats than wheat, and so on.

Just think of any item you've purchased recently, and I'm sure you'll recall feeling overwhelmed in considering the myriad choices. In some cases, consumers resort to such publications as *Consumer Reports* to find the recommended "Best Buys", in the process saving much research time. Schwartz's sensible suggestions include accepting items that are good enough, rather than over-deliberating and wasting time worrying over rejected options. Perhaps it might help to lower expectations, and practice an "attitude of gratitude" for having sufficient options from which to choose. (Yet, we can't help but wonder how our lives would be greatly simplified, if we could be assured that all food products were safe and healthy, and didn't require our reading posted labels to determine the contents, including additives; also that all marketed items, especially toys, were free of lead or other dangerous chemicals.)

So the reality is that most of us have numerous possessions that, instead of making our lives easier, actually add to our workload by overwhelming us with responsibilities related to organizing, storing, cleaning, maintaining, and using most items. So, what can we do to assure good stewardship of our possessions and make our lives simpler? My simple answer is: a lot!

Dealing With Clutter

While most people live with a certain amount of clutter in their homes, offices, and vehicles, some go overboard. Scientists theorize that the compulsion to stockpile things, some with little or no useful function, is a natural and adaptive instinct (Deunwald 2004). Most creatures have an instinctive drive to hoard certain things, especially the necessities for survival, such as food, clothing, and other essentials. In the animal world, for instance, the arctic gray jay is an avid hoarder, ensuring its winter food supply by storing over 100,000 mouthfuls of berries and insects over a wide land area. On the human side, those of us whose parents struggled through the Great Depression years of the 1930s are well aware that many of that generation had a propensity to hoard items, based on the logical assumption that certain items might be needed some day. I think most people go through such a phase at some point in their lives. I know we did, but not to our parents' extent.

My mother certainly fit the hoarder's profile, as she rarely threw things away, especially in her final two decades, when she lacked the energy or the motivation. Her motto: "When I'm gone, my children can keep or throw away anything they don't want". Kay, my good-natured caregiver sister, shouldered most of the burden of disposing loads of inherited junk, along with a few desirable items family members requested.

It seems that humans are the only species that take hoarding to pathological extremes, compulsively filling their living and working spaces with so much stuff that navigation is hampered, not to mention the impossibility of finding items buried under a pile of disorganized stuff. The extent of this pathological disorder in society is unknown, as hoarders tend to be secretive about their habits. Some psychologists suggest there might be a genetic link, or perhaps the compulsion is just a modeling effect that exists within families.

In addition to being intelligent and well educated, chronic hoarders often share the common trait of a strong emotional nature, with a tendency to place irrational sentimental value on most possessions, including mundane items. They also have difficulty making decisions, often bouncing from one activity to another. Moreover, they tend to be excessive talkers, generally supplying more detail than listeners desire or need to know. In many ways, because of the pleasure it provides, compulsive hoarding is similar to compulsive gambling. Treatment for compulsive hoarding disorder is mostly limited to cognitive therapy sessions with a trained psychologist, because unlike obsessive compulsion disorder, compulsive hoarding doesn't respond to medication.

A particularly outstanding model of a wealthy packrat, Karl Lagerfeld is a celebrated Chanel fashion designer who dwells in an 18,000 square-foot Parisian mansion that's loaded with disorderly accumulations of valuable possessions and piles of the typical materials of daily life, including magazines, newspapers, and the like. For his 1,000 square-foot office, he bought three extra desks to handle work-related materials that overloaded his one single desk. One complete room is filled with clothes, including 200 pairs of fingerless gloves, hundreds of belts, dozens of pairs of jeans, and numerous shirts, and another room contains approximately 500 suits. Because the mansion was getting too crowded with stuff, he's purchased a 200 year-old, two-story building overlooking the Louvre, with one floor dedicated to 21st-century art and furniture, and the lower floor with 18th and 19th century décor, including a vast art deco collection (Colapinto 2007). So, not only is Lagerfeld a master hoarder, but he's also a profligate consumer and waster of resources. His response: "Normal people think I'm insane". On this point, I think he's probably right.

One benign form of hoarding may be the tendency of people to collect certain things, primarily as a hobby. Up until a few years ago I never considered myself a collector type, but the fallacy of my thinking gradually hit me. In the past thirty or more years I've clipped and saved hundreds of articles I've read in professional and news magazines on a wide range of subjects related to health, philosophy, arts, singing, environment, investing, and other topics. These articles have been filed according to subject matter and stored in three four-drawer filing cabinets. Because most of the collected materials have been used in my teaching and book writing, including articles used for this book, I like to believe my collector's habit has a tangible worthwhile purpose. Besides, I periodically (once per decade) go through files, culling outdated or unimportant material and depositing it in the recycling bin.

I've also collected numerous recordings (from LPs to CDs) professional books, music scores, and music equipment, much of which I've donated to students and colleagues, with opera recordings going to the school opera program. Most of my remaining professional materials are stored in a classroom closet at the University of Minnesota School of Music. Soon I will donate portions of this valuable collection to worthy educational institutions, and the remaining materials will be hauled home for future use.

Compounding the clutter problem, my wife may also be considered a collector of sorts, mostly of books. She's an avid reader, and I'm fortunate to have her serve as my book-reading advisor. Thanks to her positive influence, I now read 50-60 non-professional books annually. As we continue aging, we'll need to hone our collections down to a more manageable level. We finally disposed of our 1964 set of Colliers Encyclopedias, after moving them into our condo and placing them in a closet. We've decided that we rarely used them, especially since Web-based encyclopedic information and computer programs are easily accessible and take up no physical space.

It's not easy letting go of favorite possessions, but a simple test for making a decision is to ask how often an item is used. The clutter police advise getting rid of anything not used within a certain time frame, such as five years—unless the item has very special psycho-emotional value, as happens with owning familiar heirlooms or keepsakes, such as prized family photos. According to the philosophy of *feng shui*, the Chinese practice of furniture placement and energy flow (chi) in a home, clearing away clutter is the first step. In her book *Clearing the Clutter for Good Feng shui* (2001), author Mary Lambert proposes the best way to clear one's home of energy blocking clutter is to retain only the most essential, well-loved items. Though I have difficulty accepting all the New-Age tenets of Feng shui, I certainly agree with the basis of this concept, which proposes that any inhabited space needs to provide a natural flow of movement and an aesthetically balanced arrangement of furnishings.

Primary essential possessions include items associated with shelter, clothing, food, personal care, education, recreation, transportation, and the like. In the following section, we look at a variety of possessions, with an eye for determining what is truly needed in providing a satisfactory lifestyle.

Creating a "Home, Sweet Home" (I)

Because everyone needs a place to call home for a multitude of uses, it seems logical to begin with considering shelter needs. Between the extremes of homeless folk sleeping in makeshift cardboard boxes and affluent citizens dwelling in mansions, we have an enormous housing gap, with most people living in shelters of modest to moderate means. What typifies the average or median U.S. dwelling and which features are the most desired? Everyone's tastes will vary somewhat, but I think most middle-class folks, especially older Americans, prefer homes that have the following features:

• A convenient location, with nearby public transportation, shopping areas, and public parks, accessible by walkways.

• A safe neighborhood, with well-maintained homes and properties, and respectable neighbors.

• Exterior green space that is properly landscaped, affording pleasant views of trees, plants, grass, etc.

• An attractive, well-designed exterior appearance that blends in well with surrounding architectural and landscaping designs.

• A structure that is well-designed and constructed, safe, energy efficient, low maintenance, temperature controlled, and well lit, with plenty of natural lighting in daytime hours.

• An attractive interior design that allows a variety of spaces for specific functions—eating, sleeping, bathing, recreating, and socializing—all connected attractively and conveniently to allow for efficient movement patterns and privacy, when needed.

• Available sheltered spaces to park one or two vehicles, plus a shop/hobby area, an exercise facility, and storage space for seldom-used household items.

• Seniors also benefit from having one-level dwellings equipped with wide doors, hardwood floors, balancing bars and easy-access showers or tubs in bathrooms, and counters, cabinets, and shelves that can be accessed easily.

As to the size of the "sensible" house, it seems that a properly designed 2,000-2,400 square-foot home should be sufficient for a family of two adults and two children (more than two is not justified in today's overpopulated world), providing sufficient space for most activities. The size-creep in the average-sized new home construction has gradually increased from around 1,000 square feet in the early 50s to more than 3,000 square-feet today. From my senior citizen perspective, large homes are not worth the extra costs and time involvement it takes to furnish and maintain them, and I marvel that it took us so long to realize this truism. We were able to negotiate all the rooms in our former home easily, even when traipsing to the tuck-under garage on the lower level, forgetting something, and having to return to retrieve it. We could move between all rooms on the main floor quickly, and the lower level, with its compact bedroom, bath and living/kitchenette area served as a private guest suite. Our condo unit is even more negotiable, as it's 100 square-feet smaller and is all on one level, with the exception of the basement garage and the exercise room, which we consider an extension of our unit, for we rarely encounter anyone exercising when we use it.

What changes would we make were we to start over again with designing and furnishing either our former or current home? In the interior of both we've been relatively satisfied with the results of earlier decisions. Regarding furnishings, we've tried to keep furniture at modest sizes so as not to overwhelm their spaces. So many of the current trends are toward producing overstuffed and oversized furnishings, ostensibly for the larger homes on the market. Of course, there remains a sizeable market internationally for furnishings that suit smaller home spaces, such as apartments and condo units; Ikea is one company that services such a market. Americans seem to be impressed with oversized items, as reflected not only by super-sized food and drink portions but large vehicles, homes, and furnishings—even gigantic beds. In our lifetime we've seen twin and full-size beds give way to queen and king-sized beds, in conjunction with mattresses increasing in depth to the point that older or frail individuals might need assistance getting in and out of beds that are at least a foot higher than normal. Even the bathroom towel is a victim of over sizing. The full-sized towel of the 50s is now the size of a large hand towel, so our solution when showering is to use more hand towels, which are easier to handle.

Although our former home was still in good overall condition overall, after 20 years of maintaining the original interior and exterior surfaces, we were at the point of considering some remodeling and repairs. The timing seemed right to consider options for how we wished to live in our old age. Building a one-level home on a small urban lot was one option, but we didn't relish the idea of searching for a lot and living through another home-building experience. The old Apache Mall (one of the first in the U.S.) and its surrounding business area was being razed, and a combined residential-business development was under construction. We visited the sales office, liked what we discovered, and decided to take a chance on a condo in the first building, which was only a blueprint at the time.

Architect Sarah Nettleton's book, *The Simple Home: The Luxury of Enough*, describes the kind of home that provides a base for a balanced lifestyle. She lists guidelines when buying, designing, or remodeling a home: keep it simple, flexible, thrifty, timeless, and sustainable. She also discusses eight common denominators and hallmarks of simple homes:

- The floor plan and form are straightforward and uncomplicated.

- The style, whether traditional or modern, is timeless.

- The interior is human-scaled, functional, uncomplicated, light-filled, and open.

- Rooms serve more than a single function.

- The design expresses a practical aesthetic intention.

- Room layouts offer natural light, ventilation, and flowing access.

- Details and finishes tend to be simple and unadorned.

- Storage is well located and often built-in to minimize freestanding furniture.

If you're an empty nester or looking toward retirement, I urge you to begin thinking, planning, and acting proactively regarding the type of home you want to spend your remaining years in, and the sooner the better. We thought we had our retirement home in 1985, but in our mid 50s at the time, we didn't foresee inevitable health problems or our eventual declining interest in home and lawn upkeep. And this brings up the importance of considering the lot or location your retirement home might occupy.

A Lot of Lot Can Be Too Much

The size of the lot or acreage a home sits on plays a significant role in overall homeowner satisfaction. On the small end there are the tiny outdoor spaces surrounding older city town-homes and the modest-sized homes of less than 1,000 square feet in subdivisions that sprung up all over the U.S. following WWII. And on the large size, there are outer-tier suburban spaces populated with lots the size of an acre or more, with a variety of home sizes and styles, from mobile homes to palatial dwellings. At various times throughout our married lives we've entertained thoughts of living in both urban town-homes as well as in rural settings. Both options offer special amenities, the downtown lifestyle featuring all the advantages of city living—excitement, culture, access to shopping, freedom from lawn work, etc.—and a rural setting, which typically provides a more laidback, and perhaps less expensive but more isolated lifestyle.

The compromise for us—a middle-ground option—has been to live either in a middle-class city neighborhood or a first-tier suburban neighborhood. This goal we've managed well since moving in 1970 to the Twin Cities, a large metropolitan area with many cultural and civic amenities. Over the past four to five decades, several rings of suburbs with a wide variety of medium-sized homes had been built around St. Paul and Minneapolis, with convenient access to both the metropolitan area and to outlying rural areas. For those preferring new home construction, it's sometimes possible to find a lot in older neighborhoods, as was our experience in the mid 1980s when we built our former home. Even today, with spaces developed, new land is occasionally being made available for new home construction, as was the case when the decrepit Apache Mall was redeveloped into an integrated community consisting of various residences (condos, cottage homes, apartments), businesses, and parks, a concept that we bought into rather quickly. In selecting where to live, we've always tried to heed the popular top three criteria for selecting a home—"Location, location, location!" And we've always been pleased with our choices of middle-class neighborhoods rather than more upscale upper-middle class communities. In terms of property values, this might have been a mistake, but in terms of preferred lifestyle, we're confident we've made the right choices. The one exception might have been our first Minneapolis home, which was comfortable and charming, but also older and required more maintenance.

As we grew older in our former New Brighton suburban home, we began to think how much easier it would be to have a smaller lot and a new one-level, compact home. We greatly enjoyed the privacy and the interesting view of the backyard marsh pond and its wildlife, but there were always issues associated with the encroaching vegetation, including many proliferating weed trees—several towering cottonwoods, silver-leaf maples, and box elders. Also, there was a rash of other invasive plants, such as buckthorn shrubs, vines, and creeping charley. Every spring I'd slip and slide on the steep bank sloping down to the marsh pond, struggling to extricate hundreds of seedlings and trim trees and shrubs, all the while suffering scratches on exposed skin. I was extremely relieved to finally get rid of this ongoing responsibility, especially because of my recurrent back problems.

In the last few years of living with a marsh pond environment, we successfully simplified some lawn and landscaping work. Our basic strategy involved reducing the amount of annuals and vegetables planted, plus eliminating some undesirable shrubs and trees. We seriously considered hiring professionals to take over more lawn and home maintenance, but previous experiences in securing dependable service providers, and overseeing their work, still required more responsibility than we wished to undertake.

For anyone determined to build a retirement home, I strongly recommend making wise choices for plantings, including shrubs and trees. I learned my lesson about trees, and I would certainly be very discerning about the types and numbers of shrub and tree plantings. Trees to avoid are fast- growing junk trees, such as Box Elders, Silver Leaf Maples, and Cottonwoods. Also, any trees I would plant would grow no taller than midsized, as large trees can be dangerous and very expensive to trim and cut down. I finally learned the extreme disadvantages of planting any trees near the foundation, preferably no closer than 20 feet, as the constant threat of spreading roots, and falling limbs, leaves, and bird-droppings on the roof—plus providing ready access to squirrels and mice that subsequently find their way into attics to create havoc—is ample reason for planting trees and tall shrubs at a safe distance.

In determining what size lot to own, a small or midsized one is simpler to maintain. People should consider the true cost of outdoor amenities. For instance, an outdoor tennis court or swimming pool may be a good investment for a family using them regularly for exercise and entertainment, but for a family using them occasionally they are a costly luxury.

Creating a "Home, Sweet Home" (II)

As mentioned earlier, health issues played a significant role in prompting our move into a condo, including my prostate cancer surgery in 2002, and a chronic lower-back condition, with sciatica-like symptoms, that lasted for six months in 2004. Though I'm now in good physical condition and cancer free, I remain ever vigilant in managing my back by observing proper moves associated with bending, stooping, and lifting. The only house work I have that taxes my back is vacuuming, but I seem to manage well enough. Bettye's incipient osteoporosis condition also precludes her from undertaking any hard physical tasks, which is why I handle the vacuuming.

As we gained greater awareness of our old-age frailty, we realized we would welcome a more age-appropriate living situation, so we decided to take a proactive approach. The first option was our former two-level home, which was fine at the time, but we didn't want to be caught in an untenable living situation as we aged. We considered ways to retrofit it for old age (elevator, wider doors, etc.), but the projected costs ran higher than we desired. Another home option was to build or buy a ranch-style home on a small suburban lot, but this option required considerable searching, as our criteria were very strict. The third option was to investigate one-level townhomes, cottage homes, or patio homes, the major drawback being the lack of one-level construction in the type of urban or first-tier suburban neighborhoods we prefer.

Having considered the options of a one-level new home and townhouse living, the remaining option to explore was the condo lifestyle, something we had never seriously considered before. We began by checking out several new condo developments in the downtown areas of St. Paul and Minneapolis. We discovered that, in addition to being very expensive, most condo developments are typically located near industrial facilities or in redevelopment areas in high-rise buildings over four stories. And, most importantly, none are located near compact shopping areas that contain a variety of essential services—grocery, hardware, and department stores, restaurants, banks, gas stations, and the like. Moreover, a large portion of new condo units are two-level lofts, smaller than we prefer, lack appropriate floor plans for seniors, and have uninteresting views that look out on other condo buildings and minimal green spaces. The developments with the best views—luxurious condo buildings that overlook the Mississippi River, city lakes or parks—fetch a very high premium, beyond our comfortable purchase-price range.

As luck would have it, we were following the news about a large redevelopment area that's located halfway between our former home in northeast Minneapolis and our New Brighton home, slightly more than a mile away. It was proposed as a replacement for the aging Apache Mall, one of the first shopping malls in the U.S. Built in the 1960s, the mall was strategically situated at the northwest corner of St. Anthony Village, adjoining the three municipalities. Although the mall was booming when we arrived in 1970, a nasty tornado in 1982 precipitated its eventual demise (and missed our northeast Minneapolis home by four blocks). By the time the mall was rebuilt a year later, most regular customers had begun shopping elsewhere, so the mall gradually declined, eventually was closed, and sat vacant for a few years.

When the final development plans for the area were circulated in local newspapers and open meetings were held at the town center to publicize the new development plans, we became very interested and sought to learn as much as possible about the residential buildings, which at the time advertised three-level townhomes, four condo buildings, and a very large luxury apartment building with one wing designated for people age 55 and older. We weren't interested in the three-level luxury town-homes (which were eventually changed to one-level cottage homes), but the condos seemed worth investigating. At first, Bettye was lukewarm about condo living, but was willing to satisfy my curiosity. So we visited the sales office, viewed all the floor plans, listened to low-keyed but enthusiastic sales pitches by very congenial representatives who described all aspects of the development, including the business area of the village, the small park and ponds, and so on.

We both became very excited over the prospect of living in such a unique environment, and it didn't take long to decide this was an opportunity we couldn't pass up. At the time the venture seemed a bit risky, because the condominium building wasn't under construction, but we trusted the information and the people who supplied it. In researching the developer and builder—and meeting them—we became confident that we should go ahead and reserve a unit while we had first crack at the larger ones that featured views of the village. At first we selected a second floor unit, but later decided the third floor unit would have a slightly better view and would receive more winter sunlight, since the second building (south side) blocks sunshine from midday to late afternoon in January.

The reason for offering so many details about our move from a traditional home to condo living is simply to offer assistance to readers who might not be well informed about condo living. There are many details to consider, including:

- A *convenient location*, preferably within a short commute of a city's main attractions, including museums, concert halls, dining, and cultural amenities.

• A *convenient shopping area* that provides most of the normal goods and services an aging person needs, including emergency health care, and preferably within walking distance.

• A *nearby public park* featuring a pond or lake, walking paths, a playground area, and open spaces for various activities.

• *Access to public transportation*, with convenient, sheltered bus stops, and access to most of the area's major attractions, including principal shopping areas and a major airport.

• *Well-designed construction*, preferably no more than four stories, with a variety of individual units and serviceable floor plans.

• *Double-wall construction* between units for sound insulation, and large double or triple-glazed windows for sound proofing and providing as much light and pleasant views as possible.

• *Aesthetic landscaping* that provides plenty of greenery, including grassy areas and a variety of shrubs, flowers, and trees (that grow to medium-height).

• *Reasonable association fees* that cover a variety of services, such as: building maintenance; water and water treatment (if needed); insurance to cover replacement of all construction (with the exception of the interior of individual units); lawn and landscaping maintenance; snow removal; cleaning of common building areas; garbage/recycling; and perhaps some combination of cable TV/internet/telephone connections.

• *Efficient management*, which is usually provided by a professional company, at least for the first few years, until most units are filled and home owners form an official association.

• *Special common facilities*, such as a community room for social events and meetings, an exercise room with a variety of equipment, a lending library, a guest room for visitors that can be rented for a low fee (ours is $30 per night, and it's equivalent to at least a $100-plus hotel room), a hobby room or shop, and perhaps a swimming or lap pool.

• *Neighborly residents*, preferably of mixed ages, but with enough older residents to form social groups with special interests, such as clubs for reading books, traveling, playing cards, and so on.

• *Resale value*, a major concern for most folks, which is why all the above criteria should be seriously considered before making a purchase.

I suppose my enthusiasm for condo living is obvious, especially for seniors and professionals who don't have time for house and lawn work. Aside from the convenience advantage, there are serious environmental and financial advantages. First, it's been proven that many people living in a single multi-unit building is more environmentally friendly in comparison to an equal number of people living in single-family homes, at least in terms of land space and the amount of building materials, labor, and energy involved. And the monthly association fee, which scares off some would-be buyers, not only provides more convenience, but is actually less expensive when considering the time and expense involved in hiring qualified workers to provide essential services. In short, when I put pen to paper to compare what we were spending or would have to spend to cover all the services provided, the condo association fee proved to be less expensive. The building insurance alone reduced our interior coverage to around $150, which was a big savings. Finally, another plus is a respectable reduction in heating and cooling expenses, especially for units sandwiched between other floors below and above, which serve as extra insulation, in addition to providing some heat gain from lower units. On some sunny days in mid winter we've not had to turn up the thermostat, relying instead on solar heat to warm up our unit to a comfortable 68-70 degrees (we set it on 68 most of the time, especially on cloudy days). Our southwest corner unit receives the morning sun in profusion, and a good bit of the afternoon exposure, the drawback being a need to use the air conditioner more often on hot days.

I don't think it's necessary to elaborate on what it was like going through the entire experience, from selecting the unit we wanted, along with the many choices for fixtures, colors, flooring, and so on. Our philosophy was to keep our unit simple, and to avoid oversized, ostentatious furnishings. The basic design itself featured more than enough impressive qualities, including large windows, 9-foot-high ceilings, angled walls, and comfortably sized rooms. In making selections for the interior, we generally selected from among the basic options, such as standard counter tops in lieu of granite, chrome bathroom fixtures instead of gold or brass, standard tile selections for entry hall and baths, white kitchen appliances instead of polished steel, and so on. We did choose to upgrade the light fixtures, carpets, and carpet pads. We also selected a natural-looking stain for the kitchen wood flooring, all wood trimmings, and the kitchen and bath cabinets, which we had installed without handles, which are unnecessary. And we had to have a super-quiet dishwasher. As for wall color, we stuck with our preference of off-white paint throughout, which we find is easier to maintain over the long term. (Our former home's similar colored paint lasted 21 years, with only the entry hall needing a fresh coat, and it still looked fine when we sold it.) In sum, all of our choices were based on the principle of simplicity and good-but-not-luxurious quality. A principal concept was to create a home that was easy to maintain and filled with as much light as possible, a decision based partially on providing sufficient light for our eventual weakening eyes. At night our unit admits enough village and street lighting through closed white blinds to illuminate our unit, allowing us to move about without turning on any lights.

So far we're very satisfied with our decisions, including the big one: to move into a more suitable senior living situation. If interested, you can check out Silver Lake Village's official website (www.silver-lake-village.com) to see for yourself.

Getting Around

As far as automobiles are concerned, I've always been a auto admirer, ever since my folks bought me a used 1940 Ford during my junior year in high school. My general philosophy about owning a car is that it must be in top condition, mechanically and esthetically, and it should provide safe, dependable, and relatively economical transportation. Age is not a major factor, as long as it fits these criteria. An older vehicle of any kind in prime condition is a thing of beauty, and this explains my enthusiasm for viewing all the types, models, styles, and ages of autos that proud owners parade around the area during annual summer car shows in the Twin Cities.

In terms of economy, I agree with the financial wisdom and logic of buying a two to three-year-old vehicle, preferably with low mileage, when the depreciation is maximized. For various reasons we don't always follow through with this enlightened car-buying strategy. Ideally, if we were to own one consummate automobile, it would be a stylishly designed crossover hybrid of medium size, combining the interior space of a minivan, with sufficient engine power for hauling five to six persons, and capable of maneuvering safely and securely on normal streets and highways. Moreover, it would be suited for light off-road excursions, should we decide to take off into the semi wilds. Off-road driving requires four-wheel or all-wheel drive, which usually means lower gas mileage, but I'm hoping the auto manufacturers will soon develop a hybrid gas/electric engine powerful and economical enough to improve the gas mileage of such a vehicle to the 25-35 mpg range for overall driving. Some vehicles are approaching these criteria, and I expect the right one will show up in the next few years. Unfortunately, waiting until one reaches the two-year depreciation point in order to get a good deal will slow our plans down a bit. Incidentally, this ideal vehicle doesn't need a lot of fancy gadgets, such as a built-in television set, electronic seats, map guidance system, or multiple-CD changer. We still haven't mastered all the controls on our 2001 Hyundai XG-300L, and though the automatic climate-control system seems to work well enough, some of the more esoteric devices are very seldom used, and are dispensable.

In thinking about the most practical basic car we've owned, I think we'd have to nominate our 1983 Volvo DL-240, which had roll-up windows, manual seat adjustments, and an underpowered but dependable four-cylinder engine, its major drawback. Everything functioned well and the controls were simple and easy to operate. The one item it lacked, which I consider indispensable for long highway trips, was a cruise-control mechanism. Other than that, this trusty Volvo transported us for 15 years and 120,000 miles, and looked terrific when we traded it in (for a used 1994 Nissan Altima SE, which our eldest son owned for several years). Of course, the winter road salt encouraged rust after several years, requiring annual minor bodywork and paint touch-up. Because of the Volvo's hardy nature, I occasionally referred to it as our yellow "tractor".

Overall, for getting around conveniently and quickly, the lifelong habit of driving autos simply overwhelms other transportation options for most in-town and road trips. The one rationale that might cause many city and suburban residents to sideline their autos, including us, is the growing traffic congestion on city streets and high-ways—plus the rising cost of gas. Overall commuting time is lengthening and stress levels rising, notably in the Twin Cities where prime-time commuters are experiencing some of the nation's highest traffic-level increases. And the much publicized collapse of the I-35 bridge over the Mississippi River in 2007 severely (though temporarily) complicated the traffic movement from our home to points south.

Instead of owning a car, there are other auto transportation options, including leasing, particularly if annual mileage is kept to fewer than 10,000 miles. But the pros and cons of leasing seem to fluctuate, depending on economic supply and demands of the auto industry. Renting a car for long trips is another excellent option, as we've done on certain occasions, figuring that using someone else's vehicle might prolong the use of our car. When using some of the dirt roads in obscure scenic areas in the western U.S., we've been glad not to be driving our car. Another enticing option, especially now that we're living in a condo, with lots of other folks, is to create a cooperative auto service, whereby the association purchases a car or two that can be used by residents depending on demand and availability. Of course, policies would be needed to determine expenses associated with the car(s), including users paying mileage or hourly use fees, but I can foresee this as a future possibility for us. A similar plan is already being used in many places, including universities and colleges.

With driving an automobile growing more risky every day we age, knowing when to cut back or quit becomes a key concern. We wonder if we'll know when it's time to stop driving, for the safety of both others and ourselves.

Well, thankfully, there are other viable options we can consider, beginning now.

An aging person can usually rely on cabs or shuttle-buses for dependable transportation in high-density metropolitan areas, but less so in spread-out cities such as Dallas/Ft. Worth or the Twin Cities, where cabs can be expensive. Besides, one never knows who the driver will be or the condition of the car. I've never been very comfortable using cabs, though I realize they are the only feasible way to travel in certain situations. However, finding a cab driver who speaks understandable English is a growing concern in large cities, as a majority of cab drivers tend to be recent immigrants with limited English-speaking skills.

So what about public modes of transportation, such as buses, one of the least expensive and carefree ways to travel? We've enjoyed some memorable tours on buses, especially in college days with college choir trips, and one-day sightseeing tours in various vacation areas. On a recent trip to Yucatan in Mexico we traveled exclusively by bus, from express buses to second-class and city buses, and they all were safe and dependable. As a child I regularly took the city bus in Jackson, Mississippi, to school for a couple of years. Yet, it's embarrassing to admit that I've used the Twin Cities' metropolitan bus system only three times in the past 37 years of living here, and the first time was in the mid 70s when commuting to the University. I recall that the bus commuting worked quite well, but because we owned two cars, and I had an annual parking pass for a campus ramp, I opted to commute via auto.

In summer 2007 we decided to take a bus trip downtown to visit the new Minneapolis library, and we were very pleased with the overall experience. Seniors can ride the bus inexpensively during off hours, and there's no traffic or parking challenges to manage. Both economically and environmentally, it certainly makes sense for us to use public transportation whenever feasible, and we do anticipate using the bus system more as we age, as it's very convenient, with a bus stop located a short half-block from our condo. The bus also connects with the light-rail system, which goes to the airport and the Mall of America, a decided advantage for metro area travel. We used it recently in traveling to and from the airport, were pleased with the service, and will use it for future trips. For aging Americans accustomed to using automobiles exclusively, we recommend giving city bus transportation a trial, with several trips over an extended period, just to get the hang of it.

Travel by rail is an attractive option very much worth exploring. Were we to have dependable, fast-speed commuter railway system in the Twin Cities, with a station nearby, we would gladly use it for some trips. One can only hope that the U.S. will eventually create a national and international (Canada, Mexico) interconnecting railway system similar to the networks used throughout Europe. If major U.S. metropolitan areas were to aggressively develop subway and commuter lines similar to those found in New York City, Washington, D.C. and other major world cities, it would not only alleviate transportation woes, but would also save valuable energy resources.

Although the initial investment of constructing commuting systems will be astronomically expensive, creating efficient high-volume public transportation in high-density metropolitan corridors makes excellent sense long-term, both environmentally and economically. In addition to the Twin Cities' commuter line running from downtown Minneapolis to the International Airport and Mall of America, other lines are being planned, including one connecting the downtown areas of St. Paul and Minneapolis, and between St. Cloud and the Twin Cities. So public transportation plans are moving in the right direction (pun intended).

For other long-distance public transportation needs, the airplane remains the fastest, least expensive mode of transportation—at least before oil prices shot up so high. As airplanes become more fuel-efficient and quieter, flying will be even more attractive. On a negative note, the threat of terrorism worldwide will probably continue affecting the amount of air travel to at-risk countries, but on a positive note, a decline in air travel will reduce aircraft pollution and energy consumption.

Many aging persons tend to postpone foreign air travel until they have more time and money, and aging parents and grown children are settled. In the meantime, wanderlusts might be satiated using other means of transportation (bus, train, auto) to visit local and regional areas, and neighboring countries. For rapid, far-distant transit, a well-functioning network of international airline service is essential for accommodating the needs of international business and recreational travelers; so let's hope the ongoing woes of the airline industry are ameliorated long term.

Before moving on, just in case you're wondering how all the above discussion relates to caring for possessions, perhaps a brief explanation is needed. Briefly, the fewer vehicles we own, the less we have to worry about maintenance and the overall costs incurred. And the less we use our personal vehicles and rely on public transportation, the longer they will last, the less they will cost to maintain, and the more value will be passed on to future owners. It seems we have a moral imperative to take good care of our vehicles, so they will remain safe, provide dependable transportation, get optimal fuel mileage, and serve all owners reliably. And, finally, all of these measures reduce the amount of CO_2 emitted into the air, as well as conserve dwindling energy reserves. With the exception of some older persons who travel extensively by auto, the overall tendency of seniors is to drive autos less frequently, which is good for the environment.

244 / Caring for Possessions

Inventorying Other Possessions

What else do we need to keep our lives in harmonious balance as we age? Since furniture is so critical in providing places to sit, lie down, write and work, or store stuff, we need to give careful attention to items we may own for the rest of our years. As is the case with most seniors, we've collected a potpourri of moderate-level furnishings that span our entire married lives; for example: some 1960s Danish modern walnut furnishings—a bedroom suit, a coffee table, two book shelves, and a lamp; some 19th-century American pieces—an oak hall tree, a maple hutch, and three oak commode-style chests (which we donated to our sons); and Scandinavian teak pieces—a bedroom suit and a dining room set. I suppose our taste in home furnishings might be labeled eclectic, representing a variety of styles, textures, and types of items that help create an interesting mix in the overall décor. With the exception of individuals accustomed to upscale model-home décors, our home décor will probably appear average, neither particularly interesting nor terribly dull. However, we're satisfied that we've achieved a sense of balance that projects our values and aesthetic objectives.

What about artwork, which provides a good insight into one's aesthetic tastes? Like most Americans, we own no expensive artwork, but several original paintings grace our walls, including one of mine from earlier years (creation of a nebulae), one small flower painting by my mother, three paintings by Minnesota artists, some framed photos from vacation trips, two Craig Blacklock photos of Lake Superior, and four colorful Asian prints. In addition, we have a Chinese wall-scroll featuring a flower, two framed posters, two framed Gregorian chants (sheets from ancient song books), and several minor wall decorations. When we moved, we decided to eliminate several wall artworks, with the idea of simplifying our décor.

We're open to replacing some of our artwork with original works by reputable artists, but only if we find something we would love to have for a specific place in our home. For certain, we're not interested in paying large sums for a piece of art simply because a prominent artist created it. In this regard, it's somewhat amusing to observe that some wealthy art patrons surround themselves with expensive artworks by celebrity artists, not necessarily for aesthetic reasons, but more for purposes of matching their interior décor or displaying their art trophies. I don't really understand why some people associate the quantity and quality of their possessions with their innate self worth, but this tendency seems awfully strong. Having said this, I think I understand the motivations of genuine collectors—those who love artworks and think of collecting them as a hobby or investment.

Finally, everyone owns a variety of favored personal items, including some inherited from loved ones. Most of the personal items we've purchased, such as jewelry, wristwatches, and clothes, are simple in design, of moderate monetary value, and intentionally unobtrusive. The same holds true for our clothing, which for the most part is functionally simple, and mostly of a subdued nature, with the exception of a few colorful items. We generally prefer informal or casual clothing, and my preferred typical daily outfit in winter is a pair of comfortable jeans and a sweatshirt, and in summer it's shorts and T-shirts. Of course, we try to dress appropriately for various social events and performances, but we're grateful that such occasions don't occur too frequently.

Unashamedly, I confess that some of our favorite shopping occurs in thrift stores, such as Savers and Unique Thrift, a Vietnam Veterans' sponsored store, to which we've donated many carloads of possessions. Both stores are nearby, and when we go on Tuesdays, which is seniors' day, everything is discounted 25 to 40 percent off the already bargain-priced items. Often we find brand-new items at a fraction of the original cost. Are we embarrassed in admitting this? Not in the least. We consider it good sense to buy quality items at low prices, and we're proud of our frugal buying practice of recycled items. Perhaps if we couldn't afford to buy items at regular retail prices we might feel differently. I suppose a little reverse snobbery comes easier to those who have options.

Downsizing and Moving On

As one grows older, the concept of downsizing tends to become more and more attractive. For us, it seemed best to make a move while both of us were still active and in good health, a lesson learned from observing and hearing about older family members, friends, and acquaintances who waited until serious health problems or a crisis arose before they (or loved ones) were forced to pare down their possessions. My parents didn't get rid of much at all before they died. But Bettye's folks — in their early 90s — moved into a one-level ranch-style home similar in size to their former home, so as to be near her brother and his wife in Brookhaven, Mississippi. At that point in their lives Bettye's parents were able to scale down their possessions to a manageable level. But they were lucky—and so were their grown children! Within two years of moving her father died, thoughtfully leaving his personal affairs in good order.

Moving from a family home into more compact living quarters and having to get rid of many possessions can be emotionally stressful for anyone, but especially for the elderly and persons who have accumulated many cherished possessions. Emotional memories connected with favorite memorabilia are difficult to part with, but at least givers can be comforted in the knowledge that other persons will use and appreciate most items. Passing along favorite items to family members or close friends who will enjoy using them while the giver is still alive certainly has merit. Because of digital-transferring technology, treasured photos, videos, letters, documents, and old-technology recordings can be preserved in formats that take up very little space. Almost everyone has prized possessions they want to keep in good condition and preserved for posterity. This is one well-intentioned project we have yet to tackle, and we can only hope we get around to it before something happens to one or both of us. In addition to passing on family photos, videos, letters, and such, special creative works of family members need to be preserved. For instance, I'd appreciate someone holding on to some of my creations, including single copies of my books, songs, selected recordings of performances, and even my few art projects.

Authors Linda Hetzer and Janet Hulstrand provide some practical suggestions for letting go of possessions in their book, *Moving On: A Practical Guide to Downsizing the Family Home.* They encourage everyone anticipating a move to allow plenty of time to go through everything, based on an overall plan, perhaps beginning with large items such as furniture and saving the most cherished memorabilia for last. Because most memorabilia such as photos, jewelry, letters, and the like take up little space, they can be moved to the new home or a family member's home for storage until getting around to going through them. We proceeded with this tact in mind, and I'm finally getting around to transferring family VHS videos to DVD formats. When finished, copies can be made and distributed to each son.

It pays to think long-term in preparation for the possibility of being incapacitated, or worse: dead. As mentioned earlier, dividing up certain possessions in advance is sensible, responsible action, as well as discussing with heirs the particular items each would like to have, and making a written record to be shared with all heirs. Certain items may need to be appraised for their monetary value, so that each heir receives a fair share. Finally, when it comes to items most heirs would like to own, it might help to create an "open shelf", with heirs drawing straws and taking turns selecting items. If the items are to be retained until the giver's death, color-coded stickers can be placed on items to identify who is to receive them. This type of give-away provides a festive, no-nonsense, unsentimental way of passing things on to loved ones, and I think the idea is worth considering.

In closing, there needs to be some mention regarding non-material possessions—the ideas, beliefs, principles, and values that each of us holds dear and lives by. Too often we are reluctant to discuss profound topics with others, so most people with whom we are close don't have a deep understanding of who we are. When we fail to share our innermost thoughts about our beliefs, including our views on death, we withhold something far more precious than the material possessions we leave to our heirs. Cultivating and caring for these non-material possessions—which own us as well—are also a vital part of our legacy, based not only on what we owned during our lives, but who we were as human beings, and how we coped with life. This topic is discussed in a later chapter, when aging, dying, and death are the main topics, but I thought it should also be mentioned here, just as a reminder that our legacy of giving involves both material and non-material entities. As it says in the Bible, *For where your treasure is, there will be your heart also.* (Luke 12:34)

10

Optimizing Life

According to Yang Yang, a University of Chicago sociologist, oldest Americans are the happiest age group of all. In a long-term study involving periodic interviews of 28,000 Americans aged 18 to 88, contentment and happiness increased 5 percent with each passing decade. Seniors seem to feel greater happiness due to lowered expectations, acceptance of personal achievements and failures, and increased coping skills based on life experience.

Other studies suggest that older creative persons—drawing on a lifetime of experiences—function well as "experimental innovators". The accumulated knowledge and experience of older persons helps create problem-solving skills that can be used in solving ill-defined problems. A broad perspective gained over decades, plus practical intelligence, works to a senior's advantage. As we age, we also learn to compensate for any loss in mind-body characteristics. Although speed, memory, and reasoning powers decline steadily after age 20, vocabulary increases up to age 50 or more. It seems that we older persons compensate for such shortcomings with clever coping strategies. For example, older typists learn to look ahead at texts-to-be read during any pauses, a tactic that makes up for slow-down in their ability to type texts as they read. (For me, it's a matter of typing slower than I think, as I constantly have to correct mistakes due to hasty typing.) Fortunately, medical advances are improving mind-body functioning in the elderly, primarily by treating such ailments as high blood pressure, diabetes, and heart disease, the key factors in depressing mind-body function.

Taking Some Preventive and Corrective Measures

The best predictor of longevity is a good set of genes. Thomas Perls, a professor at Boston Medical Center, directed the 1994 New England Centennial Study, which included more than 1,500 centenarians. Perls found that wealth and education play insignificant roles in longevity, and for those living to 88-93 years or older, the factors are mostly genetic. Centenarians appear to have a gene for vascular protection, helping prevent clogged arteries leading to heart attacks, the leading cause of death in the elderly. Longevity seems to run in families, with the offspring of centenarians having a 20 percent reduced mortality rate (Duncan 2005).

Other than genes, some behaviors help to postpone the ravages of aging—and these were covered in earlier chapters. To review, these measures include engaging in aerobic, anaerobic, and muscle-stretching exercises regularly, eating well-balanced meals, taking recommended vitamin supplements and essential medications, receiving regular medical checkups and vaccinations, wearing seat belts when driving and helmets when biking, avoiding exposure to harmful substances, reducing stress through simplifying our lifestyle, obtaining sufficient rest, sleeping at least 6-7 hours daily, and staying mentally engaged, informed, and creative. In addition to preventive measures, seniors need to take any requisite measures for maximizing key mind-body senses, particularly eyesight, hearing, and movement. If eyesight is failing, it may be due to cataracts, which can be surgically removed, or it may be simply a case of getting new eyeglasses. For loss of hearing, a simple ear cleaning to remove impacted wax will help, a preventive strategy I use annually. For more severe hearing problems, perhaps the latest model of hearing aid or penetrating auditory brainstem implant (PABI) will provide improvement.

For improved body movement due to chronically ailing joints, surgery to implant artificial replacement parts is an increasingly popular option. For rehabilitating serious injuries, physical therapy techniques have proven effective. When specific diseases, such as arthritis, are the primary problem, medications may bring relief. Finally, to avoid the increased chances of an immobile, sedentary lifestyle, technical devices may be used to assist mobility, such as canes, walkers, and wheelchairs. The important point is to take corrective measures rather than give in to any loss.

Thomas Withers, an active 87-year-old from Springfield, Missouri, wrote in *Newsweek* that his wake-up call came at the age of 50 when he first discovered he had high blood pressure and then witnessed a close friend suffering a stroke that landed him in a nursing home. He then set about to change his eating habits following the USDA's diet guidelines, and a weekly exercise regime that included biking 10 miles, walking 3 miles, or climbing the stairs in a 10-story building. As a result, Withers boasts that he is rarely sick and has only minimal medical expenses. In his words:

> *My biggest payoff, however, is not the money I save, but in the way I feel. Now, just after my 87th birthday, I can still say, "What's a headache? Constipation? Arthritis?" When I'm in the drug department of a supermarket, I feel like the bewildered Texas cowboy in a Dallas department store. When a clerk once asked, "Is there something wrong?" I drawled, "No ma'am, I've just never seen so many things in my whole life that I don't need."*

Perhaps Wither's exceptional health may be due to his healthy genes, as well as his good luck. But there's good reason to believe his proactive lifestyle choices and strong commitment to pursuing positive health habits have contributed greatly to his longevity and high quality of life.

And it's also highly likely his relatively youthful wife, Rue (age 56), might help stimulate his youthful feelings.

Regarding diet issues, in the 1930s a few individuals in the scientific community entertained the concept of calorie restriction as a method for prolonging life, but because certain scientific knowledge was missing, the idea was shelved. Then, in the mid 1980s researcher Leonard Guarente, professor of biology at MIT, proposed to study the biology of prolonging life through calorie restriction. As happens with similar far-out proposals, the scientific community tended to ignore him. But in recent years, with the increasing research involving cell life and DNA, several prominent researchers have gradually reached the conclusion that one of the surest ways to increase life span is to drastically reduce calorie intake, possibly as much as 30 to 60 percent (Guarante 2005).

Restricting calories has several positive effects, such as preserving bone mass, skin thickness, brain function, and immune function, while also providing superior resistance to heat, toxic chemicals, and traumatic injury. Why this happens had been controversial, but it is now thought that several likely mechanisms might account for it, including natural chemicals known as *sirtuins*, a family of proteins. One significant protein is *resveratrol*, which is better known as the substance that provides the major rationale for touting red wine as healthful (Carmichael & Ozols 2005).

Another likely mechanism is the oxidation process that occurs in cells. As *mitochondria* (the power plants in cells) release food energy, they produce corrosive, unpaired electrons known as free radicals. In reacting with nearby fats, proteins, and nucleic acids, these tiny vermin promote various problems, from cataracts to vascular disease. It appears that caloric restriction slows the production of free radicals, and helps the body counter them more efficiently, and, in addition, may also shield from the damaging effects of *glucose*, the sugar generated by carbohydrates we consume. When glucose molecules enter the bloodstream, they hook up with collagen and other proteins to damage nerves, organs, and blood vessels. One noted advocate, Dr. Roy Walford, a 77-year-old pathologist at the University of California, Los Angeles, subsisted for two years on a daily diet of 1,750 to 2,100 calories (compared to the average recommended level of 2,500), as a participant in Biosphere 2, and expects to maintain it (Cowley & Davis 2001).

Keeping brain cells active and alive takes some conscientious and deliberate effort, as the general tendency of aging is to slow down, largely due to a gradual decline in physical energy. Therefore, in order to have good mental and emotional health, it's imperative we give serious attention to physical health issues—exercise and fitness, diet and nutrition, rest and relaxation—all of which we covered in earlier chapters. Likewise, in order to have good physical health, it's equally important we pay heed to developing and improving our psycho-emotional lives through developing a positive mental attitude, calming the mind and emotions through meditative practices, and improving learning skills through ongoing cognitive development, or learning.

Exercising our brains by using a variety of mental tasks is a necessity, and one computer program—Brain Fitness 2.0 from Posit Science (www.positscience.com)—has demonstrated positive gains, in some cases improving brain activity by up to ten years in tested subjects. According to Henry Ford, "Anyone who stops learning is old, whether 20 or 80. Anyone who keeps learning stays young. The greatest thing in life is to keep your mind young."

Strategies for Ongoing Mind-Body Stimulation

Some of the ways I manage to stay mentally active are by reading, writing, composing (simple songs and lyrics), teaching, and singing. My reading includes a variety of topics found in both fiction and non-fiction books, in addition to several magazines, newsletters, and a local Sunday newspaper, with the goal of staying abreast of current events and news, For general coverage, I depend on *Newsweek, The Week,* and newspapers; and for scientific and technological developments I peruse *Discover* and *Scientific American* magazines for a superficial overview of scientific and technological developments in a variety of disciplines, from the most recent cosmological theories and discoveries to the newest electronic nanotechnologies. To keep abreast of a wide variety of human concerns that require critical thinking, I read *Free Inquiry.* For keeping informed about investment and money-related news, I have depended on *Business Week* and *Money,* but now rely on two financial newsletters. To remain informed about the latest news and knowledge in my vocal music field, I subscribe to two professional voice journals. Bettye also reads most of the same publications, in addition to *The New Yorker* magazine, which is passed along by a son, and I peruse *The Economist* and *National Geographic* magazines passed to us by a good neighbor. We've tried to cut down on magazine subscriptions, but this is about as far as we can go at present.

Though I don't pursue my interest in composing songs and lyrics as frequently as I should, I do find it enjoyable—and very challenging intellectually. The first major project I attempted occurred in 2002 (age 65) when I created an all-original, one-hour long lecture/demonstration titled *Vocal Explorations: the Bad, the Good, and the "Other",* the second half of which concludes with *The Best Loving Tenor Contest,* a parody of voice productions and both pop and classical styles. I developed the concept, and wrote the entire script, song lyrics and melodies. My faithful collaborator, Bettye, harmonized all songs and recorded the accompaniments, and in 2003 a vocal music colleague (and former student), Tim Almen, created the synthesized accompaniments, recorded everything, and produced a CD. I've had great fun performing the work on many occasions, though I'll probably retire it in the next few years.

For the past several years I've developed a curiosity about crossing over from classical singing to pop singing, and an invitation to perform for a summer concert series in our intimate village park's amphitheater prompted us to consider performing a program of pop music. As products of the 1950s, an impressionable decade that included our years attending junior and senior high schools and under-graduate college, we were compelled to consider a retro move that resulted in our creating a program titled "Hit Songs of the 50s". Along with our three grown sons, two playing guitar and one on percussion, and two guest performers, Bettye and I (age 70) debuted as *The SilverTones* in June 2007. We've also performed some of this repertoire for retirement homes and a family reunion, and we hope to continue performing retro pop music, as we have very much enjoyed this new adventure. Even our sons have admitted to liking "our music"!

So, Bettye and I share many of the same interests. Of course, she manages to read twice as much as I do, partially because of gaining extra reading time occasionally in the early morning hours when suffering from insomnia. In addition, she's devoted to working on challenging crossword and Sudoku puzzles, a hobby she's passionately pursued in recent years. At first her goal was simply to maintain her intellectual skills, but she has since grown addicted to it, spending considerable time occupying the master bathroom while working away at her puzzle. She's gradually worked her way up to puzzles published in the *New York Times*, which I understand are among the most challenging. For reasons unknown, I've never desired to work puzzles or play most board games, with the exception of Monopoly, which I've always enjoyed. Oh, and she also relishes spending an hour or so in the evenings playing challenging word and brain games on the computer.

Travel is another way to keep one's mind expanded, and we're pleased to have traveled a good bit over our lifetimes, including visits to all 50 U.S. states, many foreign countries (most Western European countries, with the exception of Spain, Portugal, and Finland), and four Eastern European countries. I've traveled to Japan and Korea to teach and perform, and we both enjoyed three weeks of business/pleasure travel throughout New Zealand. Because of health and safety reasons, we've avoided third-world countries (with the exception of Mexico's Yucatan peninsula, which is quite safe now) though we're receptive to traveling with a touring group. Like many seniors our age, we've been blessed with parents who lived long and productive lives (Bet's mother is still doing well at age 97), but trying to be available for them in the past few years has placed a hold of sorts on extensive long-range travel plans.

Travel experiences have enriched our lives immeasurably, broadening our appreciation of other places and cultures, and opening new avenues for growth. The British Isles have had the most lasting influence on us to date, most likely because of our combined Scots-Irish-English heritage. Heretofore, we've seldom returned to places we've ranked high on our list of favorites, simply because we felt it was important to keep exploring unknown places. In 2007 we celebrated my retirement — and new-found freedom to travel in early fall — by taking a car trip to the Canadian Rockies to Prince Rupert, B.C., where we traveled roundtrip by ferry through Alaska's Inland Passage to Juneau, with a return trip through the Canadian Rockies to Waterton Lakes-Glacier National Park and, finally, to home. I've discovered that it's my role to take the lead as "travel instigator", although Bettye is a willing travel partner. If we were to revisit the British Isles, Ireland, or Hawaii, she'll probably volunteer to make travel plans and most arrangements. Otherwise, it's up to me, and, unfortunately, my enthusiasm for foreign travel is not what it used to be.

Up until our 50s we were willing to travel independently, making all travel arrangements and plunging into foreign cultures with little hesitation, but, increasingly we find ourselves hesitant to strike out on our own. Flying to a single city and remaining in one accommodation for the entire time, with daily excursions of limited length and duration to interesting sites might still work well for us, for instance, visiting historical cities, such as Paris or London, but whirlwind tours involving long flights and train rides through several countries, with brief stays in various cities, is no longer likely. Our travel pace will definitely have to slow down for us to be able to handle it comfortably. For instance, in February '08 we spent a week in Yucatan (Mexico), principally to view Mayan ruins, with lodging stays limited to four cities—Cancun, Playa del Carmen, Chichen Itza, and Mérida, all within a comfortable bus range. In the future we might try a similarly scheduled escorted tour that includes a few stops, with 2 to 3 days in each location; for example, an escorted tour to Greece that includes 2 to 3 days in Athens, bus trips to two other land-based cities of at least two days each, and a boat cruise of several days.

In recent years we've been content to take spring break and summer trips to interesting places in the U.S., primarily to enjoy natural scenery and to take day hikes. In March we've concentrated on visiting the lower states, where the weather is warmer. Our favorite region for spring trips is the arid and temperate southwest, notably Arizona, New Mexico, Nevada, and Southern California. In 2004 we varied our spring trip by traveling to Charleston, South Carolina, for a cultural tour, and then driving up to the mountains in the vicinity of Asheville, North Carolina, to visit relatives and hike. In fall 2008 we finally visited Florida, beginning with a ten-day sightseeing tour of south Florida in conjunction with three university teaching engagements, and capped by our first cruise (a four-day Bahamas trip).

During the summers we prefer mountainous terrain and contact with fewer people, so we've spent many weeks traveling through most of the mountainous regions in the U.S., from Alaska in the north to Utah in the southwest, and from northern California in the west to the Black Hills of South Dakota and the Appalachian Mountains in the east. We've also traveled the mountainous areas of western Canada, from Calgary, Banff, and Jasper to Whistler, Vancouver, and Victoria. Our main objective has always been to enjoy the fantastic scenery, principally by hiking on beautiful mountain trails. In 2001 we managed to average ten miles per day for seven days in Wyoming's spectacular Grand Teton National Park and nearby Wind River Range, our all-time record for any single hiking expedition. Since then our hiking trips have become less strenuous, though we should be able to continue our hiking hobby for several more years, as long as we're willing to drive shorter distances, take shorter trails, allow more time, and take more rest stops along the way. The days of hiking up a mountain with few stops are long gone, so our challenge will be to pace our levels of activity.

All of this travel talk, in addition to providing me an outlet for recollecting fond memories, is aimed at stressing the importance of travel for aging adults, for as long as possible, and that applies to foreign travel, too. Aging travelers just need to plan accordingly, by taking flights that aren't too long and taxing, and are broken up with stopovers along the way. For instance, if we ever travel to Australia, we'll likely arrange a stopover in Hawaii or Fuji, or perhaps Taiwan, another country we'd like to visit.

Undertaking Meaningful Work

The importance of undertaking meaningful work as we age needs to be stressed, whether it be for monetary gain, altruistic voluntarism, or simply to continue pursuing personal interests. Projections suggest that by 2012, people over 55 will comprise over 20 percent of the workforce. Moreover, 75 percent of boomers say they expect to work in their retirement years, with a majority preferring new, second careers that promise to be more fulfilling and helpful for the greater good of society.

Traditionally, the most popular concept of work is something we do to take care of life's necessities (shelter, food, clothing) and to keep ourselves secure and comfortable. And, indeed, this is essential business. The so-called Protestant Work Ethic has been blamed for the American obsession with working hard, ostensibly for its own sake, but also to achieve power, prestige, and wealth. As Don Hall, author of *Life Work*, says (Hall, pp. 25-26):

> *We work to please the powerful masters who are parents, who are church, who are custom or culture. Not to work is to violate the contract or to disobey the injunction, and to displease the dispensers of supper and love, of praise's reward. Not working becomes conviction of unworthiness. We prove ourselves worthy by the numbers of work.*

Thankfully, the traditional view of work is gradually fading as boomer generation retirees come on the scene, most seeking meaningful work. Marc Freedman, a social entrepreneur and founder/CEO of Civic Ventures, has written three popular books. The most recent book—*Encore: Finding Work that Matters in the Second Half of Life* (2007)—provides a detailed analysis about the types of meaningful work or "encore careers" that boomers increasingly seek following their primary careers. An encore career is not defined as a retirement job or as a transitional phase to a life of leisure, but rather as a new stage of purposeful work made possible partly by today's longer life spans. Longitudinal studies show that persons who work beyond age 70 are 2.5 times more likely to live to age 82 than those who had retired cold turkey, a 250-percent correlation that is hard to disclaim.

The word "encore", which is usually associated with artistic performance, indicates a performer's response to an audience's request for an additional performance. In this case, the audience may be interpreted as anyone serviced by a worker (performer). As such, we can think of two types of encores: a repeat performance related to the performer's former line of work; or a performance signifying a different or new line of work. Obviously, some older workers might prefer performing a modified version of the career-long work for which they've developed expertise, while others will prefer to pursue new challenges, including tabled or postponed projects. It seems that more retirees are turning to new lines of work, in some cases concentrating on the favored aspects of their old careers, and avoiding former unpleasant aspects. I've chosen this tactic, by writing on subjects of special interest, becoming more active in favorite causes, performing the type of music I prefer, and teaching on a limited basis, preferably in group formats, rather than one-on-one weekly lessons.

Many new retirees elect to spend a "sabbatical year" following retirement, allowing time for reflection, research, and deciding what to do with the rest of their lives. Although I'd already spent considerable time during my five-year phase-out retirement of quarter-time teaching, I found the strategy of considering the first full retirement year as a sabbatical extremely worthwhile. After all, I felt I had earned one year of slacking off a bit from the ongoing grind of "produce, produce, produce", the mantra of professorship in a research institution.

Freedman has called for government policy changes, including programs for older workers that would allow them to buy into Medicare, provide earlier access to tax-advantaged savings and pensions, and a "national sabbatical" for providing work-training programs. This "new social compact" might ease the transition of aging baby boomers to socially useful encore careers, with available time freed to tackle some of society's major challenges.

In sum, those who have a passion for their life's work, and wish to maintain and share their acquired skills and knowledge, are strongly encouraged to keep doing it, though perhaps at reduced levels. There's plenty of evidence that continuing to work throughout retirement years results in healthier, more independent seniors, most likely because of ongoing social contact and mind-body activity. So, many American retirees find a laidback retirement lifestyle intolerable, preferring instead to remain actively engaged with others doing productive work. Demographically, as many highly qualified and experienced boomers retire from the work force, replacing them with equally skilled workers will present a distinct challenge. The solution, of course, is for more retirees to continue working part time. Moreover, senior citizens who continue working will help support and sustain the gigantic social programs of social security, Medicare, and Medicaid, and the projected improvements in medical care will help seniors maintain mind-body health for a longer time.

In addition to income-producing work, there are numerous options for seniors to remain active as contributing citizens, including serving charities as volunteer helpers in various capacities. Although old age is a time for reflection and recreation, it's also a time to be of service to society. Finding a balance between pursuing personal interests and serving society requires a judicious use of one's time, but it can be done. Several websites provide information about opportunities for seniors to stay active, including: Retired Brains (Civic Ventures and Your Encore); My Next Phase, which contains a variety of information, including the latest statistics related to retirees, and Vital Aging Network, which provides a wide range of information, services, and forums on aging.

Aging Positively and Creatively

With the political clout of nearly 8,000 baby boomers reaching the senior age of 60 daily, the social status of aging persons is gradually improving. The American Association of Retired Persons (AARP) is a mammoth organization with 3,200 chapters representing the fifty-five and older population, and there are other influential organizations that represent seniors. The political and economic clout of the existing and approaching generation of older Americans will definitely alter the current youth culture that's been in vogue for the past few decades. Though U.S. seniors may never achieve the venerable status afforded the elderly in other cultures, especially in the Eastern countries, health concerns for the boomers (the last cohort turned 40 in 2004, including our youngest son) will continue creating a public image of seniors as active and productive citizens. Sara Davidson, author of, *Leap! What Will We Do With the Rest of Our Lives?* (2007), believes her boomer cohort may turn old age into undiscovered country by refusing to slow down, and it's likely she's on to something.

Along with senior status come retirement situations for a majority of aging boomers, and many will face a variety of potential challenges. An AXA Equitable Retirement Survey (www. axaonline.com) reveals a rise in stress levels among seniors, with a 19-percent jump from 2005 to 2006. The two obvious concerns focus on health and finances. Half of middle-income retirees are worried about money issues, and 77 percent expect to continue working once retired, but only 16 percent *are* working. Fortunately, the majority of American retirees are well off, more so than any other country's senior citizens. U.S. retirees' outlooks are also upbeat overall, with workers viewing old age as beginning in the late 70s (AARP *Bulletin*, 3/7/07).

While retirement age offers opportunities for personal growth and development, many seniors pursue activities that lead to personal problems, such as gambling, which is becoming one of the most popular activities for seniors. With extra time on their hands, feelings of uncertainty and loneliness, no exciting hobbies or special interests, financial concerns, and dreams of winning the jackpot, seniors are particularly vulnerable to the packaged activities offered by casinos, including free busing, discounted meals and rooms, plus special awards and prizes. As more and more seniors are swept into the gambling craze, they squander their life savings, suffer depression, and grow ill. (See: www.ncpgambling.org) Persons who reach age 60 do so because of strong genes, common sense, respectable behavior, and good luck. But living to a ripe old age in good mind-body health requires extra special vigilance, notably regarding ingesting potentially harmful substances, such as alcohol and drugs.

Positive Steps for the Long Run

Cultivating a positive mental outlook and improving one's emotional intelligence are crucial to successful aging. According to Deepak Chopra (1993, p. 225):

> *By increasing your inner intelligence, by enhancing your happiness and fulfillment, you can defeat aging in a lasting, meaningful way, without chemicals and their potential side effects. The responsibility for changing this awareness lies with each individual.*

In 2005 Bettye and I took a class called "Aging Positively" meeting twice weekly for five weeks at Plymouth Congregational Church in Minneapolis. One of the assignments was to list all the positive and negative aspects of growing older; surprisingly, the group's pros outnumbered the cons. Some of the most-often-mentioned positives were: having greater wisdom; having more independence;

behaving less conventionally; being more outspoken, without fear of censure; having more freedom and time for family, friends, and hobbies. The one aspect that struck a chord within me is the growing freedom to express what I really think about things, which is the main reason I'm finally writing this book. Poet Sara Teasdale poignantly summarizes some positive thoughts of aging:

> *When I have eased to break my wings*
> *Against the faultiness of things*
> *And learned that compromises wait*
> *Behind each hardly opened gate,*
> *Grow calm and very coldly wise,*
> *Life will have given me the Truth*
> *And taken in exchange—my youth.*

As we get older, remaining creative is perhaps the most significant strategy for positive aging. Research shows that pleasurable mental activity gives rise to alpha-wave brain patterns typical of "restful alertness," a relaxed but mental state of awareness found in meditation, and certain desirable neurotransmitters such as *serotonin* also increase. It is highly probable that creative activity may enhance the structure of the brain itself.

Psychologists who study creativity say that artists and writers often produce more new ideas in their sixties or seventies than in their twenties. Some exemplary models of older creative geniuses include Picasso, Shaw, Michelangelo, Tolstoy, and the incomparable composer, Verdi, who wrote *Falstaff* at the age of 80. Eliot Porter, one of America's premier landscape photographers, published his first photograph after age 50, and Julia Child became a TV celebrity when she was past midlife. Architects I.M. Pei and Frank Lloyd Wright both remained very creative, Wright up until age 91, when he was building his final monument, the Guggenheim Museum in New York. Fortunately, it seems that the later one takes up any creative pursuit, the more likely it will continue into old age.

Older people excel in wisdom, a "software" program used by people to outwit biological limits. Arthur Rubinstein, who played piano concerts up through his nineties, cited three wise strategies he used for handling demanding performance stress: perform fewer pieces; practice each piece more frequently, and to compensate for loss of speed and manual dexterity—slow down for a few seconds just before the music enters a particularly fast passage, effectively making the playing sound faster than it really is. Jonas Salk defined wisdom as "the capacity to make judgments that when looked back upon will seem to have been wise." In short, as a form of holistic knowing, wisdom is largely what a person *is*, not what he or she can *do*.

Living Accommodations for the Elderly

Forgive me for repeating myself, but some things bear repetition. In addition to simplifying one's life—getting rid of unnecessary items, and making preparations (wills, living trusts, etc.) for the "final transition", so as not to burden family and friends—aging folk might consider moving into a residence facility designed for the elderly. The condo my wife and I have moved into is designed for a variety of ages, but is particularly well suited for elderly people, as all feature one-level units, wide doorways, and other features designed for older folks like us. We like the fact that our building—and an identical one—attracts a variety of ages, a desirable feature for us. We are not ready to be surrounded primarily by people our age, though we certainly anticipate making friends among those who are. Residences for persons 55 and older are proliferating everywhere, notably in metropolitan areas, and it's inevitable that smaller towns and cities will be providing them as the huge numbers of boomers retire.

As far as long-term care residences are concerned, replacing the existing 17,000 old and rather bland, institutional facilities in the U.S. is increasing, with numbers of upscale residences and family-size nursing homes undergoing architectural and cultural makeovers. The trend is now focused on providing homey, family-type environments that include the removal of nursing stations, the addition of plants and pets, and the development of positive staff-elder relationships.

Dr. Bill Thomas, a geriatrician at SUNY Upstate Medical Center, has a mission to revolutionize long-term care. In the 1990s he launched the "Eden Alternative", and today his objective is the National Greenhouse Project, which provides a radical shift from large, impersonal institutions to homes accommodating up to ten residents each. The first project was the Cedars Health Center in Tupelo, Mississippi, which features 6000-square-foot single houses, each with a driveway, entry door, and lawn. Residents get to select and help prepare their own meals, and participate in a wide range of group activities and personal hobbies. And the residents are not the only satisfied people, for the caregivers tend to be more satisfied with their work, so they tend to remain longer on the job. Finally, in comparison with the average long-term care facility's $5,000 monthly price tag, the Tupelo Green Houses run around $4,500, proof that the upgrade to resident homes isn't prohibitively expensive. And, for most residents with modest financial resources, Medicaid covers the cost (Kalb & Juarez, 2005, pp. 46-47).

Learning From Centenarians

While the traditional life paradigm tells us we become less fulfilled as we age, Chopra (1993) proclaims a new paradigm based on life as a process of constant transformation, full of unlimited growth as we age. In support of his thesis, Chopra points to studies of centenarians, of whom approximately 85 percent are women and 75 percent widowed, with 50 percent living in nursing homes. According to the U.S. Census Bureau, the highest percentage of centenarians in the U.S. is found in Iowa and South Dakota, respectively, while the lowest percentage is found in Utah and Alaska. The longest living role model is Frenchwoman Jeanne L. Calment, believed to be the oldest person in the world when she died in 1997 at age 122.

In *National Geographic* (November 2005), the secrets of longevity are explored, with concentration on three societies known to produce longer-living populations: the Sardinians in Sardinia, Italy; the Okinawans on the island of Okinawa, Japan; and Seventh Day Adventists in Loma Linda, California. Dan Buettner, author of *The Blue Zone: Lessons for Living Longer From the People Who've Lived the Longest*, produced a follow-up study published by National Geographic (2008). He collaborated with the National Institute on Aging in developing a methodology to help understand each region's culture of longevity, which was then substantiated with epidemiology studies. This study added the inhabitants of Nicoya Peninsula in Costa Rica to the three described below:

- Isolated in mountain villages for hundreds of years, the Sardinians have developed a lifestyle based on basic foods prepared simply, home-grown red wine, plenty of exercise, and close connections with family and friends. Of the 17,865 people born between 1880 and 1900, 91 have reached 100 years of age, a rate twice that of the average for Italy.

- Elder Okinawans who grew up before WWII have never learned to overindulge in eating—unlike younger generations, with a greater reliance on fast-food consumption, which has earned the current youth recognition for having one of Japan's highest obesity rates.

In conjunction with their lean diets, elderly Okinawans maintain their traditional simple lifestyle, which involves regular physical activity and active social lives.

• Seventh-Day Adventists in Loma Linda, California vow that their longevity can be attributed to their traditional religious beliefs regarding: the avoidance of harmful substances (alcohol, drugs, caffeinated drinks, tobacco); consuming healthy food and drink, mostly vegetarian; powerful religious belief system and spiritual life; and congenial social life with their church-member friends and family.

Studies show that the physical characteristics of centenarians include: moderate weight throughout their lifetime; good muscle tone and grip; youthful skin appearance; and ongoing physical activity. Likewise, centenarians' psycho-emotional characteristics include superior native intelligence, good memory, freedom from anxiety, optimism, adaptability, satisfaction with life, and spirituality. In addition, their diets are low in fat and high in protein, they are early risers (averaging 6-8 hours of sleep), they share no uniformity in drinking and smoking habits, they use medication sparingly, and the majority are coffee drinkers (Chopra 1993).

In his book, *The Longer Life* (2006), Maurice Ernest examined biographies of centenarians across many European cultures and centuries back to ancient times. Ernest concluded that understanding just a few physical processes would extend our lives to 100 or 120 years. His prescriptions include: frugal eating; exercising and fresh air; having a congenial occupation; developing a placid or easygoing personality; maintaining a high level of personal hygiene; drinking wholesome liquids; abstaining from stimulants and sedatives; getting plenty of rest; having a bowel movement once a day; living in a temperate climate; enjoying a reasonable sex life; and getting proper medical attention in case of illness.

Though Americans are not generally considered ideal models of aging, the pursuit of constructive mind-body improvement strategies is a trend that will undoubtedly increase with the approaching horde of Boomer retirees. Asian countries lead the way with active, robust seniors, as can be observed in most Chinese city parks during daylight hours. In Beijing, for example, with the opening of city gates at 6:00 a.m., streams of elderly people pour through the gates lugging their day's paraphernalia, including chessboards, music instruments, tape recorders, radios, fans, and birdcages. Soon a group begins breathing exercises, followed by Tai Chi Chuan movements. Another group begins dance practice, involving the use of red fans. Other groups play chess, chat, and gamble. In sum, they are socially, mentally, and physically very active, thanks in large part to a tight-fit, family-network society, with a tradition of revering and supporting elders. But a future problem looms that will adversely affect the outdoor activities of future Chinese elders; namely, the ever increasing polluted air in China, especially Beijing.

Senior Role Models

Although there are numerous seniors who exemplify admirable lifestyles, I'll mention only a few, beginning with my mother and father-in-law, and two men who love their life-long work, the type that would be anathema to many seniors. Finally, I'll mention a more prominent senior who continues making valuable contributions, leaving a legacy that is hard to match in his various fields of expertise.

My mother, Edna Blount Ware, was a salt-of-the-earth woman, a middle child of twelve siblings in a highly respected family in the small town of Decatur, Mississippi. Before marrying my father, Durward, a civil engineer (who didn't fare too well in his final years), she taught school for a year, though her only preparation was one year attending a teacher's college. In 1940, when I was age 3, my folks, tiring from moving around the state to accommodate Dad's ranging work assignments as a state surveyor, decided to settle in Jackson, the state capitol. Soon thereafter, my mother initiated her small-business career by leasing a corner grocery store in a predominantly black residential community that was interlaced with some non-shopping type businesses. It occurred to me rather belatedly—in my middle age—that having had a working mother at that time was not typical, even though many women were working in industries producing war materials. She was definitely a can-do person, demonstrating over the years that she could accomplish just about anything she set her mind on.

After ten years of managing the grocery store, plus a year or two of owning an adjoining hole-in-the-wall café, she decided to sell the business and move home in order to spend more time with my ten-year younger sister (Kay) and me. Well, that lasted a decade, until we were both able to fend for ourselves, which was more common in those days—before "helicopter parents" were created. Then, in midlife, she converted one of their two small rental homes into her Gift House and Florist business. For the remainder of her life—up to age 88 (she died a year later)—she rarely missed a day driving to the store and checking on things, including flowers and green plants that required lots of TLC. Even on Sundays she delivered flower arrangements to client churches, including hers.

For a few years her delivery vehicles consisted of station wagons, but for almost 20 years she drove a 1969 Volkswagen van that our family called the "Booboo Wagon". When that vehicle was on its last tires, it caught fire and burned up. She then switched to a 1989 Chevy Blazer that was stolen and later recovered. (Soon after she entered an assisted living home, she gave it to me, and I drove it for four years before passing it along to our eldest son.) After the 1989 Blazer was stolen she bought a 1992 Blazer, but soon afterwards the older model was recovered. She couldn't resist buying it back in an auction, so she had it repaired and thus ended up owning two Blazers that she drove on an alternating basis, each for a week at a time, primarily to keep the batteries charged.

I mention my mother as an example of aging well because she lived a very full life up until her last year, when the cancer she'd been fighting for several years invaded much of her body. Throughout her final years she flagged in strength but rarely in spirit, and she never ceased staying busy, including attending her regular Sunday Bingo socials with friends. I didn't learn until recently that she was a highly respected confidant for relatives, friends, and associates. The fact that she never divulged the personal information shared with her by so many people, including some gay florists she knew well, attests to her personal integrity. If she had received the appropriate educational training, she might have enjoyed a successful career as counselor or perhaps even as a psychiatrist. Of course, there are untold numbers of individuals who never fulfill their human potential due to lack of educational opportunities, and this was especially true of my folks' depression-years generation.

My father-in-law, Sam Oldham (or Daddy O, as we called him), was an unusually active 94-year-old until the last few months of his life, even maintaining his gardening hobby and lawn up until age 92. Upon his retirement from the paint company he founded (as a trained chemist), he became an avid reader, a habit that contributed to a noticeable broadening of his interests and worldview. If fact, in his latter years both he and his wife, Jean, evolved into far more interesting, broad-minded persons, and outstanding models of graceful aging. After much coercion from his grown children, Sam even learned to use a computer at

272 / *Optimizing Life*

age 88, at first somewhat reluctantly but increasingly with growing enthusiasm. Corresponding with him weekly via email was a highlight for me, as he always wrote exactly the way he spoke, using colorful expressions. When Sam (Daddy O) died, I began corresponding weekly with his widow, Jean, or Mommy O (MO) as she's affectionately addressed. At age 97 (in 2008), Mommy O remains mentally alert, in relatively good health, and mostly independent, living with part-time assistance in a home she and Sam moved into in 2002 to be near their eldest son and his wife. I consider both parents-in-law exemplary senior role models.

An interesting incident occurred in Sam's mid 80s that lead him to an epiphany of sorts. On one of his weekly forays to the supermarket, he encountered an elderly gentleman struggling to open the main door. Sam rushed to assist, and the grateful fellow expressed his appreciation with a "Thank you, good sir". Sam replied, "No problem. I just hope I can get around as well as you when I reach your age". "Yep," the fellow said, "being 75 is no fun". Sam was absolutely flabbergasted, as he was almost ten years older than the decrepit fellow. Actually, he was very pleased to discover he wasn't as old as he had figured, thanks to good genes, a healthy lifestyle, and a positive, optimistic disposition.

Senior Workers

Having presented three personal role models, I'd now like to introduce a few seniors who demonstrate how love of one's work can be a life-fulfilling pursuit in old age. Three seniors were featured in local newspaper articles in 2004 and 2005, and others are personal acquaintances.

John Nardi, a rarity in the modern workplace as an octogenarian, has been selling cars at Downtown Jaguar in Minneapolis since 1970. While many Americans strive to retire at 62 or 65, Nardi is thankful that he can still do something he loves. "I didn't take my Social Security until I was 70. And I only took it because they made me take it," Nardi said. "I've always worked," the World War II veteran said. "As long as I'm healthy and I'm able to walk and navigate, I'm going to keep on working. Dr. James Allan, his physician and friend describes John as a man blessed with a vocation he loves, which proves that not retiring can prolong life. Nardi is even a disciple of the work ethic when he visits with his old World War II buddies at POW reunions. He says, "I always tell them to go out and get themselves a part-time job." He and his octogenarian wife, Gerri, celebrated their 60th wedding anniversary in April 2007.

Lyle Baker, an 82-year-old from St. Paul, Minnesota, has served as a Fuller Brush salesman for 46 years. He wears a tuxedo, primarily because he thinks of himself as a first-class professional, and bristles (pardon the pun) at any mention of retirement. He's slowed down somewhat in the past few years, currently working five to six days per week for six months annually. In his typically upbeat mood, he says, "In my heart and mind I'm a very professional person." Characteristically, he claims he'll only retire when he dies.

Emma Shulman, age 93 (in 2005), was a veteran social worker who put in up to 50 hours weekly recruiting people for treatment at an Alzheimer's clinic at New York University of Medicine. Her psychiatrist boss, Steven H. Ferris, claimed it would take three persons to replace her if and when she retires. Shulman complained that one problem was her excessive energy, which sometimes drove her nuts.

As a vocal musician and teacher, I know many colleagues who never completely retire from their musical lives, electing to continue playing, singing, and teaching as long as they can, with little anticipation of total retirement. The following three seniors are standouts:

• Oksana Bryn, an octogenarian colleague with a lovely soprano voice and a fine reputation as a voice teacher, has maintained a very active teaching schedule at the MacPhail Center for the Arts in Minneapolis, despite painful arthritis and impaired mobility. Her desire to continue learning has been evident in her attendance to numerous vocal events, including workshops, when she eagerly asks questions and offers insightful comments.

• Geneva Eschweiler, another octogenarian voice-teacher and pianist colleague, manages a private studio of 45 students, and is active in several local Twin Cities' musical organizations.

• Mary King Osterfield, a viola performer and teacher living in Moorhead, Minnesota, continues teaching into her 90s. She attributes her longevity, good health, and energy to her ongoing teaching, which includes dozens of students. When asks about retirement, she bristles, saying she's never going to retire, as she wants to continue playing or doing something worthwhile, rather than sitting and staring out the window.

And now we consider a very extraordinary role model, a cut far above the ordinary. In 2004 public television produced a program featuring Peter Ferdinand Drucker, one of the most fascinating people I've ever had the pleasure of learning about. The professor taught his last course at Claremont Graduate School in California at age 93 in 2002, and died three years later in November 2005. Drucker, a native Viennese, worked in Germany and England prior to moving to America in the 1930s, when he became a U.S. citizen. His contributions to business education have earned him the honor of being called the Father of Management. One of Drucker's most important accomplishments was his consulting work with Japanese corporate management in the early 1980s, which resulted in Japanese companies becoming powerhouses for economic change, consequently making Japan one of the top economies in the world.

Drucker has produced 38 books—the latest, *Managers in the Next Society* (2002)—all of which reveal his uncanny ability to discern trends based on keen observation, creative thinking, and gut intuition. For instance, he foresaw the powerful trends that pointed to the knowledge-based economy that now dominates all of society, especially in the media, commerce, and education. Another trend was the popular one-stop mega-church phenomenon, a combined religious/social institution that offers a plethora of programs and activities for persons of all ages and persuasions. Above all, Drucker claimed that education should be a central social concern, with an emphasis on continuing life-long education. Moreover, he insisted that the business of all institutions is the development of people and creating community, as opposed to making and selling products, or promoting selfish concerns. One of his wise sayings, "Don't confuse motion with progress", is meant to emphasize qualitative goals over quantitative concerns, people over things. His stress on simplicity and reducing everything to essentials was intended to define principles that set the stage for creating efficient processes to achieve worthwhile goals.

Another favorite male role model is Andy Rooney, who at age 86 continues creating insightfully critical and entertaining commentaries for the 39th season of CBS' *60 Minutes* in 2008, in addition to producing a weekly syndicated newspaper column. He also recently completed his fifteenth book, *Out of My Mind* (Public Affairs), and a collection of essays written over the years is stored on his computer, potential fodder for another book. He says, "I can't stop myself from writing. I have all this stuff in my brain and I have some sort of drive to put it all down on paper." Good for him!

A few outstanding examples of aging women celebrities should be mentioned, some of whom have died in recent years: opera diva Beverly Sills, who retired from a professional singing career, then took on the directorship of the New York City Opera, continued working on behalf of arts organizations; dancer/choreographer Martha Graham, who danced until age 76, choreographed for another 20 years with her world-famous dance company; actress Katharine Hepburn, who continued acting into her 80s; religious leader and humanitarian Mother Teresa, who worked tirelessly on behalf of the impoverished and sick until her life's end; visual artist Georgia O'Keefe, who painted well into her 90s, despite failing eyesight; and primitive artist Anna (Grandma Moses) Robertson, who sold her first painting at 79, and kept producing works for another two decades.

Women today who are in their 80s and 90s grew up in a society governed by men, especially in such fields as politics, business, science, medicine, and sports, arenas that currently lack large numbers of outstanding senior women representatives. However, as the boomers gradually reach old age, the scene will begin to change, with more women and minorities becoming widely recognized for their long-term, significant contributions in a wide range of fields formerly dominated by men.

Though we can't all be as brilliant and productive as the aging celebrity models mentioned above, most of us can relate to the average Joes and Janes, persons like Edna Ware, Sam Oldham, John Niardi, Lyle Baker, and Emma Shulman. Of course, the measure of one's life achievements is determined more by one's depth of character, spirit, and positive contributions to society than to any amount of publicity disseminated by the media.

Before closing this section on senior workers, it is relevant to mention that the American Association of Retired Persons (AARP) has started a pilot program called Work-Search to assist able-bodied seniors in locating work, by matching their skills and interests to companies hiring senior workers. The program is currently connected with AARP's Senior Community Service Employment Program (SCSEP), in collaboration with the U.S. Department of Labor, and operated by the AARP Foundation. Information can be found on the AARP website (www.aarp.org).

11

Anticipating Death

Death, be not proud, though some have called thee
Mighty and dreadful, for thou art not so;
For those whom thou think'st thou dost overthrow
Die not, poor death; nor yet canst thou kill me.
   —*John Donne (1573-1631) Holy Sonnets*

At the outset we should distinguish between dying, the processes that lead to death, and death, the actual cessation of life. In earlier chapters we looked at the effects of aging on mind-body processes, particularly aging effects that eventually lead to a decline in mental and physical functions, and typically culminating in various forms of disease, illness, and painful suffering. Though death sometimes comes quickly, as in accidents, natural catastrophes, and violent human encounters, most of us exit life slowly over a period of years, months, days, and hours. The disturbing aspect of dying is that it's rarely pleasant for the dying person or for loved ones, though the possibility of an individual having greater control is increasing. But we'll delve more into this topic later.

Demystifying Dying

Experts in fields associated with dying and death have leveled some justifiable criticism of Americans and other first-world citizens for the general tendency to avoid and deny death. As proof, they point to the use of such euphemisms as "succumbed", "passed on" or "passed away" when speaking of someone who has died. Historically, when life spans were shorter due to harsh living conditions, death was more visible in the community. In contrast, today we're mostly sheltered from suffering, dying, and death, with the exception of the visual media's increasingly very impersonal and explicit fictional and actual scenes of death. Ever since death moved from the home (family or tribe) to the hospital (professionals and institutions), a trend that accelerated throughout the previous century, the subject of death gradually became a taboo topic in polite conversation. We Americans, and other first-world citizens, have generally avoided dealing with death, increasingly referring the final details associated with death to designated professionals and their institutions. In other words, death has become socially, politically, medically, and religiously bureaucratized.

In September 2000 PBS aired a special program on dying titled *On Our Own Terms: Moyers on Dying*, a four-part series focusing on the issue of how our society treats dying persons. The primary goal of Bill and Judith Moyers was to demystify the qualitative experience of dying in the U.S., which is understandably given a lower priority than living. A growing interest in death is generated in large part by swelling numbers of middle-aged boomers as they reach retirement age, with attendant increases of illness. As one expert exclaimed: "People are finally awakening to the realization that the death rate has remained unchanged, at one per person." Another wake-up call was announced with the AIDS epidemic in the 80s, a disease that touched everyone in some way, and prompted more concern and care for the dying.

Though more insurance and government money is being used to promote research and care for dying patients, most attention has been focused on the final 30 days of life, usually when a patient is confined to an intensive care unit in isolation from loved ones. Thankfully, there's a growing consensus that perhaps it might be more humane for the dying patients to be stationed comfortably at home or in nearby hospice accommodations where they can receive specialized hospice-supported care, receive pain-relieving medication, and be comforted by loved ones.

Anticipating and Reflecting on Death

The process of demystifying death begins with thinking and talking about it, as a prelude to eventually gaining understanding and acceptance. Beginning in the early 1970s, a steady stream of books on dying and death was published by experts, such as Elisabeth Kübler-Ross, (1926-2004), author of *Death: The Final Stage of Growth* (1975). Thanks to her pioneering efforts, the dialogue on dying and death has made considerable headway, though decades of entrenched public denial must yet be overcome.

Trying to understand death and make sense of it is the first step in learning how to cope effectively. Ideally, the sooner each of us begins preparations the better—before actually facing an illness that foreshadows death. Sherwin Nuland, author of *How We Die: Reflections on Life's Final Chapter*, informs us that death should not be construed as a confrontation, but simply a natural event in the sequence of life's ongoing rhythms. He claims that the real enemy is disease, and that every triumph over a major pathology is merely a reprieve from the inevitable end.

I prefer the concept of dying as a natural process, the final life adventure that culminates in death. Why not anticipate and prepare for dying and death, if not happily, at least with a sense of wonderment and curiosity? As humans for thousands of years have experienced, dying is a natural process, and for some rare individuals it can even be a positive experience, a joyful celebration of successful aging. And for those who suffer chronic pain, death can be a welcomed release. In *The Tibetan Book of the Dead*, dying persons are called "the triumphant." In certain ancient societies, for instance, in parts of Japan, when old people sensed their eminent death, they voluntarily went into the mountains to die alone, as Eskimos are also known to have done in the solitude of icy landscapes. Though not very common, this same self-death concept has carried on through the ages, even up to modern times. Wendell Berry, writing in his novel, *The Memory of Old Jack*, has his title character allude to a similar mode of death (p. 24):

> *His mind, he thinks, would do well to settle down and be quiet, for pretty soon he is going up on the hill for the long sleep that most people he knows have already gone off to, and there is not a lot that a man's mind can do about that. He has no fear of death. It is coming, there is nothing to be done about it, and so he does not think about it much. It is the unknown, and he has come to the unknown before. Sometimes it has been very satisfying, the unknown, but sometimes not. Anyhow, what would a man his age propose to do instead of die? He has been around long enough to know that death is the only perfect cure for what ails mortals. After you have stood enough you die, and that is all right.*

In a similar spirit of self resignation, Thomas Jefferson wrote a letter to John Adams in which he said: "There is a ripeness of time for death, regarding others as well as ourselves, when it is reasonable we should drop off, and make room for another growth. When we have lived our generation out, we should not wish to encroach on another." (Coincidentally, both Jefferson and Adams died on the 4th of July, 1826, the fiftieth anniversary of the Declaration of Independence.)

Historically, the practice of voluntary self-deaths was partly motivated by altruism, in part to relieve the burdens of social groups in caring for weakened elders under harsh living conditions. Most people don't want to die alone, but rather in the company of loved ones. I'm not condoning such a practice, but I do recognize that under certain conditions it might be a benevolent, selfless way to exit this world. Today, it's still possible for a dying person to decide when he or she is ready to go, simply by making wishes known to all caregivers that a natural death be allowed, a topic to be discussed later on.

The fear of dying and death is a common response to a natural process that few of us are psycho-emotionally prepared to encounter. In facing both the mystery and reality of dying, it helps to maintain a sense of humor, which can enable us to cope more effectively in relieving the psycho-emotional burden of excessive, unproductive worrying. I particularly enjoy viewing a cartoon I discovered in *New Yorker* magazine (Dec. 8, 1997). An elderly couple is sitting in rocking chairs on the front porch of their country home, discussing the topic of death. The aging husband responds to an assumed query from his wife regarding his wishes to enjoy a longer life: "No, I don't want to live forever, but I damn sure don't want to die forever, either." I imagine most people share a similar perspective.

Accepting the Concept of Dying

We learn how to die more gracefully by participating in the dying process of others. Gerda Lerner, in her book, *A Death of One's Own*, says that, in experiencing the deaths of others as fearlessly and as feelingly as possible, we share, learn, and discover that, like life, dying is untidy, mixed up, tormented, and even transcendent. Finally, we *must* accept it, because, as finite beings, we have no other choice. Another writer, Ganga Stone, in her book, *Start the Conversation*, puts it in graphic terms:

> So the body is a shit factory—that's the bottom line. And we can't even give the stuff away, much less sell it . . . Nobody gets out of here alive. There's a lease, with

terms, obligations, and an undetermined termination date. Our bodies can be reclaimed by the manufacturer (God) at any time . . . The truth of the matter is that the mortality rate of the human race is 100 percent to date. That means all the children, all the women, all the men. We have no reasonable expectation of getting any body out of here alive. No body gets out of here alive. If you think you are some body, this is very bad news. If you already know that you are not this body, it's no big deal.

Undertaker Thomas Lynch, in his book, *The Undertaking: Life Studies from the Dismal Trade*, agrees, commenting: "This is the central fact of my business—there is nothing, once you are dead, that can be done to you or for you or with you or about you that will do you any good or harm: that any damage or decency we do accrues to the living, to whom your death happens, if it really happens to anyone. The living [survivors] *have* to live with it. You don't."

When we first learn that a loved one is inflicted with a serious, terminal illness, or has been involved in a violent accident, or has died, the initial shock is like a private earthquake. Ganga Stone's advice is to quakeproof ourselves in advance, using such comforting thoughts as:

• *My beloved is not destroyed, but is taking a transcending journey to the destination of his/her dreams.*

• *The container of my beloved is the physical body, but the essence is the spirit.*

• *Memory is like a movie that never ends.*

Among the neurological mechanisms we have for inhibiting reactions is fear, which is permanently wired into the brain for survival purposes. So we must learn to adjust this instinctive response to fear to suit the reality of any situation, including dying and death. Primarily because of negative social conditioning and a lack of understanding, we are unable to perceive death in positive ways, for example, comparing it to a sound night's dreamless sleep, or thinking of fear as exhilaration and excitement that's filtered through a sense of insecurity in facing the unknown.

In preparation for death, we can more effectively cope with fear and grief by understanding beforehand that the essence or spirit of a dead person is not annihilated, extinguished, or destroyed. The positive response is melancholy or sadness—minus the burden of grief, which can be destructive to survivors. Fear aggravates pain, and pain stimulates more fear. Other fears associated with dying and death include separation from loved ones, home, and work, being a burden, losing control, being dependent, and leaving things undone. Whatever the fear, the emotional pain can be lessened by admitting and sharing one's honest feelings.

In an exclusive AARP *Modern Maturity* survey involving 1,815 interviews of Americans 45 and older, it was revealed that the older we are, the less afraid we are of dying, and of suffering pain at the end of life. Over a lifetime, it seems that people gradually adapt to the eventual reality of aging, suffering, and death. In practical terms, many older people have fewer financial concerns, such as depleting family finances to pay for medical care. Somewhat surprisingly, women reported being more fearful than men of painful suffering, as well as having their death prolonged by artificial means.

Octogenarian Dr. William Ackerman, a retired research geneticist from the U.S. National Arboretum and author of *Beyond the Camellia Belt* (2007), exhibits a positive attitude with these thoughts (Ackerman 2008, p. 13):

I am now in my mid-eighties, and I feel that I have had

*my full allocated time and space in this world, beyond
that of many of my kindred. Perhaps soon will be my
time to rest. I do not feel any apprehension of its coming,
only of the possible suffering that may proceed it. I should
be well satisfied with a deep sleep for the rest of eternity.
Sleep is the pacifier of all anxiety, a thing to be cherished,
for in sleep there is absolution from feeling and pain. I
have no ambitions of going through another life. This one
is quite enough.*

Coping With Grief

Grief, or profound sorrow, is a natural response to any
significant loss, including an anticipated loss, as happens
when one receives a dire medical diagnosis portending a
painful, terminal illness. In this section we consider the
effects of grief on those who are terminally ill, as well
as survivors of those who have died. Studies show that
intense grief can be debilitating, especially when it lasts
for a long period. Ganga Stone says that "Grief is not logical, not appropriate, not necessary, and in my view, not at
all beneficial. But sadness makes all kinds of sense".

Perspectives among professional grief counselors vary.
Psychologist Stephen Levine advises dealing openly with
grief, allowing it to happen, while Norman Klein claims
that standards for grieving may be arbitrary and culture
dependent. According to cross-cultural studies of 73 societies, the obvious variable was the form and intensity of
expressing grief. In 72 societies, people weep at death, but
the Balinese laugh to avoid crying. In 32 of 60 cultures, both
sexes cried equally, and in the others it was the women who
cried the most. In 18 of 32 societies self-mutilation occurs,
led by women. In sum, death evokes an incredible variety
of responses in societies, with some remaining calm, some
crying, some wailing, and others mutilating their bodies.

And the length of mourning also varies, some lasting for months, and some only for a few hours.

In the mid 1970s Dr. Kübler-Ross proposed Five Psychological Stages of Dying, in conjunction with coping mechanisms during a terminal illness (Kübler-Ross 1975):

- Denial and isolation ("No, not me; it can't be true.")

- Anger-rage, envy, resentment ("Why me?")

- Bargaining ("If you'll . . . then I'll . . . ")

- Depression ("What's the use?")

- Acceptance (the final rest before the long journey)

Taking issue with these five stages, Edwin S. Sneidman recognizes the stages but doesn't agree that everyone goes through these exact stages in any particular order, as the main tendency is to alternate between acceptance and denial. What he does see in his psychology practice is described this way (Fulton 1981, p. 182):

A complicated clustering of intellectual and affective states, some fleeting, lasting for a moment or a day or week, set, not unexpectedly, against the backdrop of that person's total personality, his "philosophy of life" (whether an essential optimism and gratitude to life or a pervasive pessimism and dour or suspicious orientation to life).

My experience leads me to posit a hive [shelter] of affect, in which emotional stages seem to include a constant interplay between disbelief and hope and, against these as background, a waxing and waning of anguish, terror, acquiescence and surrender, rage and envy, disinterest and ennui, pretense, taunting and daring, and even yearning for death—all these in the context of bewilderment and pain.

Ganga Stone has developed 10 questions for determining a person's level of grief or sadness. If answers are "yes" to the first five and "no" to the last five, the person is experiencing sadness rather than grief. For self-examination, simply substitute "you" for "they".

1. Can anything make them laugh?

2. Can they talk to someone about how they feel?

3. Do they talk about their feelings?

4. Are they crying readily off and on?

5. Does their food taste all right?

6. Does everything seem awfully difficult?

7. Are they having trouble getting to sleep?

8. Are they having trouble waking up?

9. Does everything seem terribly flat?

10. Has everyone let them down?

Stone also offers advice regarding ways of relating to dying or grieving persons. First, slow down and collect yourself, possibly by using meditation-type strategies. Second, connect with the person by touching, preferably by holding hands. Throughout the grieving period it's important to avoid engendering feelings of guilt in self and others, and forgiveness of any committed wrongs is essential. In sum, friends can help grieving persons by just being present and showing concern, sharing in the grieving process (crying), and continuing to give moral and physical support as long as it's needed. So *doing* something for grieving persons is less important than just *being* with them.

In keeping with the idea of minimizing overt action, Stone believes talking may not be needed. But when it is needed, there are some statements she suggests avoiding: "You'll get over this." "It's better now because he's at peace". "Don't question God's purpose". Or "I know how you feel". On the other hand, it is acceptable to say: " Would you like to talk?" "It must be difficult for you". And "How are you adjusting?" One way to think about grief is to consider it an extended conversation, not only with others, but primarily with one's self.

The question of whether an extremely ill person should be kept informed of any near-death status is a crucial one. Most professionals would answer affirmatively. Understandably, physicians regret having to convey bad news, buoyed with the belief that hope should always be extended. I side with the option of open disclosure. It seems important that a dying person know when the time is near, in order to prepare psycho-emotionally, and to bid farewell to loved ones.

The Ways We Die

Of course, there are many ways to die, and the most violent means are by horrific accidents and murders, both during peacetime and war. Death by violence is largely associated with young persons, and for Americans below the age of forty-four, trauma (physical injury or wound) is the leading cause of death, accounting for more than 150,000 annually. An additional 400,000-plus persons are disabled, and sixty percent of the mortality rate occurs within the first twenty-four hours following injury. In half of all auto accident fatalities, alcohol is involved. The primary causes of death are brain damage and bleeding, in a sequence of events that might include hemorrhage, cardiac arrest, moments of agonizing pain, and clinical death. In contrast, the common denominator in most deaths is the choking off of oxygen and nutrition.

Although suffering occurs in conjunction with many deaths, Stone offers a more positive outlook for the dying, based on the following scenarios:

• *Sudden or instantaneous death* is usually painless, eased greatly by the body's release of automatic pain-killers (endorphins) into the bloodstream, causing an obvious calm to come over the anesthetized victim.

• *Gradual death* may not be painful, if it comes in a few minutes to a few hours to persons who are properly sedated. In most cases, due to a lack of oxygen, the dying person experiences drowsiness or stupe-faction, and welcomes sleep. Though a sense of panic will aggravate the situation, physical pain is usually not evident.

• *Death following a prolonged illness* is more difficult, but taking sufficient dosages of appropriate medication can alleviate debilitating pain. Unfortunately, the most common form of medical drug abuse may be attributed to minimizing use of pain medication. Since rest is hampered by pain, patients and loved ones should not hesitate in requesting painkilling medication.

To die with a lack of dignity is the ultimate insult to a good life. With the exception of violent deaths due to accidents, murder, strokes, or heart attacks, most people have time to prepare for a dignified death. Although many people avoid anguished death passages, others remain in distress up until the final breath. Sherwin Nuland, M.D., describes a worst-case scenario (1995, pp. 141-149):

Denying the probability of a miserable prelude to death

is deluding, for the truth is most of us will die wondering what we, or our doctors, have done wrong . . . Septic shock can be extremely painful, with a series of lethal events, from fever, rapid pulse, to respiratory distress, with the patient being shuffled around in emergency procedures, from the intensive care unit to X-ray to MRI, etc. All organs begin to fail, dialysis may be tried, etc . . .

By now, if not before, the anguished patient, providing he/her can still orient his/her thoughts, has begun to wonder what is being done to him/her. Although he cannot know it, his doctors are starting to wonder the same thing . . .

A process of depersonalization sets in, with the patient becoming every day less of a human being and more a complicated challenge in intensive care, testing the genius of the most brilliantly aggressive of the hospital's clinical warriors.

Thomas A. Preston, writing in his book—*Final Victory: Preparing for the Best Possible Death*—states that we need to be prepared for high-tech dying, since approximately three-quarters of Americans die in hospitals or medical facilities experiencing excessive and aggressive treatment. In fact, more than eighty percent of American deaths now occur in hospitals, having risen from fifty percent in 1949. Moreover, of all dying patients submitting a "do not resuscitate" request, less than half have their wishes honored. Moreover, a majority experience severe, minimal-treated pain, and nearly 40 percent spend at least 10 days in an intensive-care unit.

In his latest book, *The Mysteries Within* (2000), Sherwin Nuland criticizes medical doctors for their end-of-life care. He explains that most doctors are highly competitive individuals, not accustomed to losing. So, when patients are in serious trouble, physicians view their challenge as making them well. The attitude is "I must conquer this disease, which is the enemy", rather than "I must do whatever I can to make my patient's suffering and pain more humane and tolerable."

This attitude helps explain why some physicians appear uncompassionate, and may seem to lose interest in treating terminally ill patients. Last-resort patients may be viewed a lost cause, and physicians may be needed by those who have a chance at living. Perhaps at such a time the patient can be assigned to another physician, a specialist more qualified in working with terminally ill patients through administering pain medication and collaborating with other medical workers in making the patient's end-of-life more comfortable and meaningful.

Nuland believes that pursuing heroic treatments can be a disservice to patients, blurring the borders of candor and revealing a fundamental schism between the best interests of patients and families versus the interests of physicians. He insists that dying persons are the central player in the death drama, not loved ones and medical personnel, who are supporting cast. To paraphrase his thoughts:

> *I will not allow a specialist to decide when it's time for me to let go. Instead, I will choose, or at least state my preferences so clearly, verbally, and in writing, that, should I be unable, those who know me well can make the decision. The conditions of my illness may not permit me to die with the dignity I optimistically seek, but given the limits of my ability to make a final decision, I prefer not to postpone dying for the senseless reason that a technologically skilled physician does not understand my wishes.*

Nineteenth-century American poet Emily Dickinson summed up the wishes for a dignified death succinctly:

The heart asks pleasure first,
And then, excuse from pain;
And then, those little anodynes
That deaden suffering;
And then, to go to sleep;
And then, if it should be
The will of its Inquisitor,
The liberty to die.

A very sensitive moral and political issue is the cost of prolonging life. George Lundberg (2001) argues that, since we are genetically programmed to die, it doesn't make good sense to spend billions pretending we can stave it off forever. He points out that in 1950 the U.S. spent $12.7 billion, or 4.4 percent of the gross domestic product (GDP) on health care, whereas in 2002 the cost was approximately $1.54 trillion, or nearly 14 percent of the GDP. (And in 2007, total national health expenditures rose nearly 7 percent—twice the rate of inflation, with total spending of $2.3 trillion ($7600 per person), which is 16 percent of the GDP.) Most of the increase from the 1950s was due to medical treatment of last resort, which statistically extends the average life of dying people incrementally, typically by a few months, all the while prolonging undue pain and suffering.

In sum, Lundberg's belief is that we need to put health care costs in the proper perspective, balancing in relation to other social needs, such as education, housing, and defense. Also, instead of spending on expensive life-saving measures, more funds might be allocated for disease prevention, humane palliative care, and lower-cost alternative and complementary medical treatment, the latter of which receives only one-half percent of the National Institute of Health's budget.

Physicians and family members aren't the only persons influencing end-of-life decisions, for a large segment of the public shares conservative attitudes regarding the right of an individual to determine his or her own death. It's ironic that most passionate pro-life advocates believe that only God, not human beings, should determine the point of death. Yet, they also expect—even demand—that medical experts make exhaustive efforts at prolonging a dying person's life, even when it's likely he or she will survive only in a vegetative state.

In such critical situations, do we really want to ignore and dishonor the natural process of dying? And who's really in charge of the process: God or humans? Typically, life-at-any-cost advocates posit that God uses humans as instruments in sustaining human life. To these good folk, the quality of a person's life doesn't seem to matter much, even though he or she may be experiencing great suffering, or that medical staff and loved ones are strained to provide care, or that the costs to society of prolonged, impractical treatment are detracting from other crucial social needs, or that, most importantly, the unnecessary prolongation of life is perhaps in opposition to the dying patient's profound desire to "let go" and move on.

It's worth noting that Pope John Paul II chose to remain in his Vatican residence rather than return to the hospital during his final week. Throughout his papacy, a recurring theme was the compatibility of faith and science, the explainer of reality. It can be surmised that he relied on medical science to treat his dying body, but eventually resorted to his spiritual beliefs in facing death. Although the pope encouraged the use of feeding tubes for persons in vegetative states, he also said it was acceptable for patients to refuse drugs that cause unconsciousness, or to reject extraordinary medical measures leading to a "precarious and burdensome prolongation of life." As the most vocal pro-life advocate in recent years, Pope John Paul II came to understand that an individual has the right—as well as the responsibility—to accept death as a natural event.

Here's another interesting observation about pro-life advocates. In most cases they hold passionate opinions about an afterlife, a heavenly realm that presumably offers a superior existence over this earthly life. To me, the belief in life at any and all costs seems to contradict the traditional concept of a transcendent "other life", presumably the ultimate goal of true believers. I can't help but wonder if such beliefs are sincerely held, or merely professed expressions of an individual's faith.

End-of-Life Care

A dignified death may mean deciding to forego hospital confinement and extreme life-saving measures in the last days. When suffering a terminal illness, many people elect to avoid hospitals, instead remaining at home in the care of family, and using professional assistance as needed. If and when home care becomes impractical, the dying person may be moved into a hospice facility, where optimal comfort and treatment can be provided. The important point is that the dying person is allowed to continue living as normally as possible, with the devoted support of family, friends, and caring professionals. As Nuland says (p. 243):

> *A promise we can keep and a hope we can give is the certainty that no man or woman will be left to die alone . . . For it is the promise of spiritual companionship near the end that gives us hope, much more than does the mere offsetting of the fear of being physically without anyone.*

Suffering is perhaps the greatest concern of the dying. A *Modern Maturity* survey revealed that 77 percent of respondents want controlled substances for pain control, while 71 percent don't want expensive health treatments,

50 percent support voluntary euthanasia for the terminally ill, and 46 percent would allow physician-assisted suicide. Two legal treatments include a steady dose of morphine or a "terminal sedation" prescription, which may include barbiturates or other drugs. Again, to quote Nuland (1995, p. 257):

> *When my time comes, I will seek hope in the knowledge that insofar as possible I will not be allowed to suffer or be subjected to needless attempts to maintain life; I will seek it in the certainty that I will not be abandoned to die alone; I am seeking it now, in the way I try to live my life, so that those who value what I am will have profited by my time on Earth and be left with comforting recollections of what we have meant to one another.*

Finally, we should reemphasize that a primary strategy for assuring a dignified death—in keeping with one's wishes—is to issue an advance directive that's witnessed, signed, and notarized according to the laws of one's state— while one is healthy. Painful stories of long-term comatose, vegetative-state individuals continue to drive home the necessity for individuals to prepare self-directives as soon as possible, and this goes for young people as well.

In 2005, 41-year-old Terri Schiavo, who survived in a vegetative state for fifteen years, died 13 days after having her feeding tube removed, as directed through legal proceedings instigated by her husband, Michael, who claimed Terri would not want to continue living in a vegetative state. Taking a strong opposing stance were Terri's grieving parents, Bob and Mary Schindler, who undertook every available measure to assure her survival. Both viewpoints were taken up as banners by the public, with particularly aggressive actions instigated by pro-life advocates up until the bitter end.

Anna Quindlen addressed this issue in her regular *Newsweek* column "The Last Word" (April 4, 2005), with a potent commentary titled "The Culture of Each Life". In this article she claimed that the "culture of life" arguments associated with Terri's case were not appropriate when applied to individual cases. Her heartfelt response:

There is no culture of life. There is a culture of your life, and the culture of mine. There is what each of us considers bearable, and what we will not bear. There are those of us who believe that under certain conditions the cruelest thing you can do to people you love is to force them to live. There are those of us who define living not by whether the heart beats and the lungs lift but whether the spirit is there, whether the music box plays . . .

There are many ways this case has been played up in public: spouse vs. parents; liberals vs. conservatives; and secular vs. religious. But it is truly about that thing that defines free human beings: the right to self-determination instead of a one-size-fits-all approach in private matters, in those issues that take place in bedrooms and kitchens and hospices. It's a primal demand for a personal sense of control in the face of intrusive government, intrusive medicine and intrusive strangers who think holding a crucifix like a blunt instrument makes them righteous when it only makes them more sanctimonious.

I heartily concur with Ms. Quindlen's compassionate interpretation, which reemphasizes the need for individuals to create an advance directive that explains in clear terms one's wishes. Advance directive documents and specific information can be obtained from Choice in Dying (www.choices.org).

Suicide: The Last Resort

In speaking of euthanasia, or physician-assisted suicide, we enter a very sensitive area, one that separates progressive liberals from conservative religious activists. Though taking one's own life is almost always a wrongful, desperate action, Nuland believes there are two circumstances that may allow for some flexibility in making such a decision (2000, p. 151): "The unendurable infirmities of a crippling old age, and the final devastations of terminal disease".

Personally, I think that keeping terminally-ill elderly patients alive against their wishes—when they have no hope for recovery or a decent life—is cruel and inhumane punishment, especially when the patient is ready to die, and has made out a health directive to that effect, explicitly requesting medical staff not to undertake heroic lifesaving measures.

So what about genuine suicide, the taking of one's own life when confronted with a terminal illness? Ganga Stone draws an analogy of a suicidal person to that of a terminally ill person living in his dilapidated home. The owner no longer cares for the building, and has stopped paying taxes and utilities. Eventually, life becomes so miserable that the owner decides it's time to move out, and considers taking his or her own life.

Whatever may be a person's motivation for committing suicide, there are several well-recognized methods for committing the final act. Nuland describes the major methods his book, *How We Die* (pp. 157-162).

Societal support for suicide has been evidenced in many cultures, including the traditional American Indians, who allowed ailing elders to play a major role in deciding when it was time to die. In many situations, when extremely ill and on the brink of dying, the elder would be escorted to some natural setting where it was believed the dying person's spirit could wander free when released from the body. Then, they would simply lie down and die, sometimes slowly but most likely within hours.

Euthanasia, or assisted suicide, remains a highly controversial and emotionally charged topic. Jack Kavorkian, M.D., is widely recognized as the most notorious "death doctor" in the U.S., if not the world. In 2007, he was released from serving prison time for defying laws that he determined were immoral and unreasonable. What's important in explaining his position is a contention that the terminally ill people he assisted with suicides approached him willingly, supposedly of rational mind and in good faith.

I'm not condoning Dr. Kavorkian's behavior, but I can understand his thinking of himself as a benevolent assistant rather than a cold-hearted killer. I daresay many physicians and terminally ill persons would also understand his motivation and his actions, though perhaps questioning his defiance of legal issues.

Not surprisingly, the U.S. is not a leader in advocating euthanasia. Oregon is the only state officially condoning it, but only under severe medical circumstances. A comprehensive poll conducted by Harris Interactive in April 2005, shows that 70 percent of Americans believe "the law should allow doctors to comply with the wishes of a severely distressed dying patient who wants to end his or her life."

This percentage is a big jump from 1982, when a similar poll found that 53 percent of Americans agreed with that statement. Moreover, 67 percent of Americans taking the Harris poll would favor a law similar to Oregon's Death With Dignity Act in their state. Of course, religious conservatives, including many conservative-minded physicians, are strategizing to overrule the majority opinion. A third of the American Medical Association strongly opposes physician-assisted dying, but, again, this is a minority opinion (Jacoby 2005, p. 8).

Outside of the U.S., guidelines have been drawn up in the Netherlands that allow competent and fully informed patients to have death administered in carefully regulated circumstances. The usual method involves the administering of deep sleep with barbiturates, followed by an injection of a muscle-paralyzing drug to cause cessation of breathing.

Derek Humphrey, founder of the Hemlock Society, has written a book, *Final Exit,* which provides some measures for suicide. Also, organizations providing information about medically assisted deaths are listed in the resources and reading section at the end of this chapter. (Note: These materials are offered for informational purposes only, and not as an endorsement.)

A strong argument can be made to have physician-assisted suicide upheld on grounds of one's religious or spiritual beliefs. Perhaps I'm missing something, but I can't discern the difference between parents of Christian Scientist or Amish religious persuasions withholding medical treatment for family members (or themselves) solely on religious grounds, and a dying person making an equally significant decision for him or herself. If I wish to be spared pain, as well as to spare loved ones undue suffering, and I hold this belief on religious and spiritual grounds, shouldn't I be allowed the same respect as those withholding medical treatment?

In sum, it seems that assuming certain religious beliefs are valid, while other beliefs are not, is an intolerant attitude. Moreover, denying this basic human right can be construed as a violation of a dying person's beliefs and personal rights. Litigation over religious freedom has been fought and won on many occasions, so it seems that challenges to physician-assisted suicide can also be overturned in a court of law.

The Meaning of Death

The dying process might be the most challenging experience we mortals have to endure, as it is typically drawn out over years, with a gradual decline in health. Typically, the dying process speeds up near the end, with death coming rather quickly in the final days, hours, and minutes of life.

We will now focus on the final moments leading to death, and death itself, beginning with a consideration of what death means. In her influential book, *Death: The Final Stage of Growth*, Elisabeth Kübler-Ross has much to say about the meaning of death:

> *Death is the key to the door of life . . . All that you are and all that you've done and been is culminated in your death . . .*

> *We must allow death to provide a context for our lives, for in it lies the meaning of life and the key to our growth . . . death does not have to be a catastrophic, destructive thing; indeed, it can be viewed as one of the most constructive, positive, and creative elements of culture and life . . .*

> *If you can face and understand your ultimate death, perhaps you can learn to deal productively with each change that presents itself in your life. Through a willingness to risk the unknown, to venture forth into unfamiliar territory, you can undertake the search for your own self—the ultimate goal of growth . . .*

> *And through a lifetime of such commitment you can face your final end with peace and joy, knowing that you have lived your life well . . . death may be viewed as the curtain between the existence that we are conscious of and one*

that is hidden from us until we raise the curtain.

Exemplars of Dying Well

Cardinal Joseph Bernardin (1928-1996) was a "born again" priest, who spent the first part of his career as a worldly, self-indulgent church bureaucrat. In the early 1980s he made a momentous decision to commit to a holy life, which included giving away money, objects of art, and other possessions he felt were more materialistic than spiritual. In 1982 he was appointed Archbishop of Chicago, and six months later Pope John Paul appointed him as a cardinal. He was greatly respected within the Catholic community, and extending as well to non-Catholic religious communities locally, nationally, and worldwide.

The death alarm went off in 1994, when Cardinal Bernardin learned he had pancreatic cancer. Following surgery, he assumed he was on the road to recovery, but cancer cells had spread to his liver, which portended death. In his final three months of life, suffering from spinal stenosis and severe osteoporosis, he promised to live his dying openly and in continuing service to others, which included visits to comfort and counsel fellow terminal cancer patients at Loyola University's Cancer Center, now named after him. He confessed that there were lessons of faith yet to be learned and lessons of dying yet to be taught, and the result was that he learned to accept death as a friend.

In a letter responding to the *Newsweek* article, "The Art of Dying Well" (Woodward & McCormick), Judy Tomlonson of Warrensburg, Missouri wrote:

I read the article on Cardinal Bernardin with great interest. I, too, am dying, and may have at most one more year. I have ALS (Lou Gehrig's disease), so before I die I will be unable to speak, move, eat or breathe on my own.

I have discovered, however, that dying is all right. I can honestly say with the apostle Paul, "I have learned in whatever state I am therewith to be content." I have had great joy and rewards in my life, and if I didn't question my right to those, why should I question the opposite?

While, at the age of 57, I wouldn't choose to leave this world so soon, dying isn't what's frightening—it's the leaving I regret. I'll not see what my five grandchildren do with their lives or what will happen in the lives of my children. I'll not see the year 2000, or what amazing advances will be made in medicine and technology that may, hopefully, see us learn to live together with understanding and tolerance.

An admirable approach to dying is to continue working. As a writer, I appreciate author Don Hall's dedication to writing while battling his terminal cancer of the liver. In his book, *Life Work*, he discusses the value of work to ward off suffering, and the fear of death in stimulating work:

When I went to the hospital I brought work with me, and in the last two days before I went home I started writing again.

When I began to recover, still anxious about recurrence, I worked with manic prolixity [wordiness]—not well—and knew in my heart that I worked against death. What's more, I realized that I had always worked—the real thing, the absorbedness—in defiance of death . . .

If work is no antidote to death, no denial of it, death is a powerful stimulus to work. Get done what you can.

In a *New York Times* interview (Rosenblatt 1993), Lewis Thomas, physician and biologist, spoke from personal experience when he confided that dying felt like a general weakness, causing him to lose respect for his body [while gaining respect for his mind].

The good news is that many dying persons have time, energy, and opportunities to settle affairs, including completing projects, serving others, and healing personal relationships. Dr. Ira Byock, president of the Academy of Hospice Physicians, writes in his book, *Dying Well*, that good deaths can be understood and fostered, with the patient repairing strained relationships, and allowing time and space for transcendence and "letting go". Medical staff can assist by respecting patients' integrity, helping them live as fully as possible, including the reduction of pain.

The Final Countdown

In the days leading up to death, it's important that loved ones and close friends maintain communication with the dying person. Some suggestions from experts may prove helpful in most circumstances:

• Remain close at eye level, and don't be afraid to touch. Let persons talk and don't be afraid of silence.

• When dying persons say they going to die, don't contradict them. Allow for acceptance, anger, guilt, and fear, without trying to "fix" things. Just listen and empathize.

• Give them as much decision-making power as possible, as long as possible. Allow for talk about unfinished business, and offer to help with it.

• Encourage happy reminiscences, humor, and laughter.

• Never pass up an opportunity to express love or say goodbye. Don't fret if you don't get the chance. Just do your best.

The final symptoms associated with the final days of life are common knowledge, but bear mentioning again. According to information provided in the AARP magazine, *Modern Maturity* ("Start the Conversation." Sept/October 2000, pp. 51-58), there are five major characteristics:

• *Depression*, which should be treated with a combination of medications and psychotherapy.

• *Anorexia*, the unwillingness or inability to eat, has a protective effect, releasing endorphins that help contribute to a sense of wellbeing. Force-feeding can create discomfort and cause choking.

• *Dehydration*, the result of refusing drink is normal in the last days, another protective mechanism that releases helpful endorphins.

• *Drowsiness and deep sleep* is similar to a coma-like state. During such time the patient may be able to hear conversation, so all conversation should remain positive and encouraging.

• *Agitation and restlessness* (moaning and groaning) or "terminal delirium" occurs when the patient's level of consciousness is markedly decreased near to the point of death, and is usually not a sign of great pain.

When a person is severely injured or near death, peptide hormones (endorphins) are released by cells in the hypothalamus and pituitary gland, attaching themselves to the cells responsible for feeling pain. For the last time, the patient's pupils widen into still, black circles, the skin takes on a grayish pallor, and one by one, cells cease to function. Life flickers out, and the dying process ends.

The final determination of death is a point of controversy, which explains the vociferous debates among close kin and medical staffs regarding appropriate action to take when a dying person goes into a coma. The two opposing viewpoints:

• A person who is brain dead *is* dead—medically, legally, and philosophically.

• According to current medical practice, a patient whose entire brain is destroyed may be mortally wounded, but not yet dead.

In sum, when dying persons exist in vegetative states, family members and medical personnel may take opposing sides regarding the simple question of whether or not the patient should be considered dead. In such cases it's clear to me that any decision to "pull the plug" should be founded primarily on the patient's wishes, as predetermined in written and oral directives.

When self-directives are not available, however, I favor decisions made in accord with the position that it is the death of the brain (mind) that determines death, rather than ongoing primal body functions. This approach validates and substantiates the concept that one's mind (spirit) is of higher significance than one's physical body. Hence, we should rejoice in the comforting thought that the dying person is allowed to die peacefully, with a graceful transcendence of this earthly life. Isn't this what most people desire?

12

Managing Pain and Suffering

The truth that many people never understand, until it is too late, is that the more you try to avoid suffering the more you suffer because smaller and more insignificant things begin to torture you in proportion to your fear of being hurt. —Thomas Merton

Religious Beliefs about Pain and Suffering

Ninety percent of Americans have a religious outlook on life, which according to one writer (Law 2005) provides four explanations for God's role in our pain and suffering:

• *Free will.* As suggested in the Biblical accounting of Adam and Eve, God has given us free will, including the ability to make either good or bad choices. God has set everything in motion and abides by a non-interference mode of operating.

• *Character-building.* By causing or allowing pain and suffering, God helps us grow morally and spiritually, as suggested in the Biblical accounting of Job.

• *Good and evil.* God had to include suffering and pain to exist in order to balance out major qualities of goodness. For instance, the positive qualities of charity and sympathy require needy, suffering persons.

• *Mystery quotient.* God works in mysterious ways, so it's arrogant of us to suppose we can comprehend the mind of an infinite power and wise being. Suffering and pain are to be borne for our betterment, not to be fully understood.

Personally, I find none of these explanations very satisfactory in helping me cope with the pain and suffering I've experienced. Of course, I'm fortunate in that I've never suffered long-term, ongoing pain at the high levels commensurate with persons who experience chronic health problems. Hence, I really can't grasp the full extent of the chronic pain many people suffer, such as back or joint problems, upper respiratory-tract dysfunction (asthma, allergies, etc.), certain diseases such as shingles, or a host of equally disruptive ailments. Moreover, my pain and suffering have been experienced periodically, lasting anywhere from a few intense days to a few weeks or months, depending on the malady. As with most people, I've experienced bouts of headaches, gastrointestinal problems, various cold and flu bugs, and the typical childhood diseases. In addition, I've survived three surgeries (hernia, appendectomy, and prostatectomy), a broken foot, and off-and-on back problems, including a six-month stint with sciatica. I imagine my luck will run out some day, but so far, so good. In short, I simply can't imagine coping with the kind of persistent, debilitating pain that so many good people suffer.

Like everyone, my perspective on pain and suffering is based on everything I've learned and experienced over my entire life. I do believe in free will, but not in the concept of a supreme being who ordained free will specifically for humankind. As for pain and suffering, I think most people accept that any adversity can make one aware of what's truly important in life, and appreciative of life in general. There are many examples of long-suffering people who've learned to cope, and in the process developed stronger character and a more meaningful existence. Regarding good versus evil, most people readily acknowledge the existence of these opposing forces, although interpretations vary widely depending on an individual's peculiar life experiences, including the influences of nature and nurture.

It's a fact that some people are genetically predisposed to feel pain more acutely, and others develop chronic pain through prolonged conditions that are not ameliorated by medical treatment, including medications. According to the latest brain research, chronic painful conditions can cause brains to develop strong neural pathways that habituate and reinforce pain circuits, with the unfortunate effect of extending the pain indefinitely, as my father experienced with a long-term debilitating bout of shingles. Of course, like my father, some people apparently enjoy the sympathy and attention their maladies cause, in turn becoming hypochondriacs.

Speaking to the fourth explanation offered above, everyone acknowledges that life is full of mystery. Yet, in spite of any pain we may suffer, it behooves us to continue learning as much as possible about life's mysteries, as we seek a deeper understanding and a more meaningful existence. Ken Wilber addresses suffering from a spiritual position that stems from a metaphysical perspective (Wilber 2004, p. 73):

> *A person who is beginning to sense the suffering of life is, at the same time, beginning to awaken to deeper realities, truer realities. For suffering smashes to pieces the complacency of our normal fictions about reality, and forces us to become alive in a special sense—to see carefully, to feel deeply, to touch ourselves and our worlds in ways we have heretofore avoided. It has been said, and truly I think, that suffering is the first grace. In a special sense, suffering is almost a time of rejoicing, for it marks the birth of creative insight.*

In sum, I suppose we can say that the ability to accept one's condition—whatever it may be—as a fact of life, and not merely as a state imposed by a supernatural being, takes a great deal of faith in our ability to reason and learn from our experiences. I believe wisdom is the term that best suits the quality we all strive to achieve. Thus, the main challenge for each of us is to find an effective psycho-emotional strategy for dealing with pain and suffering, one that allows us to maintain our integrity, and to continue developing as psycho-emotional or spiritual beings, even though our physical bodies may be declining in vitality.

Pain, Treatment, and Healing

Regardless of the level of care we afford ourselves, pain is inevitable, particularly as we age. Pain, whether temporary, acute, or chronic, alerts us to mind-body harm, so regardless of how much we dread pain, it provides a beneficial mind-body warning response. The effects of pain can vary greatly among individuals, the result of several predispositions, such as genetic makeup, psycho-emotional constitution, physical conditioning, cultural conditioning, and life circumstances. Of course, our personal reaction to pain largely determines how well we are able to manage it.

One stirring example of an individual who suffered extreme mind-body stress and learned to cope effectively is Trisha Meili, also known as the "Central Park jogger", a 28-year-old investment banker who was savagely attacked, beaten, and gang raped in 1989. For 12 days she barely existed in a comatose state, with a dire prognosis. Though she eventually managed to snap out of the coma, she was extremely incapacitated, including not being able to walk, talk, or think clearly. But she did survive, and has even thrived throughout the long and painful healing process, making a steady and courageous comeback. She still suffers some long-term aftereffects, such as double vision when tired, minor balance problems, loss of the sense of smell, legs that fatigue faster, and some loss of mental acuity. But thanks to her positive, optimistic attitude, excellent medical care, ongoing physical activity, and youth, Meili is able to function well in her new career of motivational speaking and volunteering to talk about her healing process to medical and mental health organizations, patients, and anyone recovering from traumatic changes. Psychologists are increasingly using the term "positive psychology" in explaining how humans can develop crucial coping skills in the pursuit of happiness. Some guidelines for creating resilience to extremely stressful life events are a "can-do" optimism that includes goal setting, an ability to focus on what's happening in the present, a determination to face any issue head-on, a willingness to accept help from others, a spiritual awareness, and a sense of gratitude for one's good fortune.

Fortunately, I've never suffered the type of horrific trauma that Meili experienced, but I have endured various levels of pain on many occasions, including the normal toothaches, flu attacks, childhood diseases, and minor accidents that most people encounter. The most memorable pain events I associate with a scarlet fever episode in childhood, an appendicitis attack in 1980 (I vividly recall lying in a curled up position writhing in pain at first, then a subsequent three-week hospital confinement due to severe infection); prostate surgery in 2003 (lower abdominal pain); and most recently, chronic lower-back pain in 2004. The chronic back pain, which lasted only six months, with sciatic-like symptoms, has gradually proven manageable. Overall, this illness represents the longest continuous span of chronic off-on pain I've ever experienced. I'm very grateful that the generally low-grade pain now occurs only intermittently, striking sometimes completely unexpectedly, as when making a simple motion, like making up a bed. I generally manage to keep it under control by performing the special exercises recommended by my physical therapist, in addition to the series of other exercises mentioned in the previous chapter.

These personal ailments are mentioned as a catalyst for continuing to discuss various approaches, methods, and techniques for self-treatment and healing. Most people place primary responsibility for treatment and healing on medical professionals, together with reliance on high doses of medication, which can lead to other health problems. Who hasn't heard of senior citizens having been overmedicated by their trusted, well-meaning doctors? My father-in-law, age 93, had been taking several medications for heart-related problems, but when a new doctor ordered him to stop taking several pills, he started feeling better within a week and the symptoms he had been experiencing disappeared. Upon the recommendation of a new doctor, my mother-in-law also stopped taking various pills and some of her symptoms disappeared. Such stories are more common than we would like to think.

Although I've always sought medical consultation and treatment whenever needed, in addition to annual physical exams, I long ago accepted responsibility for working with medical professionals in managing my health and healing processes. Although I depend on professionals for guidance, I figure it's up to me to be an informed patient, beginning with researching any ailment and all recommended exercises, medications, and other treatments prescribed by medical practitioners, and then faithfully executing their orders or advice. Should physical conditions persist, I believe it's appropriate to seek alternative treatments, including non-traditional alternative therapies and medications. In general, I'm open to considering methods or treatments that have proven successful through testing, such as chiropractic care, hypnotherapy, acupuncture, and several kinds of massage. Of course, the effectiveness of treatment is largely due to the expertise of the practitioner, whether he or she is a medical doctor, a chiropractor, an acupuncturist, or a massage therapist.

312 / Managing Pain and Suffering

My self-treatment philosophy is largely attributable to having been a university voice teacher for over four decades, in the process learning some important lessons. Since a voice teacher's one-on-one time with students is usually limited, from a half hour to an hour weekly, a teacher can only diagnose, prescribe, encourage, and cajole students to do whatever it takes to master the myriad complex skills associated with high-level singing. Students shoulder the primary responsibility for teaching themselves during the remaining six to twelve hours of weekly study time needed to fulfill all academic expectations and requirements. Understandably, almost without exception the students who accept responsibility as "collaborators in learning" are the ones who excel in making progress. This experience has taught me that a similar approach can be used in managing personal healthcare and healing processes.

This line of reasoning leads to my belief and commitment to the first line of defense in health care: taking proactive preventive measures. As mentioned previously, most of my adult years I've maintained a proactive approach to preventive health maintenance, by avoiding harmful habits (smoking, drugs, etc.), exercising regularly, and ingesting nutritious foods and drink. Though I've had my share of illnesses, I believe my ability to heal and recover within a reasonable time span has been hastened by my general physical conditioning and psycho-emotional attitude.

When undergoing surgeries in 1980 and 2004, I was in overall good physical conditioning, and was mostly mentally prepared for any eventualities, including negative prognoses. For three days during my three-week hospital stay for complications from appendicitis, the tentative diagnosis was pancreatic cancer. In 2003, when I learned I had the beginnings of prostate cancer, I endured another close call with surgery that proved successful, though I must continue having PSA tests every six months until fall 2008, and annually thereafter. Finally, the chronic back pain that suddenly appeared and gradually worsened in 2004 led to a number of visits to medical specialists and several medical exams, including an MRI, another bone scan, and specific blood and urine tests, ostensibly to determine if the "Big C" was present, the result of my prostate cancer. So, my psycho-emotional state has at least been put to a good test, providing my wife and me a few weeks contemplating the potential of my having a serious illness and an early demise—at least earlier than the projected life span for a person of my age and physical condition.

In developing a balanced approach to life and integrating the mind and body, I am committed to maintaining good health through regular physical exercise, balanced nutrition, and adequate rest and recreation, in addition to addressing psycho-emotional or spiritual concerns. Though some healing strategies may appear far out, as well-intentioned New Age quests, many have proven valid over great time spans. Eastern therapeutic strategies— yoga, Tai Chi, Qigong, acupuncture, imaging techniques, and various types of meditation and prayer—have proven effective in helping people treat themselves. The use of scientific measures to test the validity of all holistic therapies may not always be possible, although brain scans do show, for instance, that meditation and prayer alter brain activity in specific areas, and yoga has been proven to help reduce heart rate and induce greater powers of concentration.

Strategies for Managing Pain

On a practical level, suffering is usually the result of physical pain, and learning how to manage it is essential to one's well being. In addition to pursuing mind-body strategies such as various forms of meditation, physical exercise (yoga, Tai Chi, etc.), and perhaps hypnosis, there are numerous painkilling medications, most of which are tinged with controversy of some sort. The news reports about the safety and effectiveness of various types of drugs can be very confusing, as findings vary from study to study. This isn't the time or place to discuss the pros and cons of specific drugs, but suffice it to say one should exercise extreme caution when taking any medication, by learning as much about it as possible, including how it may interact with other drugs one may be ingesting.

Briefly, the major types of pain drugs are: topical therapies (capsaicin cream); acetaminophen (Tylenol); NSAIDS (Aspirin, Ibuprofen, Naxoproxen); nonacetylatd salicylates (subclass of NSAIDS); cox-2 inhibitors (Vioxx, Bextra); and opioids (codeine). With the exception of topical therapies, which are intended for localized pain, all others have their pro/con characteristics. In sum, exercise caution when using any of these painkillers, keeping their use to a minimum, whenever possible.

Most people are not interested in spending a lot of time dwelling on the subject of pain and suffering, which is an inevitable by-product of getting old. Even more unsettling is the prospect of long-term suffering that typically precedes life's final curtain. With more people living into their 80s and even 90s, it's estimated that approximately 40 percent of the population are spending their final years in severely debilitated states, suffering from dementia or Alzheimer's disease, and dependent on caregivers. Bettye and I have witnessed the deteriorating mind-body effects of aging and illness on elders, including our parents, which in two cases involved considerable suffering, with home confinement and several weeks of hospitalization.

Prior to moving into a nursing home for her final year, my mother spent several weeks confined in a hospital in treatment for complications associated with spreading cancer. My father, who suffered from a severe case of debilitating shingles for more than 15 years, was progressively confined at home. Eventually, in the final life-stage that typifies what happens with many elderly Americans, he spent several weeks in a hospital suffering from various mind-body complications. As soon as he was relatively stabilized, he was moved into a nursing home, where he died within a few weeks.

These parental experiences have taught us that, as relatively young seniors, we must prepare for the inevitable accumulation of ailments that accompany aging in life's final stages. Hence, we are determined to do all we can to assure our last years will be as qualitatively tolerable as possible, and that our eventual deaths will occur as humanely as possible.

Rev. James Gertmenian, in a sermon titled "Innocence: Found and Lost" at Plymouth Congregational Church in Minneapolis, set forth a particular pet peeve regarding a "religious nostrum" that he considers more protective than perceptive: *"God never gives us any more to deal with than we have strength* [to manage]". His explanation:

> *Put aside for a moment the implausible notion that God is up there somewhere handing out good experiences and bad ones, treasures and troubles. Isn't it a fact of our experience that sometimes people are dealt an unplayable hand? That sometimes people do receive burdens that are more than they can carry? That sometimes we buckle under the weight of what the world gives us? The redeeming truth here is not that we cannot be broken, but that beyond the breaking—beyond even death— there is healing, and new life. Not that we were given burdens that we cannot bear . . . but that even when we are incapable of bearing whatever weight it is, we are still valued, still loved.*

Most people who live to old age have had close calls with intense suffering, encouraging them to think about death in a new light. Thanks to good fortune, a healthy lifestyle, and the high level of modern medical care, many people are alive who would surely have died in earlier eras. I've previously alluded to some of my ailments, but the one that "put the love (not fear) of God into my heart" was in 1980 when hospitalized for three weeks with an unknown illness that turned out to be a ruptured appendix. For three days the tentative diagnosis was pancreatic cancer, so when my team of doctors finally diagnosed appendicitis, a far less life-threatening illness than deadly pancreatic cancer, we all rejoiced. The second big scare was a diagnosis of prostate cancer in 2003, following a routine PSA test. Even though the cancer was small, and the surgery deemed very successful, with checkups every six months for the past five years, the threat of a recurrence has always been present. And, though a zero PSA reading has held firm for the five-year "watch period", there's no guarantee of cancer not returning. Indeed, when I suffered sciatica pains in 2005, one doctor showed some concern that cancer might have spread to my lower back in my spine's lumbar region, based on some fuzzy MRI readings. Luckily, that concern proved to be a false alarm.

So, aside from the therapeutic value gained from writing about my illnesses, what I wish to emphasize is that I've had three notable periods in my adult life when the prospect of death has been uncomfortably close. Actually, I don't suppose my situation is all that unique for a person of my age, as most people reaching senior status have encountered various maladies, including serious injuries and diseases that heighten one's awareness of aging and death. So far, I'm pleased with my ability to deal with potentially life-threatening physical conditions in a mature manner, without panicking and becoming angry, bitter, and depressed. I think the typical response, "Why me?" is irrelevant, as no one has any special guarantee of being spared serious health problems. Instead, the response "Why not me?" seems to makes more sense, as it expresses a realization that we are all vulnerable to life's misfortunes. I try to maintain this objective perspective, accepting the fact that I'm not destined to receive any special favors in the universal scheme of things, and must be ready to handle whatever happens with as much grace and dignity as possible.

I am very grateful for my long life to date, with plenty of time to accomplish many worthwhile goals. Though I have many more projects I wish to accomplish, I feel I can accept the full life I've enjoyed up to this point, and, given certain humane conditions, I believe I can accept death graciously. Most importantly, I hope I never develop a negative, groveling attitude and offensive behavior in dealing with health issues. For now, I can see no advantages to complaining or obsessing about one's health, or resorting to imploring God to bestow special favors. But I do believe that praying for strength of character in facing and dealing with suffering and pain can be a worthwhile strategy.

One thing for certain: experiencing a close wake-up call with a potential terminal illness, accident, or other ordeal, can exert a powerful influence in changing one's attitude toward life. Even older persons who have never had a life-threatening experience have probably known someone who came to a greater appreciation of life after surviving a major ordeal. I can think of one example of a fictitious character that illustrates how humans are capable of coping with tragedy. Hannah, a character in author Tami Hoag's novel, *Guilty as Sin*, learned what it means to survive a traumatic ordeal. Her son had been kidnapped, and when he was eventually returned safely, she had a renewed outlook on life (Hoag 1994, p. 305).

> *The ordeal had pared away the unnecessary in her, cut away the crap of social ceremony, leaving only the honest, the essential. Like many people who had gone through harrowing experiences, Hannah had seen how much of life is just bullshit, just meaningless ritual made important to give humankind some pretense of being*

better than the rest of the animals on the planet.

In a similar mood, but from a unique perspective, Jill Conner Browne expresses some thoughts on the "near-life" experience in her popular book, *God Save the Sweet Potato Queens* (Browne 2001, p. 242).

We all die, some sooner rather than later. We are just a breath away from it, all the time . . . Don't fear being near-death — but rather fear, dread, loathe, and do all you can to avoid near-life experiences. Nobody goes to the grave or the nursing home wringing their hands and gnashing their teeth and just wishing they'd served on a few more committees, worked a few more hours. Too often we are waiting until we (and then later, our children) finish school, waiting until the mortgage is paid off, waiting until we lose weight, waiting until we retire. We are always, as we say in the South, just "fixing to." After this thing or that one happens, then we will travel, write, play, rest, visit friends, then we will live. And, lo and behold, before any of that stuff can happen, it is over, and we never got around to living . . . No more near-life experiences, please. Whatever it is you are going to do someday, well, someday is here. Have at it. I am here to tell you, it is way better to live your dream than it is to dream it.

Suffering, and particularly the fear of dying, has always played a significant role in developing human character, essentially by providing ample opportunity for the sufferer to find an effective way of dealing with his or her pain and eventual mortality. To my mind, no one exemplified courage in the face of extreme adversity better than Viktor E. Frankl, who survived the inhumane conditions of a Nazi concentration camp during World War II. In his book, *Death Camp to Existentialism,* he provided a powerful message (Frankl 1946, 2006).

Man has both potentialities within himself; which one is actualized depends on decisions but not on conditions . . . The way in which a man accepts his fate and all the suffering it entails, the way in which he takes up his cross, gives him ample opportunity—even under the most difficult circumstances—to add a deeper meaning to his life. It may remain brave, dignified and unselfish . . . His unique opportunity lies in the way in which he bears his burden.

Frankl's solution is to learn how to make the most of one's situation, whatever it may be, by dealing with it in a positive manner. The fear of suffering, especially in the realization it could end in death, is common to most humans. As Simone de Beauvoir wrote in her book, *The Prime of Life* (1963): "A few more years more or less matters little when set against the freedom and peace of mind one achieves the moment one stops running away from death".

The best way to cope with suffering and death is by seeking as much knowledge as possible to gain a proper, realistic perspective and a deeper understanding. At the same time, we need to regret-proof our lives, by giving attention to unfinished personal concerns, such as completing special projects, nourishing and healing human relationships, and developing a philosophical and psycho-emotional outlook about life, aging, suffering, and dying. Also, we need to make all necessary physical preparations far in advance, including preparing and filing a living will, drawing up an estate will or living trust, organizing all financial papers, throwing or giving away unessential material possessions, and arranging appropriate living accommodations.

We've tried to tend to such matters, and most major items listed above are covered, including preparation and filing of a living will. Of all documents associated with suffering and death, this one tends to be overlooked by most people. The chances of suffering from a debilitating illness or accident increase significantly in the last three decades of life, so most experts concur with writing a living will as soon as possible. Most guidelines suggest making the living will explicit by spelling out exactly what care you want at the end of life, as well as what medical services you want withheld. One copy should be filed at home, with other copies distributed to your doctor, your local hospital or health care organization, and your adult children. An advocate should be chosen, usually a designated family member, friend, or attorney to insist that your wishes be honored, should a hospital or doctor act reluctantly. Living Will Registry (uslivingwillregistry.com) offers a free registration of living wills and even sends a copy to a hospital upon request.

Based on everything learned thus far, perhaps the secret to aging well is no secret at all. We can encapsulate all information using this simple guideline:

Do everything possible to achieve and maintain mind-body vitality, by remaining physically active, mentally curious, and emotionally balanced. A positive mindset and proactive life strategy include accepting one's mortality, living fully in the present, and adopting an overall attitude of gratitude for life's many blessings.

13

Confronting Death

I intend to live forever—so far, so good.—*Steven Wright*

Public Rituals

The primary character of any death is the feeling of loss and grieving experienced by survivors. Yet, in any death, particularly when the deceased person has lived a full and happy life, tied up all loose ends in advance, and died well, the spirit of the occasion can be more like a celebration, a gathering of loved ones, friends, and others to pay tribute and honor to one whose life touched them all in various ways. Though survivors need private time to sort out their feelings and think about the occasion, sometimes they also need to be surrounded by supportive persons.

Friends and relatives close to the family typically observe the etiquette of helping out in various ways: notifying significant persons; procuring, preparing, and serving food at home, at the visitation, and following the burial/memorial service; serving on clean-up crews; and transporting people. Meanwhile, the bereaved should be sure to notify the public (paid newspaper announcement), encourage as many persons as possible to participate in the services, pay all professional persons involved, and acknowledge all kind services in good time.

Cultural and religious groups vary considerably in how they acknowledge and treat death, though most follow accepted rituals and procedures. Generally speaking, in the U.S., professionals now manage details associated with most deaths, while loved ones have little if any contact with the deceased person's body. In contrast, some socio-cultural groups observe bedside formal rituals, such as bathing and dressing the corpse, and leaving a watchful guard or guards to protect it, a former practice that might have been the beginning of the wake service, which is now held in mortuaries. There is a movement afoot to encourage families to become more involved in the entire death process, from preparing the body to officiating at the funeral or memorial service, and disposal of the corpse.

A funeral or memorial service is a ritual that can help focus our emotions and bring meaning to the death experience. Such public rituals link us both to the past and to the future, giving mourners the opportunity and permission to express feelings of sadness and loss, and stimulating mourners to begin talking about the deceased, one of the first steps in acknowledging his or her death. Accepting the reality usually means viewing the body in an open-casket visitation period, which usually takes place in a home, a church, or a funeral home.

When a person is ill for weeks or months prior to death, there is time for preparations to be made, and survivors might be more involved in the overall death experience. If the death comes unexpectedly, professional assistance will more likely be needed. In any case, family members should have as much input into the arrangements as possible, especially with selecting the service contents and the participants. The more involvement on the family's part, the more therapeutic will be the experience.

Survivors can be spared decision-making when the deceased has previously provided specific requests for a funeral or memorial service. Suggested plans might include the location (indoors or outdoors, church or public building), type of public rituals (open-casket visitation, funeral or memorial service), content of the service (music selections, officiators, speakers, etc.), and disposal of body (burial or cremation). The more that can be written down and discussed before one becomes incapacitated, the better. And it needn't be too specific, just some basic guidelines, such as a suggested list of favored readings and music, as well as officiators (pastors, friends, relatives). I particularly appreciate hearing family members and close friends offer brief testimonials or eulogies about the deceased.

I've been thinking about what type of rituals and procedures I would like to have when the time comes, and to date I've decided on the following:

- *Upon death.* Hopefully, I will die at home or in a hospice, but even if it's in a hospital, the statistical probability, I would like for my family to gather around to provide mutual support and to express any final thoughts or feelings. They even have my permission to take photos as a remembrance (unless my condition is too painful to view), and to show to others who need to witness the reality of my death. Other than this public viewing, none other will be possible, as I've designated that my body be donated to the University of Minnesota Medical School for the purpose of training doctors.

- *Memorial Service.* I'm not sure where I want the service to be held, but I've narrowed it down to Plymouth Congregational Church in Minneapolis, or if the weather is pleasant, at some beautiful and quiet outdoor location, perhaps a park that's familiar to my family. The service will consist of selections made from a list of readings and music I'll provide, as of yet to be determined, though I've made a start in collecting material. Participants may include family, friends, colleagues, and former students. I want the event to be a joyful and meaningful celebration, filled with high-quality texts and music, and involving audience participation (singing, group recitation). It's of special note that some of the most creatively inspired literature, music, and art are expressions about death, so I hope to research such material in coming years. Also, I appreciate the custom of having a few (3-4) close friends and family members speak briefly about my personal characteristics, notable accomplishments, and so on (with gentility, please).

• *Reception.* Following the memorial service, it would be appropriate to have a reception, including an informal buffet meal for attendees. Perhaps, rather than in the memorial service, this would be the best time to present some brief, informal talks of a humorous nature, and to share personal memories. I think it would also be nice to have an exhibit area featuring significant photos representative of all periods of my life, including loved ones (especially Bettye and immediate family) and friends. A PowerPoint slide presentation would be ideal, and I hope to get started on such a project in the next year or so. Since music is such a large part of my life, it might be appropriate to play some of my vocal performances, including both classical and pop. I'd also like to have my creative projects featured, perhaps in photo formats, which should be easier to display.

• *Corpse Disposal.* Since my body will be used for medical studies, the university medical school will dispose of it through cremation, returning the ashes to the family for safekeeping or further disposal. Of course, there's the possibility that the university will not accept my body for various reasons, including the possibility of having too many cadavers, or because of contagious disease (I certainly hope not). In any case, my body will be cremated, and the ashes dispersed in a natural location, perhaps in our Silver Lake Village Salo Park, or in nearby Silverwood Park. My ashes can be mixed with dirt in planting a long-living, hearty tree, preferably in an open area.

Speaking of corpse disposal, a new option is entering the scene that may appear gruesome upon first learning about it, but may well become a viable future alternative. The new highly efficient disposal method is called *alkaline hydrolysis*, a process that involves placing a corpse into a pressurized, high-heated steel container filled with a caustic chemical lye. After the corpse is dissolved, the brown sterilized remains can be poured down the drain and safely disposed of in public sewage system, and any skeleton remains can be easily pulverized into dust and treated similarly to cremated body ashes. Medical researchers are already using this method successfully, and the prognosis for its use by the public is inevitable, as it makes good sense, both economically and environmentally.

As for burial, the main objection I have is of a dual nature, in both spiritual and ecological terms. Inordinate attention given to preserving the physical body seems to contradict any professed religious beliefs about spiritual reality. In other words, is a person's only identity with his or her body, or does a spiritual self exist separately—at least in the minds and hearts of those still alive? Understandably, most survivors need some concrete notion of the dead to hold fast in their memories, but when a body is buried, it's out of a loved one's sight, if not out of his or her memory.

Bettye and I have chosen to be cremated because it seems a rational option, but it's possible that we might opt for the newer alkaline hydrolysis disposal method. In comparison to burial, both methods are simpler, more aesthetic, cheaper, and better for the environment. We've mulled over the prospect of being pumped full of embalming fluid, gussied up, placed in a confined, non-recyclable container, and buried under six feet of earth, only to wither away and take up valuable ground space, and we've concluded that burial is not for us. "Ashes to ashes and dust to dust" is an ecological solution, so we prefer that our ashes be put to good use in fertilizing newly planted, slow-growing trees, perhaps twin oaks. Instead of visiting a gravesite head-stone in a decrepit cemetery, our loved ones may someday pay homage to two donated trees planted in a designated natural open area. It's comforting to envision loved ones visiting the site to view our side-by-side trees. It might even be possible to enjoy a family picnic under its shady branches, or perhaps individuals might find it a suitable spot for solitude and refection, with awareness that we are there, too.

Expenses and Estate Concerns

The types of expenses associated with death are worthy of consideration. Lisa Carlson was dealing with her husband's death and body disposal in 1981. Faced with expenses she couldn't afford, she took matters into her own hands. Instead of paying the $700 cremation fee quoted by a prominent funeral home director, she shopped around until she found a company within commuting distance that would do it for $85, and the hands-on experience of handling the disposal was a therapeutic experience. As a result of her experience, she founded the nonprofit Funeral and Memorial Societies Association (FAMSA) and its sister organization, the Funeral Consumers Alliance (www. funerals.org/), operating from her home in Hinesburg, Vermont. Although there are reputable funeral services, she believes the 14 billion U.S. funeral industry is rife with shoddy practices, greed, and insensitivity, not to mention the latest scandal: harvesting of body organs. In her book, *Caring for the Dead: Your Final Act of Love* (1998), she offers consumers advice (Baker 1999).

In recent years, a more novel approach to corpse disposal has gained a small but enthusiastic amount of public attention. Ever since the 1950s, a certain technology has been capable of exposing matter to intense pressure and temperatures up to 3,000 degrees to create beautiful gems from various materials, including body ashes.

Lifegem of Elkgrove Village, Illinois (www.lifegem.com) has created over 500 gems for people around the country and world. They range from 0.2 carat to 1 carat and cost from $2,500 to $14,000. Eighty percent of the raw material used is derived from humans, the rest from pets, including horses. All of the remains aren't used, only a relatively small amount. As expected, people's reactions vary widely, with some excited over the prospect of knowing their loved one is safely incased in a gem that can be worn, and others completely repulsed by the idea. I don't particularly find the idea attractive, though I'm not adverse to the practice, as long as it makes the user happy.

Ideally, aging persons will voluntarily aid in the process of downsizing and getting rid of unnecessary items as they reach their golden years, especially if they are experiencing looming health issues. In their last two decades our aging parents began giving certain prized items, memorabilia, and what they considered "excess money" to family members. However, my parents, who lived in the same house for 50 years, and rarely threw anything away, left a considerable legacy of minutia that had to be disposed of following their deaths (see earlier discussion regarding hoarding in chapter 9). My forbearing sister, Kay, spent numerous hours going through disorganized boxes, drawers, and closets over a period of two years before most of the accumulated items were disposed of properly. In learning from this experience, we plan to leave our family members a minimum of unnecessary possessions, which if they can't use, will be passed on to others, including certain charities. If we do our job well, there should be little need for them to toss stuff in the garbage.

Regarding memorabilia, we plan to review all family photos, sound recordings (reel-to-reel, cassette, LPs) of special performances, and videotapes (formerly 35mm film), convert some items to digital formats, and organize others into albums or collections that can be easily referenced. We know there are many photos and tapes that can be tossed, while desirable ones can be converted to reduced formats for storage. A helpful book for such situations is *Moving On: A Practical Guide to Downsizing the Family Home*, by Linda Hetzer and Janet Hulstrand. The authors recommend that parents make a list of all special items, and make comments about who should receive them.

Religion, God, and Death

It's impossible to discuss death intelligently and thoroughly without touching upon religion, and, in particular, God's role in the scheme of things. Each of the major world religions—as well as many diverse branches, minor religions and sects—holds a formulated set of beliefs about death and a deity's role in it, with supporting rationalized dogma founded primarily on faith. As I've explained throughout this book, the primary source of my faith rests in the human capacity to solve problems rationally, based largely on using good intuitive sense and a healthy dose of skepticism in examining all aspects of any issue.

When considering any spiritual topic, we must acknowledge that subjectivity is involved, and that any interpretation is obviously influenced by one's socio-cultural and religious background, in addition to educational level and life experiences. In contrast, science is primarily concerned with the material world, things that can be observed, measured and tested empirically. While it would be neat to combine the two into a single package in studying death, there are always some questions that cannot be answered adequately, and perhaps the most intriguing query of all is why suffering and death are integral aspects of life. In short, I think that the prevailing popular belief in an omnipotent God— an anthropomorphic being who decides when, where, why and how *who* lives, suffers, or dies—is a shallow, misguided concept. For me, the simple fact is that—if such a being actually exists—He/She/It doesn't make life-or-death pronouncements or interventions of any sort. I realize this stance is in opposition to most faith-based interpretations of sacred scriptures, but it's my well-educated, sincere opinion. Thankfully, I'm in good company, as a relatively small but growing and influential population of progressive religious persons share similar views.

One branch of Christianity, the Dutch Reformed Church, has dealt with the age-old question of divine involvement in unexplained human suffering by making an official statement: "The natural order of things is not necessarily to be equated with the will of God". According to scientist and author Stephen Jay Gould, the Dutch Reformed approach makes eminent sense, as it accords respect to the scientific investigation of the material world, while recognizing the peculiar spiritual domain of religion in dealing with entities unseen and immeasurable, such as values and morality. Gould would say that science and religion are contrasting *magisterium* (realms, domains), and should not intrude upon one another's territory, but rather tend to their own peculiar time-proven issues. Gould gladly emphasizes that the leaders representing all the world religions and denominations concur with his viewpoint. Unfortunately, a large minority of fundamentalists, particularly radical adherents of Islam and Christianity, are heaven-bent (pun intended) on subordinating science to religion, and it doesn't seem to matter that such a drastic move is in opposition to the time-honored democratic separation of church and state. It's hard to imagine any progressive society that places religious controls on science, which occurs in some Muslim countries.

To present a non-religious or secular viewpoint of death, we turn to a humanist's perspective:

We [humanists] *respect the right of joyful irreverence toward dying as a human response to the old and supernatural dreads. Religion's vain and puerile attempt to deny death and provide a supernatural solution to a natural problem must be not only criticized, but [also] made an object of humor seasoned with pungent sympathies for its many unwary victims. Religion's clichés of death seem to us simplistic, cold, horrific, and pompous. Against these pretences we encourage jocularity. We accept and mourn the grim ironies and ghastly pains of dying, and, yes, the sting and victory of death. We will that religion's death-dread die, and that eupraxophic exuberance endure and prevail.*

Another humanist, Jennifer M. Hect, says that we must "remember death" in order to be happy, that death really is the end: "I think this world is extraordinary, and I also think it's a pain in the ass. I'm happy to be here, but I'm OK with not being here forever." (Grothe 2007)

Perspectives of Life After Death

There appear to be four perspectives of life after death:

- *Paradise or Hell.* Judaism, Christianity, and Islam promote the reward-punishment concept in ascertaining the quality of a person's life on earth, with the reward of a joyful paradise promised to the righteous, or, in case of the wicked, an endless hell of punishment. Of all the beliefs I've grown up with, this is the hardest to accept, mostly because of its immature win-lose stance. The idea of spending eternity in a perfect world, presumably populated with untold millions of transcendent beings (everyone who has ever lived), doesn't sound very appealing. Talk about overpopulation! Though we may appreciate the possibility of living forever with most of the people we've known, I doubt that any of us would be enthusiastic about maintaining relationships with *everyone* we've ever known. Those who believe themselves to be "saved"—according to the heaven-and-hell scenario—have reason to be thankful that the most despicable sinners will not join them in paradise. As for hell, most of us have experienced aspects of a hellish existence during our Earthly sojourn, and received ample punishment for our transgressions.

• *Reincarnation.* The belief that a person lives and dies many times, and after each death is reborn into another body, is a belief of Hinduism and Buddhism. While this may be true, I have a hard time understanding and accepting this form of predeterminism. For one thing, who wants to continue an endless cycle of birth and death, reappearing in different animate forms—one lifetime as an insect, another life as an animal, etc.? On the other hand, I *can* accept the fact that the same atoms making up my body—and perhaps even my spirit—do indeed transform throughout time, from stars to dust to various forms of life. Hence, I can accept a broader metaphorical interpretation of the reincarnation concept, but the orthodox perspective is beyond my comprehension, at least at present.

• *The End, Period.* Humanists and atheists firmly believe there is no life after death, a view they base on reason and science. While I understand and appreciate this rational approach, I find it difficult to accept an outright denial of a spiritual reality, or other potential dimensions currently unknown to us. As far as scientific theories are concerned, the theory of existing parallel universes holds promise, and it's likely that someday the spiritual dimensions humans have historically intuited might be revealed (see discussion that follows a bit later).

• *Another Possibility.* One more perspective worth pondering stems from Zen Buddhism and Hinduism.

Buddhist scriptures view suffering as an intrinsic aspect of biological existence, its deepest cause being the force responsible for the life process. The goal of the spiritual path is to extinguish the fire of life and transcend the wheel of death and rebirth. Hinduism considers death as an awakening from a world of illusion (*maya*), an opportunity for the individual self (*jiva*) to realize and experience its divine nature (*Atman-Brahman*).

The meditative traditions of Buddhism and Hinduism are based on spiritual transcendence that occurs through intense meditation, and leads to a union with what has been called Atman-Brahman, Eternal Consciousness, Universal Spirit, Emptiness, or God. I realize this viewpoint might resemble certain aspects of New Age thinking, but it seems worth exploring, and later on we will.

Near-Death Experiences

Ganga Stone criticizes the mistaken belief that *who* we are is concentrated in our physical bodies, which she says is a belief formed by fear, grief, and pain (suffering). She believes that the most prevalent and probing questions concerning life after death can be found in examining near-death experiences (NDE), as reported numerous times by those who have died temporarily and are later restored to life. One prominent pioneer in this field we met in the previous chapter: Dr. Elisabeth Kübler-Ross, a physician who interviewed numerous survivors of near-death experiences, including blind persons, who were able to describe minute details of their resuscitations. A Gallup poll in the early 1990s revealed that over eight million Americans had reported undergoing an NDE experience. Some of the reports by NDE survivors include such elements as a general sense of wellbeing, body separation, entering the darkness through a tunnel, seeing the light, and entering the light. Some people report reviewing their lives, encountering a "presence", meeting loved ones, and, finally, making the decision to return.

Another researcher who investigated near-death and post-death experiences is Janis Amatuzio, M.D., a forensic pathologist and founder of Midwest Forensic Pathology in Minneapolis. Known as the compassionate coroner, Dr. Amatuzio has been exposed to ongoing experiences of death, including follow-ups with loved ones. In her book, *Forever Ours* (2002), she relates several poignant stories of peoples' deaths, and offers some personal experiences that have helped convince her that death is not such a terrible experience, nor that it is necessarily the end of a person. One of the inspiring quotes listed in her book struck me as one that needed including here:

> *Won't you let me know*
> *that death is eternal*
> *and love is immortal*
> *and death is only a horizon . . .*
> *and a horizon is nothing*
> *save the limit of our sight.*
> —Rossiter Worthington Raymond

Offering a scientific explanation for the near-death experience phenomenon, astronomer and cosmologist Carl Sagan (1934-1996) defined the NDE tunnel experience of death as a surviving memory from the birthing process. He suggested that the struggle of moving through the birth canal reaches a climax when we emerge into a bright and colorful world filled with people who are happy to see us. In a similar vein, Sherwin Nuland explains the so-called Lazarus Syndrome (returned to life from the dead) as the result of a few million years of biological evolution, which in effect provides a life-preserving function for our species. The production of endorphins or other biochemical agents may instigate such experiences. He also suspects other causes may be involved, including: the psychological defense mechanism known as depersonalization; the hallucinatory effect of terror; seizures originating in the temporal lobes of the brain; or insufficient cerebral oxygenation. In his words (Nuland, 1995, p. 138):

> *As a confirmed skeptic, I am bound by the conviction that we must not only question all things, but [also] be willing to believe that all things are possible. But while the true skeptic can exist happily in a permanent state of agnosticism, some of us have a wish to be convinced. Something within my rational soul does rebel at the invoking of parapsychology, but certainly not of God. Nothing would please me more than proof of His [Her, Its] existence, and of a blissful afterlife, too. Unfortunately, I see no evidence for it in the death experience.*

Sagan may not have been privy to the latest studies when he stated his skepticism. An article in *Discover* magazine (July 2005) titled "Extreme States" provides a brief overview of near-death and out-of-body experiences. Through brain research, scientists are beginning to gain more understanding about near-death and out-of-body experiences, the types of astral projections reported by religious mystics in all five of the world's major religions, and in every country for centuries.

Similar reports have also been made by motorcyclists, who recall floating above their bikes, and pilots, who find themselves outside their aircraft struggling to get back inside. However, most out-of-body experiences (defined as perceptual shifts in consciousness) actually occur in normal life, as described previously, when people who have died have been resuscitated. The reports are very similar, with descriptions of entering a dark tunnel, heading into light, and feeling an all-encompassing sense of welcome, love, and peace. Along the way friends, loved ones, and religious figures are present to assure and comfort them. Some people experience a life review, accompanied by having to make a decision to go or not to go. In 1990 a Gallup poll of American adults revealed that approximately 30 million Americans (almost 12 percent) have claimed some sort of near-death experience.

More recently, Jill Bolte Taylor, a well-known neuroanatomist, had an ethereal experience that no other brain scientist has had: a massive stroke caused by a blood clot in the left side of her brain. As the attack occurred, she sensed her brain functions slipping away one by one—speech, movement, and comprehension—and all the while she was analyzing and remembering every moment. Hers is a compelling story of recovery and awareness, and how our brains define us and connect us to the world and to one another. She relates her experience eloquently and passionately in a videotaped lecture that is available on the TED TALKS website (http://www.ted.com/talks/view/id/229). I highly recommend checking out this 18-minute video, in conjunction with its accompanying transcript. The reason for mentioning Taylor's loss of left-brain function is the similarity of symptoms associated with other paranormal experiences, such as near-death. Although some of the evidence supporting such experiences remains questionable, leading brain experts are convinced there is sufficient evidence to warrant serious ongoing scientific consideration of this phenomenon.

Biological clues as to what might possibly cause out-of-body states turned up unexpectedly in the late 1970s, when the Navy and Air Force introduced a new generation of aircraft that exerted tremendous G-forces, resulting in too much blood draining from pilot's brains and causing them to black out. This phenomenon is known as G-LOC, or G-force-induced loss of consciousness. Working over a 16-year period with a massive centrifuge at the Naval Air

Warfare Center in Warminster, Pennsylvania, scientists tested more than 500 pilots using high G-forces. The tests revealed that G-LOC could be induced in 5.67 seconds, with average blackouts lasting 12 to 24 seconds. Of special note, 40 pilots experienced out-of-body experiences while unconscious. In fact, the longer pilots were blacked out, the more likely they were to have out-of-body experiences. Physiologically, this process involves loss of vision prior to blackout, in conjunction with the occipital lobe's loss of function due to compressed blood flow. The transition to blindness conforms to the tunnel vision that usually occurs in blackouts, the transition to unconsciousness resembles floating peacefully within a dark tunnel, and the feeling of peace and serenity experienced by pilots upon gaining consciousness is consistent with reported near-death experiences. In sum, these phenomena may be thought of as normal physical processes occurring during special circumstances. For example, compression of the optic nerve could cause tunnel vision; neurochemicals such as serotonin, endorphins, and enkephalins could explain euphoria states; and psychotropics, such as LSD and mescaline, could explain hallucinations.

In the 1980s, Melvin Morse, a researcher of brain cancer in children, began studying near-death and out-of-body experiences reported by children who had died and were resuscitated. In follow-up studies involving elderly people who had near-death experiences in early childhood, including his former patients, as well as a separate group, he learned that all remained absolutely convinced their lives had meaning, which was provided by a universal, unifying thread of love. Compared with a control group, they scored significantly higher on life-attitude tests and significantly lower on fear-of-death tests. They also were more generous in donating to charities and took fewer medications. In short, they were transformed by the experience, similar to Jill Bolte Taylor's unique story.

As a doctoral student in clinical psychology research-ing traumatic stress disorder at the University of Arizona, Willoughby Britton learned that persons having had a close call with death didn't seem to have the same pos-itive response as persons who had atypical near-death experiences. Britton was familiar with the pioneering epi-lepsy work of neuroscientist Wilder Penfield, who discov-ered that stimulating the temporal lobe on the right side of a subject's brain with mild electric current produced out-of-body experiences, heavenly music, vivid hallucinations, and the type of panoramic memories associated with the life preview that occurs in the near-death experience. This could also help explain why right-side temporal lobe epi-lepsy has been associated with extreme religiosity, with intense spiritual emotions, mystical visions, and aural hal-lucinations (voice of God). It's interesting to note that this right-brain stimulation conflicts with the left-brain damage J. B. Taylor suffered with her stroke—unless brain functions were switched in counteracting the effects of the stroke.

Persons trained in meditation have reported simi-lar experiences, notably Buddhist monks. Scientists have studied the brains of Buddhist monks during meditation and Franciscan nuns during prayer using SPECT (single photon emission computed tomography) scans. They've discovered a marked decrease in activity in the parietal lobes, an area in the upper rear region of the brain that helps to orient us in space, to judge angles, curves, and dis-tances, and to know where the inner self ends and the out-side world begins. The SPECT scans suggest that highly skilled meditation temporarily blocks processing of sen-sory information within both parietal lobes, causing the brain to perceive an endless self-connectedness to every-thing else, very similar to the reports of near-death experi-ences. Though this idea is highly controversial, an increas-ing number of scientists are convinced that our brains are wired for mystical experiences (Kotler and Astor 2005).

This research has expanded into *neuroplasticity*, which focuses on the brain's ability to be changed by means of thought and behavior, especially when using skilled meditation techniques requiring well-focused attention. *Train Your Mind, Change Your Brain,* by Sharon Begley, reports on several years of collaborative brain research involving neuroscientists working with the Dalai Lama and several monks skilled in meditation. When meditating on compassion, for instance, the monks' MRI brain scans revealed off-the-chart activity in the left sides of their prefrontal cortexes. In effect, deep meditation is capable of strengthening neural connections from the thoughtful two prefrontal cortex lobes to the fear-and-anxiety-generating amygdala, with brain activity shifting in the prefrontal cortex from the right side, which tends toward discontentment, to the left side, which tends toward contentment or happiness. This confirmation of brain plasticity is particularly encouraging to the elderly, as the research also has shown the brain remains malleable throughout life. Good news indeed: not only can everyone gain some positive benefits from meditative practice, but also we oldsters can even continue learning new tricks!

Notable Quotes: Life After Death

Based on all available opinion-poll data on the topic of life after death, it's obvious that skeptics represent a minority opinion. In addition to the overwhelming concurrence of belief in an afterlife by the general public, some very prominent thinkers have also voiced their belief in life after death, perhaps not always in traditional religious terms, but rather according to spiritual intuition. The following brief quotes provide some valuable insights.

> *What happens after death is so unspeakably glorious that our imagination and our feelings do not suffice to form even an approximate conception of it . . . Sooner or later,*

the dead all become what we also are. But in this reality, we know little or nothing about that mode of being. And what shall we still know of this Earth after death? The dissolution of our time-bound form in eternity brings no loss of meaning. Rather, does the little finger know itself a member of the hand? —Carl Jung *(New Age Journal)*

The sheer volume of physical evidence for survival after death is so immense that to ignore it is like standing at the foot of Mount Everest [on a clear day] and insisting that you cannot see the mountain. This evidence is of many types—accounts of near-death experiences, out-of-body experiences, and so on. —Colin Wilson *(What Survives)*

In the universal life that flows around us, any notion of death as a final end or a complete cessation is, to my mind, untenable. There is birth and there is death. They are more nearly two events in a whole life of livingness—with youth, maturity and old age, diversions in between— familiar features of human existence. Life links them all and continues beyond . . . Is there a permanent ageless "I" that survives through a greater cycle? In a sense, who and what we are has no age. There seems to be a center of consciousness in each entity that is separate from the body. How long does that exist after the body dies? What awaits it? —Helen Nearing *(Light on Aging and Dying)*

If my interpretation is accurate, the immortal William Shakespeare voiced an uncertain view of death in *Hamlet*. In comparing death to sleep, he questions whether or not we continue to live through our dreams:

. . . To die, to sleep; to sleep: perchance to dream; aye, there's the rub; for in that sleep of death what dreams may come when we have shuffled off this mortal coil, must give us pause . . .

In closing, I think it's fitting to quote some excerpts from a poem titled "Miss Me, But Let Me Go" by an unknown author. The thought expressed—that deceased persons are finally free of life's cares, and that loved ones will continue to remember and honor them is a call for celebration, rather than doom and gloom. Also, survivors should be encouraged to find a healthy balance throughout the grieving process, as everyone moves forward in facing the everyday challenges of life.

When I come to the end of the road
And the sun has set for me,
I want no rites in a gloom-filled room
—Why cry for a soul set free?
Miss me a little, but not too long.
And not with your head bowed low.
Remember the love that we once shared.
—Miss me, but let me go.
    —Anonymous

14

Inspiring Hope

Finding and inspiring hope in the face of death can be a daunting assignment, especially for those of us who are in the last decades of life. But, as discussed earlier, meaning and happiness are largely determined by our states of mind—our mental attitudes and our beliefs. If it's true that what we believe influences our behavior, and that our attitudes can influence our sense of meaning and happiness, then we best be working on improving our beliefs and psycho-emotional dispositions. It seems reasonable to suggest that only by developing an objective and positive outlook on life can we gain or inspire hope, which is an essential ingredient for living a meaningful and fulfilling life.

Hope Versus Optimism

There's a difference between hope and optimism. *Hope* is generally associated with a feeling that something desirable is likely to happen or is possible, or is something somebody desires to happen or be true. In contrast, *optimism,* a word typically confused with hope, is associated with a positive attitude based on the belief, expectation, or hope that things will turn out well, and that good will triumph over evil.

Though similar in meaning, not everyone agrees they refer to the same thing. Vaclav Havel, the Czech playwright and former president wrote "An Orientation of the Heart" in 1989, three years before the "Velvet Revolution", and his opening comments focused on defining hope, which I offer in a paraphrased format (Loeb 2004):

342 / Inspiring Hope

> *In a deep and powerful sense, hope is not the same as joy [optimism], a feeling that all things will turn out well. Nor is it a willingness to invest in enterprises that are obviously headed for success. Rather, hope is the ability to work for a cause simply because it is worthy, not because it stands a chance to succeed. In sum, It is not the conviction that something will turn out well, but the certainty that something makes sense, regardless of how it turns out. It is hope, above all, that gives us the strength to live and continually try new things, even in conditions that seem as hopeless as the current world situation.*

Mark Hertsgaard, a journalist, author, and broadcaster who writes on environmental issues, agrees with Havel's definitions of hope. He says, "Optimism is the belief that things will turn out well; but sad to say, the objective facts give little reason to expect that humanity will avoid environmental suicide. Hope, on the other hand, is an active, determined conviction that is rooted in the spirit, chosen by the heart, and guided by the mind." He adds that hope has triumphed over implausible odds on numerous occasions in recent history, as evidenced notably by the collapses of apartheid and the Soviet empire (Loeb 2004).

The Reverend Jim Wallis, editor of *Sojourners*, a Christian magazine devoted to social justice and peace, adds that "Hope is believing in spite of the evidence, then watching the evidence change." He ardently believes that faith makes hope possible, and hope is the single most important ingredient for changing the world in a positive way. He insists that faith, according to the Christian Bible, is not something one possesses, but rather practices, a belief substantiated by biblical apostle James' statement, "Faith without works is dead." A more modern slang version of "Don't talk the talk . . . walk the walk" might be rephrased to "walk the talk", that is, "Do what you say you believe".

When we consider our world's future prospects, it's not always easy to be hopeful or optimistic. The world has always been fraught with primal uncertainty and danger, especially natural disasters, And, as enlightened as we have become, we still face some major challenges: threats of global warming, global terrorism, pre-emptive wars, high-level corporate crime, escalating health-care costs, endangered social security benefits, mounting national debt, economic woes, and a consumption-oriented economy that primarily benefits the rich upper class. With so many problems, it's so easy to feel overwhelmed and impotent in making any positive changes. And, depending on our individual situations, our anxiety may appear justified. But is it in our best interests, individually and collectively, to give in to despair? I know that Deepak Chopra would answer, no, that giving in to despair tends to create negative results, whereas imaging positive future outcomes helps to guide our collective behavior toward constructive ends.

To be sure, our age is marked by a widespread cynicism and materialism, with idealistic values and the spiritual (nonmaterial) aspects of life given less priority. On the other hand, there are many diverse religious organizations, all professing allegiance to a benevolent God or Supreme Being, as defined according to each group's unique religious persuasion. As a whole, there is little argument that much good has been and continues to be accomplished within the realm of organized religion. However, the discouraging factor is what I perceive as an overall superficial religiosity and a corresponding immature worldview that's exemplified in religious fundamentalism, which a recent Gallup poll suggests represents approximately one-third of the American population. At least 15 percent of evangelicals sincerely believe in the Rapture, or the second coming of Christ, a predicted time when "true believers" are expected to shed their clothes, rise up, and join Christ in heaven. The 12 volumes of the popular "Left Behind"

344 / Inspiring Hope

series capitalize on this implausible, primarily fictional thesis.

Sadly, religious irrationality is capable of turning thoughtful people away from organized religion, and propelling them toward agnosticism or atheism. It's hard to imagine that thoughtful, compassionate people can embrace such narcissistic views of hope; yet we all know some highly respected folk who take it rather seriously. Essentially a winners-take-all philosophy, this false sense of hope appears wholly uncharitable, and un-Christian, according to the understanding and appreciation I have for the historically authentic Jesus and scholarly Biblical interpretations. Okay, now that I've gotten this off my chest, let's get back to seeking genuine hope for the future.

Promoting Hope Through Good Works

As Paul Loeb points out in his book—*The Impossible Will Take a Little While*—hope is founded on the belief, and historical evidence, that what appear to have been miraculous advances in the promotion of worthwhile causes are actually the result of many people making small, collective efforts over time. The book's title was inspired by the indomitable spirit found in Billie Holiday's lyric and World War II Army Corps of Engineers motto: "The difficult I'll do right now. The impossible will take a little while". Being aware that chains of like-minded, hopeful people exist, and that we can choose to join them, is a primary way to sustain hope, especially when our individual efforts don't seem significant enough to make a difference.

Examples abound showing how collective human efforts can make a huge difference. Within the U.S. alone over the past fifty years, we've witnessed the successes created by movements for women's rights, non-violent civil rights campaigns, anti-war demonstrations and peace initiatives during the Viet Nam engagement, environmental conservation, gay and lesbian rights, national health care, minimum wage for workers, educational reform, social security, and so on. All of these movements were, and are, the result of combined human efforts, under the leadership of highly dedicated individuals who provide inspiration and direction. Moreover, it's relevant to note that most of the people championing these historic causes were very likely affiliated with a variety of religious organizations, from liberal to moderate and evangelical persuasions.

Even more significantly, for the most part the majority of positive social reforms have been brought about by non-violent means. Just contemplate the major social reforms experienced in the last two centuries, and into your head pop such prominent names as Susan B. Anthony, Harriet Tubman, Mahatma Gandhi, Nelson Mandela, Martin Luther King, Jr., and the Dalai Lama. The leaders of the world who achieved great ends by using force are less idolized, with the exception of those who achieved peaceful ends, such as Franklin D. Roosevelt and Winston Churchill for their inspiring roles in helping defeat the imperialistic aggressions of Nazi Germany and Japan in World War II.

In confronting the many challenges humanity faces, we may find that fear can be paralyzing. And the antidote to such paralysis is defiant, resilient, persistent hope, no matter the odds. Hope may be associated with *faith*, a belief or trust in, or devotion to, somebody or something that does not require logical or empirical proof, and does not rely on human action to create a positive outcome. However, faith placed in humans—with a time-tested belief in humankind's ability to overcome adversity by taking positive measures—might be interpreted as an aspect of hope, which encourages an optimistic worldview that motivates proactive, constructive behavior, the drive to "make a difference". Creating citizens with hope in their hearts can be a daunting task in this very complex and paradoxical world. To hope is to dream, and many people have lost the will to envision a better future. As Benjamin Mays, president of Morehouse College and mentor to Martin Luther King, Jr. reportedly said:

> *The tragedy of life doesn't lie in not reaching your goal. The tragedy lies in having no goal to reach. It isn't a calamity to die with dreams unfulfilled, but it is a calamity not to dream. It is not a disgrace not to reach the stars, but it is a disgrace to have no stars to reach for. Not failure, but low aim, is a sin.*

Our Legacy and the Challenge of Younger Generations

Marian Wright Edelman, founder of Children's Defense Fund, and author of several books, raises the all-important question regarding the legacy we wish to create for future generations: How will we be remembered in the future?

• By the number of enemy killed, the number and sophistication of weapons produced, or by our willingness to destroy the prison of violence we've constructed in the name of peace and security?

• By the number of material items manufactured and sold, or by a rediscovery of more lasting, nonmaterial measures of success, such as a better overall quality of life for all world citizens?

• By how human beings are being made obsolete, with rapidly growing technologies and corporate merger mania and greed, or by finding a balance between corporate profits and corporate concern for helping workers, families, communities, and the environment?

• By how a few at the top of the income scale receive so much—at the expense of those at the bottom and in the middle—or by our development of a concept of enough for all?

- By the glitz, style, and banality of our culture, or by substantive, qualitative measures, including an ethic of caring, community, and justice in a world driven by too much money, technology, and weaponry?

Assuming we older folks do our job adequately and leave our heirs a respectable legacy, what about the current crop of young people who will be the future leaders, many of whom are our children and grandchildren? Will they be up to the task? Well-known *Newsweek* columnist, Anna Quindlen, advocated eloquently on behalf of present-day youth in an article titled, "Now It's Time for Generation Next". As demographers have named them, the "millennials" (born between 1977 and 1994) number 70 million strong, the largest cohort since their parents, the Boomers. Quindlen, whose children are of this age, describes them in glowing terms: "They are more interesting, more confident, less hide-bound, better educated, more creative and, in some essential fashion, unafraid." With pride, she claims they are the products of the world the older generations have provided them. The diversity of our population and the openness experienced in school have exposed them to a wider worldview based on tolerance, including acceptance of their own human idiosyncrasies. They have also grown up seeing and believing that women are just as intelligent and capable as men, that gay persons also have human rights, and that volunteer service on behalf of less fortunate, disadvantaged persons is an appropriate response for those so blessed.

A 1999 survey of college freshmen, the oldest group in the millennial curve, found that three-fourths of them had participated in volunteer work in the last year, including schools, hospitals, charities, and churches. The quality most admired by these students was integrity, and the people they admired most were their parents. And their minds were more open to new ideas and intellectual inquiry, with a distinct preference for Socratic discourse over rote learning and didactic instruction. They also were more inclined toward peace, prosperity, diversity, and environmental concerns than previous generations. Quindlen's view of the younger generation is most welcome, as it balances the media's predominance of negative news.

The popular TV news program, *60 Minutes,* dedicated a segment of one program (September 4, 2005) to a profile of the "Echo Boomers", the Boomers' 80 million children, a population encompassing elementary school children to those graduating from college in 2005. In addition to the positive characteristics provided by Quindlen, the program broadly profiled these youth as cultural traditionalists, team players, and technological multitaskers. Whereas TV is the major source of information for Boomers, the Internet is the chosen media for the Echo Boomers.

Two downside characteristics of this team-player generation might be a general lack of individual creativity and an inability to think and plan long-range, which leads to instant gratification. Indeed, some sociologists and psychologists refer to this youthful population as the Now Generation, and for good reasons. These youths are accustomed to being celebrated and protected by their doting parents, who, in wishing only the very best in life for them, often act as "helicopter parents", hovering over them even up through college age. The unintended result is a tendency for them to have high expectations of entitlement, as reflected by grade inflation in school, trophies for all types of extra-curricular activities, a wide range of educational opportunities, and stylish, faddish material possessions. In other words, this generation has some narcissistic tendencies that can lead to culture shock, as they wend their way through life, including dealing with careers, marriage, and rearing children.

The dress styles, body decorations, and hair styles of some youth do seem outrageous to us older folks. As a university professor, I've had occasional contact with students who sport a variety of styles, including punk or grunge, so I've had opportunities to get to know some fairly well. As a group, all have been rather decent people underneath their appearances, and I suspect their rebellious-looking apparel and body decorations will not be with them forever (or at least let's hope not, especially those low-hanging, over-sized, ground-dragging "gangsta" pants).

I shall never forget having a young woman attend one of my voice pedagogy classes as a guest singer who took lessons from a graduate student. She was dressed in a punk-style black and white outfit, and adorned with body piercings—in her nose, ears, and elsewhere—so I immediately sized her up as rock singer of dubious vocal music talent. Surprisingly, when she began singing a classical song, a beautiful natural tone quality emerged that would rival the best of our 120 voice majors. She was obviously well trained, and on a personal level going through an experimental life phase. I also found her to be well mannered and polite, for she received my feedback graciously, including my tactfully managed comment regarding her attire, which would be taboo in any classical music situation. Her mild response: "Yes, I know, but I clean up well." Thus, I was once again reminded that one should not prejudge others based entirely on their appearance.

It's highly likely that many readers have children or grandchildren who exemplify some of the stereotypical traits discussed above. I hope we can all be more understanding of any seemingly "different" beliefs and behaviors that conflict with ours. The aspect we need to pay more attention to is each person's quality of character, based on time-tested values. A young person's attire or hairstyle should not automatically cause us to think of them or treat them with less than respect. We need to remain hopeful that our younger generations will mature into respectable American citizens, as we must depend on them to assume our places of leadership, as well as enlisting their support in sustaining our entitlement programs and quality of life.

The Pew Research Center's 1999 Millennium Survey revealed that American optimism for the quality of life in the twenty-first century ran high, from 67 percent in the South and West, to 69 percent in the Midwest and a whopping 78 percent in the Eastern U.S. The most optimistic responders were also the more highly educated college graduates, at 75 percent, compared with the 68 percent of high school graduates, and 60 percent of those not finishing high school. Based on these findings, it seems that the level of education has a potent influence on one's overall life attitude, although it's also likely that corresponding financial success bolsters optimism. Large percentages of respondents expressed hope for the future regarding space travel and finding cures for serious diseases. On the negative, gloomy side: 64 percent feared a terrorist attack (a fear tragically realized on 9/11/2001); 63 percent believed there would be another energy crisis (and, indeed, there have been some serious episodes since then, and it's likely this problem will persist); 37 percent believed the U.S. will experience a nuclear war (not yet, thankfully); and 31 percent believed an asteroid will hit Earth.

The Future of Human Civilization

Though it's possible an asteroid or comet will strike our planet again at some future time, the probability for it happening in the twenty-first century is extremely remote. Unfortunately, asteroids travel so fast that, unless a telescope is pointed toward the particular portion of the sky where an asteroid can be spotted early enough, the human race may never know what happened. Similar in effect to the single offshore Yucatan blast that reportedly led to the extinction of the dinosaurs—along with most other plant and animal life—the resulting damage could be so severe that another worldwide extinction would most likely occur.

Other more likely calamities must also be considered, including the possibilities of nuclear wars, rampant diseases, natural disasters caused by extreme temperatures of freezing and overheating that produce erratic, devastating weather, and strained resources due to over-population. The chance that some of these calamities will strike during our lifetime is highly probable, and becomes increasingly so as the years pass—unless drastic solutions are found in time. I suppose the main reason for mentioning this unpleasant subject is simply that it's within our power— and our responsibility—as the oldest and wisest members of society, to do whatever we can to ameliorate the potential for any human-caused catastrophes. Rather than retiring to pursue our personal needs and interests, perhaps we can contribute something worthwhile to society, as a part of our individual and generational legacy.

Finally, according to most scientific findings, there is evidence indicating that the eventual obliteration of Earth will occur in approximately 5 billion years, as the sun expands into a giant red star. Of course, by then humankind might have disappeared, due to natural catastrophes or nuclear wars, or because of vacating an inhospitable Earth for another planet home in outer space, perhaps in some distant galaxy. Millions of years from now humans may have evolved to a higher level of intelligence and enlightenment, and a physical appearance radically different from today. Hopefully, by the time a major catastrophe is foreseen, sufficient technological expertise will be available to avert the prospect of such a calamitous finale for our planet and all life forms.

According to an article in *Discover* magazine (December 2004), far-thinking scientists are conjuring a seven-step plan for leaving Earth and the cosmos that includes:

finding and testing a theory of everything (TOE), such as the string theory, and searching for a naturally occurring wormhole, a dimensional gateway or cosmic tunnel to a parallel universe; sending a probe through a black hole and retrieving information; creating a black hole in slow motion; creating negative energy; making a baby universe, which requires a laser implosion device and a cosmic atom smasher; and sending nanobots through the wormhole to regenerate human civilization on the other side. (For details, refer to the article "How to Survive the End of the Universe", pp. 46-53, by Mochio Kaku).

Overcoming Our Past and Starting Anew

Putting aside such troubling doomsday thoughts, how do we begin to use our communal sense of hope for profound, positive changes that will enable a prosperous future for the heirs of current generations? Is it possible to sustain hope in a world that is teetering on the brink of potential destruction by our own hands? I think so, but we can only do so by rethinking who we are, and what we have the potential to become.

Contrary to the opinion many intellectuals may hold of Louis L'Amour, the renowned author of numerous adventure books, he was a profound thinker. In his book, *Education of a Wandering Man* (1989), L'Amour expresses his opinion regarding our collective human state of mind, and how it needs to evolve to a higher level of creativity:

> I believe that man has been living and is living in a Neanderthal state of mind. Mentally [psycho-emotionally], we are still flaking rocks for scraping stones or chipping them for arrowheads. The life that lies before us will no longer permit such wastefulness or neglect. We are moving into outer space, where the problems will be infinitely greater and will demand

quicker, more accurate solutions. We cannot trust our destinies to machines alone. Man must make his own decisions . . . We simply must free the mind from its fetters and permit it to function without restraint. Many of us have learned to supply ourselves with the raw materials and then allow the subconscious to take over. This is what creativity is. One must condition oneself for the process and then let it proceed.

L'Amour is suggesting we must think beyond the confines of our narrow worldviews—our boxes—which means moving beyond our individual prejudices and biases, our personal preferences, political agendas, and even our religious beliefs, to gain a worldview or universal perspective that acknowledges and honors all people, all creatures, all philosophical and religious concepts, and all aspects of our natural environment. In this regard, I'd like to offer a brief outline of my personal hopes for the future, as related to the major issues previously discussed.

Since all motivated actions are instigated through thought and emotion, we might begin by expanding the breadth and depth of our thought processes, intentionally moving beyond the mundane issues of our personal, everyday lives in a search for universal principles that stretch our limited knowledge and understanding. In practical terms, if we truly believe in the lofty, common ideals held by the world's principal spiritual traditions, for instance, the universal concept of "peace and good will for all people", then we are challenged to become more rational and constructive in our thinking, more skillful and efficient in our physical actions, and more lovingly compassionate in our relationships with all sentient beings. To become enlightened world citizens, negative or narrow-minded ideological perspectives must be discarded, particularly some forms of extreme religious fundamentalism, a topic I've addressed at various points.

Based on information we've covered thus far, it seems safe to suggest that the major fetters restraining us from developing creative solutions to worldwide problems may well be the very institutions we most respect and revere: families, ethnic groups, and bureaucratic, religious, educational, and political institutions. These powerful institutions influence us in various ways, causing us to conform— for better and/or worse—to a particular way of thinking and behaving. Though the well-meaning intention of most ethnic, religious, and socio-cultural groups is to create community cohesiveness, social order, and collective good will, the outcomes are not always benevolent. Examples of failures are visible in every society, from the growing ranks of extremely poor "street people" struggling to survive in the world's most affluent metropolitan areas, to the even less fortunate folk barely surviving in the slums of third-world countries. Harmful societal influences are especially evident in the way a large portion of extremely wealthy persons benefit from the talents and labors of a less fortunate labor class. I don't mean to sound like a socialist, but I think you know by now how I feel about extremely wealthy people, particularly those who don't share their wealth with the less fortunate, and for the good of the general public.

Though the problems we face may seem daunting, our primary intention should be to concentrate on what we *can* do, both individually and collectively, in seeking effective solutions for the potentially disastrous mega trends set in motion by the human race, trends that may ultimately destroy our environment, our civilization, and, with it, any hope for assuring a potentially glorious future for our species. Of course, creative solutions are needed, requiring a critical self-examination of who we are and what kind of relationship we should have with all living species on Earth, as well as any life forms that may exist in the far reaches of outer space.

Any solutions we seek must enhance our prospects of evolving toward a world-centric (or cosmo-centric) perspective. By improving the conditions of life for all sentient beings and the natural world that sustains us, we will concurrently promote our own interests of self-preservation. The conditions and steps for improving the quality of life on this planet are common knowledge, but for the sake of constructive repetition, it might help to list some of the major goals that will set us on a road that leads toward a hopeful future. As we proceed, we need to keep in mind that all the world's problems are synergistically interconnected and interrelated, making it difficult to clearly discern the cause-and-effect relationships associated with complex situations, circumstances, and conditions. Nevertheless, our objective is to identify the most obvious problems, propose creative yet feasible solutions, and find effective ways of implementing them, all the while sustaining hope that we or our heirs will eventually succeed. The following proposals to specific problems may seem redundant and super simplistic, but I think they are worth mentioning, for our collective contemplation and consideration.

Taking Some Practical Steps Toward Enlightenment

The first step toward realizing our potentially glorious future is for a majority of world citizens to become more curious and inquisitive, more informed and skillful, more broadminded, tolerant, and inclusive. We need to be more deeply committed to achieving peaceful ends through rational thought and reflection, creative action, open communication, and compassionate concern for all people and the natural environment. Thinking creatively will become more essential, for we can no longer rely totally on the traditional nurturing influences of orthodox beliefs and behaviors fostered upon us by our well-intentioned social, political, educational, and religious institutions.

I don't mean to denigrate our principal institutions, or downplay their significance, in providing essential public services. In general, our various institutions have fulfilled their respective roles well enough in the past, but our future survival depends on our ability to adapt our institutions to face the challenges that lie ahead. We can no longer afford to maintain a status-quo mindset. Following are three initiatives I recommend, especially for those of us who have not yet fulfilled our legacies:

• Gain accurate knowledge and fresh insights into human nature, including knowledge and experience related to genetics, history, and socio-cultural influences.

• Become better informed about our natural environment, especially our role as protectors and conservers of lands, minerals, energy resources, plants and animals.

• Implement long-term plans to assure a high quality of life for all world citizens, including safeguarding our natural environment, the source of our sustenance.

Convincing a majority of the world's population to adopt a holistic, moderate (balanced) way of thinking and acting will involve large numbers of like-minded people working cooperatively and collaboratively to achieve common goals that promote a better way of life for everyone. Some of the issues that must be addressed include:

• Reducing poverty and raising the overall standard of living worldwide.

• Promoting the concept of a simpler, less-is-more life-style regarding material possessions and energy consumption.

• Advocating educational reforms that emphasize the role and importance of learning as a means of creating well-rounded, informed, rational, creative, and moral world-centric citizens who are capable of fulfilling essential roles in society.

• Reforming our major institutions—social, educational, political, and religious—by creating the conditions and policies that assure everyone the basic freedoms that enable a full and productive life, including opportunities for personal growth and expression.

Regarding the first goal, all people deserve access to basic life-sustaining material needs, including adequate food, clothing, and shelter. It's almost impossible to achieve any quality of life without eradicating hunger and extreme poverty. In a world where 13 to 18 million people each year die of starvation, or the side effects of malnutrition or other poverty-related causes, those of us who are comfortably secure must do our part in providing the basics for the less fortunate among us. However, though it's relatively easy to donate money, food, or cast-off clothing to charities specializing in helping the poor, I think the real issue needs to be addressed on a macro scale. For example, in the long run I think we'll do more to help alleviate world hunger on a worldwide scale through broader initiatives that affect all people, such as:

• Establishing guidelines, policies, and procedures for controlling population growth, especially in underdeveloped countries.

• Providing basic health care and social security benefits, with everyone contributing to the collective income-related tax base, at whatever levels may be deemed appropriate for individuals, according to income and other significant guidelines.

• Helping everyone to obtain gainful employment (including government-sponsored service programs, such as the Peace Core, neighborhood development programs, and the armed services), based on paying a minimum wage that permits living above the poverty level.

• Providing educational opportunities that allow people to gain more knowledge and skills, to help them become more competent as workers and citizens, and more economically independent.

• Creating the type of social conditions and governing systems that grant all citizens equal opportunity and rights under law (justice), including all the basic freedoms associated with a genuine democracy.

• Sharing wealth more equitably, perhaps by increasing the tax rates on upper-income citizens, thereby narrowing the gap between rich and poor.

• Convincing everyone that the fate of humankind lies in our collective responsibility to safeguard the natural environment that sustains us.

Summary and Conclusion

The future of humankind on earth will be built on beliefs and mores inherited from past and current senior generations, particularly the G.I. Generation, and reinforced by the modern insights and contributions of our younger generations. The issues mentioned earlier need our urgent attention, but in addressing them we must first work on transforming ourselves, individually and collectively, from the inside out. Greater numbers of world-centric individuals are needed to collaborate with kindred spirits to develop and promote integral world-centric perspectives.

As suggested in the preface, a major impetus for writing—at a stage of life bordering on old age—was to undertake an intensive self-transforming exercise. In the process

I've grappled with some serious topics and issues, with a concentration on aging and dying, topics that force us to consider our authentic nature, our ultimate goals, and the positive qualities we wish to achieve before the end. In other words, we are concerned with the legacy we wish to leave to subsequent generations. Although we may be sure that the world will go on without us, we are not excused—while living—from contributing what we can.

I sincerely hope you have been stimulated to seriously contemplate some of the concepts presented throughout this mutual journey of exploration and discovery. Your journey is unique, one of a kind. Yet, it is an all-human journey, with all the fears, joys, and hopes experienced and expressed by humans for thousands of years. Whether you are in your early 50s or nearing 100, you are an aging, finite being, alive and kicking. I hope you are encouraged to make the most of whatever time is left to fulfill your innate potential—however full your life's cup may be—including:

- Finding a balance in all areas of life;

- Optimizing and maintaining mind-body health;

- Learning more about aging and dying and making preparations for a graceful life exit; and

- Continuing to contribute to society by fulfilling the kinds of worthwhile goals that create a lasting legacy.

A closing quote summarizes some thoughts about the meaning of legacy.

There are certain things that are fundamental to human fulfillment . . . The essence of these needs is captured in the phrase 'to live, to love, to learn, to leave a legacy'. The need to live is our physical need for such things as food, clothing, shelter, economic wellbeing, and health.

The need to love is our social need to relate to other people, to belong, to love and to be loved. The need to learn is our mental need to develop and to grow. And the need to leave a legacy is our spiritual need to have a sense of meaning, purpose, personal congruence, and contribution. —Stephen R. Covey *(First Things First)*

Bibliography

(Sources and Selected Readings)

BOOKS

Alexander. F.M. *The Use of the Self.* 1932 Reprint. Downey, CA: Centerline Press, 1984.

Amatuzio, Janis. *Forever Ours: Real Stories of Immortality and Living from a Forensic Pathologist.* Novato, CA: New World Library, 2007.

Arrien, Angeles. *The Second Half of Life: Opening the Eight Gates of Wisdom.* Boulder, CO: Sounds True, 2005.

Begley, Sharon. *Train Your Mind, Change Your Brain.* New York: Ballantine Books, 2007.

Berry, Wendell. *The Memory of Old Jack.* Washington, DC: Counterpoint (Perseus Books), 1999.

Browne, Jill Conner. *God Save the Sweet Potato Queens.* New York: Three Rivers Press/Crown Publishing Group, 2001.

Buettner, Dan. *The Blue Zone: Lessons for Living Longer From the People Who've Lived the Longest.* New York: National Geographic, 2008.

Burklo, Jim. *Open Christianity; Home By Another Road.* Scotts Valley, CA: Rising Star Press, 2002

Byock, Ira. *Dying Well.* New York: Riverhead Books, 1997.

Carlson, Lisa. *Caring for the Dead: Your Final Act of Love.* Hinesburg, VT: Upper Access Publishers, 1998.

Chopra, Deepak. *Ageless Body, Timeless Mind.* New York: Harmony Books, 1993.

Covey, Stephen R. *The Seven Habits of Highly Effective People.* New York: Simon and Schuster, 1990.

Covey, Stephen R., Merrill, Roger A., & Merrill, Rebecca R. *First Things First: To Live, to Love, to Learn, to Leave a Legacy.* New York: Simon & Schuster, 1994.

Cowley, Chris & Lodge, Henry S. *Younger Next Year: A Guide to Living Like 50 Until You're 80 and Beyond.* New York: Workman Publishing, 2004.

Danko, William & Stanley, Thomas. *The Millionaire Next Door.* Atlanta, GA: Longstreet Press, 1996.

Davidson, Sara. *Leap! What Will We Do With the Rest of Our Lives?* New York: Random House, 2007.

Diamond, Jared. *Guns, Germs, and Steel: The Fates of Human Societies,* New York: W.W. Norton, 1997.

Dominguez, Joe & Robin, Vicki. *Your Money or Your Life.* NY: Penguin Books, 1992.

Drucker, Peter F. *Managing in the Next Society.* New York: Truman Talley Books/St. Martin's Griffin, 2003.

Ernest, Maurice. *The Longer Life* (1938). Bel Air, CA: Hesperides Press, 2006.

Frankl, Viktor. *Man's Search for Meaning.* New York: Beacon Press, 2006.

Frank, Robert H. & Cook, Phillip J. *The Winner-Take-All Society: Why the Few at the Top Get So Much More Than the Rest of Us.* New York: Penguin Books, 1996.

Frank, Robert H. *Luxury Fever: Why Money Fails to Satisfy in an Era of Excess.* Princeton, NJ: Princeton University Press, 1999.

Freedman, Marc. *Encore: Finding Work That Matters in the Second Half of Life.* Public Affairs. New York: Perseus Books Group, 2007.

Fulton, R., Markusen, E. Owen, G., Scheiber, J.L. (editors) "Death Work and the Stages of Dying" (By Edwin S. Shneidman). *Death and Dying: Challenge and Change.* San Francisco: Boyd & Fraser Publishing Company, 1981.

Goleman, Daniel. *Emotional Intelligence.* New York: Bantam Books, 1995.

Hall, Don. *Life Work.* Boston: Beacon Press, 1993.

Hallowell, Edward. *CrazyBusy.* New York: Ballantine Books, 2006.

Hetzer, Linda & Hulstrand, Janet. *Moving On: A Practical Guide to Downsizing the Family Home.* New York: Stewart, Tabori, & Chang, 2004.

Hoag, Tami. *Guilty as Sin.* New York: Bantam Books, 1994.

Hollis, James. *Finding Meaning in the Second Half of Life: How to Finally, Really Grow Up.* NY: Gotham (Penguin Group), 2005.

Humphrey, Derek. *Final Exit: The Practicalities of Self-Deliverance and Assisted Suicide for the Dying.* New York: Dell Publishing, 2002.

Kübler-Ross, Elisabeth. *Death: The Final Stage of Growth.* New Jersey, Englewood Cliffs: Prentice-Hall, Inc., 1975.

Kübler-Ross, Elizabeth & Kessler, David. *On Grief and Grieving.* New York: Scribner, 2005.

Lambert, Mary. *Clearing the Clutter* (for good feng shui). New York: Barnes & Noble, 2001.

L'Amour, Louis. *Education of a Wandering Man.* New York: Bantam Books, 1989.

Leonard, George. *Mastery: The Keys to Success and Long-Term Fulfillment.* New York: Plume (Penguin Books), 1992.

Lerner, Gerda. *A Death of One's Own.* New York: Simon & Schuster, 1978.

Lippe, Toinette. *Nothing Left Over: A Plain and Simple Life.* New York: Tarcher/Putnam, 2002

Loeb, Paul Rogat. *The Impossible Will Take a Little While: A Citizen's Guide to Hope in a Time of Fear.* New York: Basic Books (Perseus Books Group), 2004.

Lynch, Thomas. *The Undertaking: Life Studies from the Dismal Trade.* New York: Penguin Books, 1998.

Maslow, Abraham. *Motivation and Personality* (rev. ed.), New York: Harper & Row, 1970.

Moyers, Bill. *Healing and the Mind.* New York: Doubleday, 1993.

Nearing, Helen. *Light on Aging and Dying; Wise Words Selected by Helen Nearing.* Gardiner, Maine: Tilbury House, Publishers, 1995.

Nettleton, Sarah. *The Simple Home: The Luxury of Enough,* Newtown, CT: Taunton Press, 2007.

Nuland, Sherwin B. *How We Die: Reflections on Life's Final Chapter.* New York: Vintage Books, 1995.

Nuland, Sherwin B.. *The Mysteries Within.* New York: Knopf, 2000.

Oech, Roger von. *Expect the Unexpected (Or You Won't Find It).* New York: The Free Press, 2001.

Olson, Steve. *Mapping Human History: Discovering the Past Through Our Genes.* New York: Houghton Mifflin Co., 2002.

Ornish, Dean. *Eat More, Weigh Less: Dr. Dean Ornish's Life Choice Program for Losing Weight Safely While Eating Abundantly.* New York: HarperCollins, 2001.

Osbon, Diane K. (ed.) *Reflections on the Art of Living: A Joseph Campbell Companion.* New York: HarperCollins, 1991.

Peck, Scott. *A World Waiting to Be Born: Civility Rediscovered.* New York; Bantam Books, 1993.

Piaget, Jean. *The Child's Conception of the World.* London, England: Routledge, 1998 (Reprint).

Pirsig, Robert M., *Zen and the Art of Motorcycle Maintenance: An Inquiry Into Values.* New York: Bantam Books, 1974.

Preston, Thomas A. *Final Victory: Preparing for the Best Possible Death.* New York, Prima Publishing, 2000.

Quindlen, Anna. *Blessings.* New York: Random House, 2003.

Roisen, Michael & La Puma, John. *The RealAge Diet: Make Yourself Younger with What You Eat.* New York: HarperCollins, 2001.

Rolls, Dr. Barbara. *The Volumetrics Eating Plan: Techniques and Recipes for Feeling Full on Fewer Calories.* New York: HarperCollins Publishers, 2005.

Rowling, J.K. *Harry Potter and the Chamber of Secrets.* New York: Scholastic Press, 1999.

Russell, Bertrand. *Portraits From Memory and Other Essays.* New York: Simon and Schuster, 1956.

St. James, Elaine. *Simplify Your Life.* New York: Hyperion, 1994.

Seligman, Martin E.P. *Authentic Happiness.* New York: Free Press, 2002.

Schwartz, Barry. *The Paradox of Choice: Why More is Less.* New York: HarperCollins, 2004.

Stanley, Thomas J. & Danko, William D. *The Millionaire Next Door.* New York: Pocket Books, 1996.

Stone, Ganga. *Start the Conversation.* New York: Warner Books, 1996.

Strauss, William and Howe, Neil. *Generations: A Future History of America from 1584 to 2069.* New York: William Morrow and Co., 1991.

Sykes, Bryan. *The Seven Daughters of Eve: The Science That Reveals Our Genetic History.* New York: W.W. Norton & Co., 2001.

Weiner, Eric. *The Geography of Bliss: One Grump's Search for the Happiest Places in the World.* New York: Hachette-BookGroup, 2008.

Wilber, Ken. *A Brief History of Everything.* Boston; Shambhala, 1996.

Wilber, Ken. *The Essential Wilber.* Boston: Shambhala, 1998.

Wilber, Ken. *The Marriage of Sense and Soul: Integrating Science and Religion.* New York: Broadway Books, 1999.

Wilber, Ken. *Integral Psychology: Consciousness, Spirit, Psychology, Therapy.* Boston: Shambhala, 2000.

Wilber, Ken. *Sex, Ecology, Spirituality: The Spirit of Evolution.* Boston: Shambhala, 2000.

Wilber, Ken. *A Theory of Everything: An Integral Vision for Business, Politics, Science, and Spirituality.* Boston: Shambhala, 2001.

Wilber, Ken. *Boomeritis.* Boston: Shambhala, 2003.

Wilber, Ken. *The Simple Feeling of Being: Embracing Your True Nature.* Boston, MA: Shambhala, 2004.

Wilber, Ken. *Integral Spirituality.* Boston: Integral Books, 2006.

Wilber, Ken. *The Integral Vision.* Boston: Shambhala, 2007.

Willett, Walter C. *Eat, Drink, and Be Healthy.* New York: Simon & Shuster, 2001.

Wilson, Eric G. *Against Happiness: In Praise of Melancholy.* New YorK: Sara Chrichton Books, 2008.

ARTICLES

Ackerman, William L. "Against a Personal God". *The Secular Humanist Bulletin.* Spring 2008, p. 13.

Adler, Jerry and Scelfo, Julie. "How Affluent Baby Boomers' Legacy Has Changed Us". *Newsweek* (Website). January 2008).

Arnst, Catherine. "How to Keep Your Memory Intact". *BusinessWeek.* October 15, 2001, p. 128 E4.

Asnes, Marion. "The Affluent American". *Money*. December 2003, pp. 40-41

Baker, Beth. "Fighting for Funeral Rights". *AARP Profile*. November 1999, pp. 18-19.

Begley, Sharon & Foote, Donna. "The Brain in Winter". *Newsweek* Special Issue. Fall/Winter, 2001, pp. 24-29.

Block, Sandra. "Your Money: Life's No Box of Chocolates for Today's Retirees, So Start Saving Now". Website: USA TODAY.com. November 9, 2004.

Buffett, Warren E. "Buy American: I Am". (*New York Times* online), October 16, 2008.

Carmichael, Mary. "Medicine's Next Level". *Newsweek*. December 6, 2004, pp. 45-50.

Carmichael, Mary & Ozols, Jennifer B. "A Wrinkle in Time". *Newsweek*. January 17, 2005, pp. 50-55.

Chodzko-Zajko, W. J. & Ringel, R. L. "Physiological Aspects of Aging". *Journal of Voice*, 1, 1: 18-26. 1987.

Colapinto, John. "Where Karl Lagerfeld Lives". *The New Yorker* (www.newyorker.com). March 19, 2007.

Conlin, Michelle & Hempel, Jessi, "The Secret Givers". *Business Week*. December 1, 2003.

Cowley, Geoffrey & Davis, Rachel. "The Biology of Aging". *Newsweek* Special Issue. Fall/Winter, 2001, pp. 12-13, 16-19.

Cowley, Geoffrey. "Science of Happiness". *Newsweek*. Sept. 16, 2002, pp. 46-48.

Dawson, J. "Brain Power, a Matter of Gender". Minneapolis *Star Tribune*. Feb. 11, 1996, p. A16.

Deets, Horace B. "The Graying of the World: Crisis or Opportunity". *Modern Maturity*. Jan./Feb. 2000 (p. 82).

Deunwald, Mary. "The Psychology of . . . Hoarding". *Discover*. October, 2004, pp. 30-31.

Duncan, David E. "Forever Young". *Discover.* October 2005.

Editor. "Start the Conversation". *Modern Maturity* (AARP magazine). September/October 2000, pp. 51-58.

Editor. "Sleeping Pills". *Mayo Clinic Health Letter.* January 2008, pp. 4-5.

Effron, Eric (ed.) "The Return of the Stay-at-Home Mom". *The Week.* January 26, 2007, p. 15.

Fields, Douglas R. "White Matter Matters". *Scientific American,* March 2008, pp. 54-61.

Foreman, Judy. "Revising the Idea of An Aging Mind". Minneapolis *Star Tribune.* August 19, 2001.

Foreman, Judy. "Emotional Stress May Speed Aging". Minneapolis *Star Tribune.* Dec. 26, 2004.

Gertmenian, James. "Innocence: Found and Lost" (sermon; Plymouth Congregational Church). Minneapolis, MN: May 2, 2004.

Gertmenian, James. "Home By Another Road" (sermon; Plymouth Congregational Church) Minneapolis, MN: February 6, 2005.

Goldberg, Steven T. & Smith, Anne K. "Do Good, and Do Great". Kiplinger's. March 2004, pp. 34-39.

Grothe, D. J. (ed.) "The Myth of Happiness: A Conversation With Jennifer Michael Hecht". *Free Inquiry.* August/September 2007, p. 8.

Guarante, Leonard. "Regulation of Aging by SIR2". *Annals of the New York Academy of Sciences.* December 2005.

Heirich, Jane R. "The Alexander Technique and Voice Pedagogy". *The NATS Journal,* 49, 5: 1993, pp. 16-18.

Jacoby, Susan. "The Right to Die". *AARP Bulletin.* November 2005, pp. 8-9, 31.

Kaku, Michio. "How to Survive the End of the Universe". *Discover.* December 2004, pp. 47-53.

Kalb, Claudia & Juarez, Vanessa. "Aging: Small is Beautiful". *Newsweek*. August, 2005, pp. 46-47.

Kiplinger, Knight (Editor-in-chief). *Kiplinger's Personal Finance Magazine*. January 2004.

Kotler, Steven & Astor, Josef. "Extreme States". *Discover*. July 2005, pp. 61-66.

Law, Stephen. "The God of Eth". *Skeptical Inquirer*. Sept./Oct. 2005, pp. 39-43.

Levin, Ross. "Managing Accounts". Minneapolis *Star Tribune*. November 20, 2005.

Lundberg, George D. "The Best Health Care Goes Only So Far". *Newsweek*. August 27, 2001, p. 15.

Moyers, Bill & Judy. "On Our Own Terms". PBS Broadcast (4-part series). September, 2000.

Nakazawa, Donna J. "Living Longer: Diet". *AARP Magazine*. September/October, 2006, pp. 84-88.

Ornish, Dean. "Love is Real Medicine". *Newsweek*. October 3, 2005, pp. 56.

Preston, Thomas A. "Facing Death on Your Own Terms". *Newsweek*. May 22, 2000, p. 82.

Quindlen, Anna. "Now It's Time for Generation Next". *Newsweek*, January, 2000.

Quindlen, Anna. "The Culture of Each Life". *Newsweek*. April 4, 2005.

Quinn, Jane Bryant. "The Retirement Race". *Newsweek*. March 15, 2004, pp. 65-73.

Reinan, John. "One Nation, Under Debt". Minneapolis *Star Tribune*. November 28, 2004, pp. A-1, A-16.

Remick, D. "The Last Italian Tenor". *The New Yorker*. 1993. p. 41.

Restak, Richard. "All in Your Head". *Modern Maturity*. January/February, 2002. pp. 60-65.

Roizen, Michael F. & Oz, Mehmet C. "10 Steps to a Younger You". *USA Weekend*. January, pp. 5-7, 2007.

Roof, Wade Clark. "Spiritual Marketplace: Baby Boomers and the Remaking of American Religion". Author(s) of *Review: Rodger Payne Contemporary Sociology,* Vol. 31, No. 1 (Jan., 2002), pp. 43-45.

Rosenblatt, Roger. (Interview with Lewis Thomas) *New York Times Magazine*. Nov. 21, 1993.

Saseen, Jane. "The CEO Mega-Mansion Factor". *Business week*. April 2, 2007, p. 9.

Shell, Ellen Ruppel. "X Rated". *Discover*. October 2005, pp. 42-43.

Sinclair, David & Komaroff, Anthony. "Can We Slow Aging?" *Newsweek*. December 11, 2006, pp. 80, 82, 84.

Sloan, Alan. "A Blissful Dream, a Rude Awakening". *Newsweek*. February 5, 2001, p. 45.

Smith, Jocelyn. "Why We Age". *Discover*. September, 2004, p. 7.

Underwood, Anne. "Nature's Design Workshop". *Newsweek*. September 25, 2005, p. 55.

Underwood, Anne. "A Healthy Toast". *Newsweek*. October 3, 2005, p. 70.

Underwood, Anne. "The Good Heart". *Newsweek*. Oct. 3, 2005, pp. 49-55.

Underwood, Anne. "Tracking Disease" (interview with Mary Pearl). *Newsweek*. November 14, 2005, pp. 46, 48.

Withers, Thomas. "My Turn". *Newsweek*. September 2005.

Woodward, Kenneth L. & McCormick, John. "The Art of Dying Well". *Newsweek*. November 25, 1996, pp. 61-66).

Wright, Karen. "Staying Alive". *Discover*. November 2003, pp. 64-70.

WEBSITES

Administration on Aging (AOA) (www.aoa.gov)

Adventures in Singing (www.mhhe.com/ais4)
  – C. Ware book/songs

American Association of Retired Persons (AARP)
  (www.aarp.org)

American Psychological Association (APA) (www.apa.org)

AXA Equitable Retirement Survey (www.axaonline.com)

Birch Grove Publishing (www.birchgrovepublishing.com)
  - C. Ware book

Blue Zones (www.bluezones.com/) - aging models

Centerpointe (www.centerpointe.com) - meditation programs

Character Counts (www.charactercounts.org/)

Choice in Dying (www.compassionandchoices.org)

Consumer Reports (www.consumerreports.org)

Consumers Alliance (www.funerals.org)

Generous Giving (www.generousgiving.org)

Integral Life Balance (integralifebalance.com)

Lifegem (www.lifegem.com)

National Council on Problem Gambling (www.ncpgambling.org)

National Review (www.nationalreview.com)

Noise Pollution Clearinghouse (www.nonoise.org)

Posit Science (www.positscience.com)

Ted Talks (http://www.ted.com/talks/view/id/229) – video lecture

Upper Access (www.upperaccess.com/) - funeral advice

Vital Aging Network (www.vital-aging-network.org)

Wikipedia (www.en.wikipedia.org)

Index

About the Author

Clifton Ware, Professor Emeritus of Voice, University of Minnesota, received his Doctor of Music degree in vocal performance from Northwestern University in Evanston, Illinois in 1970. His teaching career, which began in 1962 as a high school choral director, culminated in a rewarding 37-year post at the University of Minnesota.

As a tenor soloist, Clif has performed extensively in opera, oratorio, and recital venues in the U.S. and abroad. He can be heard on four recordings, including Benjamin Britten's *St. Nicolas* and *Paul Bunyan*. Since 2007, Clif has teamed up with his wife and sons in performing classic pop songs, primarily from the 1950s. This crossover experience—from a lifetime of performing classical vocal repertoire to pop songs—illustrates his continuing desire to make the most of life as a senior citizen.

Clif has written three highly acclaimed books: *Adventures in Singing* and *Basics of Vocal Pedagogy* (McGraw-Hill) and *The Singer's Life* (Birch Grove Publishing). His books reflect a dedication to helping individuals develop a holistic, integrated, and well-balanced life. Clif's Integral Life Balance website also features sections devoted to singers and voice teachers. (See page 371 for website URL addresses.)

As an artist-teacher, Clif has given numerous presentations nationally and internationally for professional organizations and educational institutions. His wife, Bettye, an accomplished pianist, organist, and piano teacher, frequently joins him as his accompanist. Together they have collaborated on many projects, including composing and arranging songs, writing song lyrics, creating recordings for the *Adventures in Singing* song anthology, and editing and proofreading Clif's books. Clif and Bettye love to travel and hike, as illustrated in the photo on the front cover of this book, taken in the summer of 2008 at Capitol Reef National Park in Utah.